Drucker
on
Marketing

Drucker on Marketing

Lessons from the World's Most Influential Business Thinker

WILLIAM A. COHEN, PhD

New York Chicago San Francisco Lisbon London Madrid Mexico City
Milan New Delhi San Juan Seoul Singapore Sydney Toronto

1 2 3 4 5 6 7 8 9 0   DOC/DOC   1 8 7 6 5 4 3 2

ISBN   978-0-07-177862-6
MHID   0-07-177862-4

e-ISBN 978-0-07-177863-3
e-MHID   0-07-177863-2

Library of Congress Cataloging-in-Publication Data
Cohen, William A.
    Drucker on marketing : lessons from the world's most influential business thinker / by William Cohen.
       p. cm.
    ISBN 978-0-07-177862-6 (alk. paper) — ISBN 0-07-177862-4 (alk. paper)
    1. Marketing. 2. Drucker, Peter F. (Peter Ferdinand), 1909-2005. I. Title.
    HF5415.C54248 2013
    658.8—dc23
                                                                              2012016985

Contents

Part IV
New Product and Service Introduction

Part V
Drucker's Unique Marketing Insights

Foreword

Peter Drucker is widely acknowledged as the father of modern management. Occasionally, I have been carelessly called the father of modern marketing. If that is so, then Peter should be described as the grandfather of modern marketing.

Bill Cohen has done us a wonderful service by faithfully combing through Peter Drucker's vast writings and weaving together Peter's thoughts on marketing. This has never been done before. Peter did not write a systematic treatise on marketing, but nevertheless marketing was on his mind when he discussed the customer-driven purpose of a company, the role of profits and leadership, the critical importance of innovation and entrepreneurship, the need to identify and research opportunities, and so on. We owe it to Bill Cohen to have taken the various strands of Peter's observations on all aspects of marketing and put them together in the 25 chapters of this fine book. Bill studied under Drucker and tells many stories that illustrate good or bad business thinking à la Drucker. As a result Bill not only describes Peter's insights and tells us many of Peter's famous company engagements and observations but also adds wonderful illustrations from his own personal experiences that illustrate Peter's thinking.

Peter Drucker has influenced many leaders in business, nonprofit organizations, and government, not to mention all the professors who pass on Drucker's insights to new classes of business students. I had the privilege of knowing Peter personally and discussing ideas with him. I would like to share here my personal experience with him, as I did first at the Drucker Forum in Vienna during the Drucker Centennial in 2009.

Before I met Peter Drucker, I was an avid reader and admirer of his sage writings. Then one day, out of the blue, I received a call from a person with a German accent who said that he was Peter Drucker. Peter said that he was calling to invite me to visit him in Claremont, California, to spend a day together. In my mind, this was more exciting than a call from any other person I could imagine. We set a date, and I flew out to Claremont.

Peter and I found out that we shared a mutual interest in Japanese art. Peter collected Japanese scrolls and screens, and I collected Japanese netsukes and tsubas. When I landed in Claremont, our first stop was to visit Peter's art gallery. Peter was not only a professor of management at Claremont College but also a professor of art. Claremont College gave him the use of a private gallery in which he could store and display his Japanese screens and scrolls. We spent the next few hours discussing the finer points of each Japanese scroll that he displayed. I learned a great deal from Peter about the Japanese aesthetic, which is quite different from the Western aesthetic. The Japanese bring a different set of concepts—wabi and sabi—to understand and judge greatness in a work of art.

After the visit in the art gallery and a healthy lunch in a nearby restaurant, Peter and I went to his home. I met Peter's wife Doris who is an accomplished physicist and who still plays a great game of tennis. I was surprised by the modesty of their home, especially knowing that Peter received in the same living room CEOs from many leading companies. Peter and Doris did not need any of the trappings of conspicuous consumption.

In the late afternoon, Peter took me to a recording studio near his home. Peter used this studio to do video conferences when he did not want to travel. (I remember attending a major management conference a few years later watching Peter's face fill a giant screen and talking brilliantly to the delegates.) In the studio, Peter interviewed me about the role that marketing can play to help nonprofit organizations improve their performance. His questions were thought-provoking. I subsequently was inspired to undertake research into the museum world and the performing arts world to really answer his penetrating questions. The research resulted in my publishing two culture-oriented marketing books, namely *Museum Strategy and Marketing: Designing Missions, Building Audiences, Generating Revenue and Resources,* and *Standing Room Only: Strategies for Marketing the Performing Arts.*

When the Peter F. Drucker Foundation for Nonprofit Management was formed in 1990 with the help of the very special Frances Hesselbein, former leader of the Girl Scouts of America, I was invited to join the advisory board. Many of Peter's longtime acquaintances and admirers were on this board. Peter didn't want the institute to be named after him. He relented on the condition that the name Peter Drucker would eventually be replaced by another title. It was eventually renamed the Leader to Leader Institute, and most recently renamed again for Frances by her trustees.

The Drucker Foundation was set up to help nonprofit organizations (NPOs) improve their performance by hearing from other NPOs, businesspeople, and scholars. I attended several annual meetings where 300 or more NPOs would attend. At each annual meeting, the Drucker Institute presented awards to organizations that created exciting and original solutions to social problems.

I saw Peter on a few subsequent occasions, each time drawing inspiration from his incredible knowledge of history and his visionary grasp of the future. I never understood how he could amass so much information about so many fields of inquiry. He had an intimate knowledge of the lives of great persons, he knew the world of music, he followed and influenced developments in religious congregations, he wrote two novels—he was a true Renaissance man. He is one of the most impressive persons that I had ever met.

Peter and I would correspond occasionally. What impressed me is that he would handwrite his notes. No typewriter, no computer. He probably used a typewriter but not in his personal correspondence with me.

Peter was an early visionary regarding the discipline of marketing. For over 40 years ago, he explained to businesspeople the central role of the customer and the company's task of value creation. If anyone should be credited with awakening us to the concept that a company must be or become customer-centered, it is Peter Drucker. In his meetings with Procter & Gamble, Metronics, Intel, and many other companies, he always put several questions to them. Leaders of these companies testify to having an epiphany when trying to answer these questions from Peter:

"What is our business?"
"Who is our customer?"
"What does the customer consider value?"
"What should our business be?"

Many of Peter's statements flew in the face of what most CEOs believed. For example, they said that the purpose of a business was to make a profit. But Peter saw this as an empty statement. It lacked the key idea on how to make a profit. That key idea was to create a customer. And you created a customer by offering superior value and satisfying that customer. From this the profits would follow. The only profit center is the customer.

As you can see, Bill's work has uncorked a flood of memories and connections. There are many more.

Peter Drucker wanted managers to see marketing as more than just another one of a half-dozen business functions. He wanted managers to see marketing as an overriding business philosophy that defines the company's best customer opportunities and directs the total company effort to capture the best opportunities. This profoundly influenced my own thinking on the nature of marketing. I couldn't accept marketing as just a function that handles advertising and the sales force. Nor could I accept marketing as only handling the four Ps, namely product, price, place, and promotion. All this is important tactical work, but it isn't the whole story of marketing. A company's marketing people must undertake the more fundamental responsibilities of segmentation, targeting, and positioning (STP). Even these three don't tell the whole story of marketing.

The whole story is that marketing must be viewed *holistically*. That's how successful companies see marketing. Marketing is the driving force in these companies. Acquiring, keeping, and growing customers through creating, communicating, and delivering value is the defining mission. Peter knew this, and Bill has put it all down in this book. I highly recommend his work to you.

Philip Kotler
Kellogg School of Management
Northwestern University

Introduction

Drucker and His Different Marketing Approach

Most marketing professors spend their entire working lives without developing or uncovering a single concept of note or generating much fame outside their own university. Yet there is one, Philip Kotler of the Kellogg School of Management at Northwestern University, who has uncovered many concepts of note and achieved fame outside his own university. Ask anyone who has contributed most to the discipline of marketing, and you'll hear the name Philip Kotler. Kotler developed new concepts in marketing including demarketing, megamarketing, turbomarketing, and synchromarketing—and much more. His textbook on marketing management has been the world's most widely used marketing textbook for many years. Ask any marketing professor at any university, anywhere in the world, who is the world's most outstanding marketing professor, and he or she will instantly answer, "Philip Kotler." Most call Kotler the "father of marketing." Yet, so insightful are Drucker's own concepts for this discipline, that Kotler proclaimed in the Foreword of this book and elsewhere, "If I am the father of marketing, then Drucker is the grandfather."

Despite Peter Drucker's extensive writings available in books, articles, and edited collections of his works, some of Drucker's marketing wisdom has never been published, and none has been collected together and published as a separate book of marketing. There is no other book like *Drucker on Marketing*. Drucker's marketing thoughts are spread over 39 books, several hundred articles, and thousands of lectures, both those open to the public and those limited to his students in the classroom or in informal settings around the world.

Drucker certainly didn't mince his words about the field. He wrote that there were two, and only two, essential functions for any business: marketing and innovation. Everything else, he said, was a cost. Of course innovation is associated with all aspects of marketing, as well as strategy and the theory of the business and the business model. Although he wrote no books on marketing, Drucker did write about marketing very often, including an article in the *Journal of Marketing* in the early 1950s. Only a year after *The Practice of Management*, his first book with management as its prime focus, was published, he wrote the article boldly predicting that "selling will become marketing." Before most companies thought much beyond sales and were still arguing that marketing was just a sophisticated term for selling, Drucker not only explained the difference between the two terms and the use and integration of marketing functions such as research, product planning, product testing, pricing, distribution, promotion, advertising, selling, customer service, and more, but he also predicted that the day would come when even small organizations would have vice presidents of marketing.[1] He was years ahead of his time.

Drucker the Genius

Peter Drucker was a genius. More than that, Drucker was a unique genius. Drucker was in a class with Newton, Freud, and Einstein, and like them, Peter wanted to see his insights and conclusions disseminated and applied. What is most unusual in this respect are the lengths he went to interact and influence those he considered worthy. These were his "students." However Drucker's students were not only those he encountered in the classroom. They also included corporate CEOs, religious leaders, and politicians from around the world.

C. William Pollard was one. For over 25 years, Bill Pollard participated in the top leadership of the ServiceMaster Company and served not once but twice as its chief executive officer. He also served as chairman of the board and was elected chairman emeritus when he retired. During his leadership, ServiceMaster was recognized by *Fortune* magazine as the number one service company among all of the Fortune 500 and was also included as one of Fortune's most admired companies. It was identified as a "star of the future" by the *Wall Street Journal* and as one of the most respected companies in the world by the *Financial Times*.

Pollard was one of a select few invited to speak at the installation of Dr. Deborah Freund as president of Claremont Graduate University, which houses among others the Peter F. Drucker and Masatoshi Ito Graduate School of Management. During his presentation, Bill told a story about an important lesson he learned from Drucker. It typifies Drucker and distinguishes him—as what I would call "a leader-genius"—from many others not only as someone who theorized and practiced, but also as a leader who dramatically influenced his students, many of whom were major corporate and organizational executives.

Peter and Bill Pollard flew together to Tokyo to make a presentation with one of ServiceMaster's partners in Asia. About 250 senior executives were expected to attend the event. When they arrived, Pollard was disappointed to learn that the one business partner had not done its job and had failed to promote the event properly. Instead of 250 attendees, only 160 had signed up, and almost all of these were from Bill's organization's efforts, not the partner's. The partner had done little or nothing. Both Pollard and Drucker gave their presentations anyway and proceeded to do their best despite their disappointment and Bill's anger at the business partner for failing to do its part.

Pollard was supposed to go on alone to Osaka by train the following day to do additional work with the partner at the company's headquarters. However at dinner with Drucker that night, he told Peter that he had decided not to make the trip. Instead he would take an earlier flight back to the States. Peter tried to dissuade Pollard from this action. He encouraged him to rethink his position and gave him his thoughts and understanding of Japanese culture. Although Pollard listened, he made up his mind that he was not going to accept his advice and he would reschedule his flight the next morning. On this note, both returned to their respective hotel rooms.

At about 10:30 that night Pollard's telephone rang in his room. It was Drucker. "Bill, come down to my room right now."

"I can't," responded Pollard, "I'm in my pajamas."

"Well put your pants on and get down here. I want to talk with you."

Pollard acquiesced and knocked on Drucker's door. "You sit on the couch and I'll sit on the bed," said Drucker. Pollard had no sooner seated himself, when Drucker began. He sat down on the edge of his bed and looked him straight in the eye. "Bill," he said, "you are suffering from the arrogance of success. It's time for you to eat some humble pie."

"I know exactly what's wrong with you," he told Pollard. "It's your ego. Even though you know that this trip tomorrow is necessary and in the best interests of your company, you don't want to go because your ego is bruised. Get yourself together and catch that train to Osaka. Go down there and do what you are supposed to do." Drucker went on to explain how quickly leaders can lose touch with the reality of their responsibility when they think their pride is at risk. He pointed out that Pollard's job was to go to Osaka, meet with his business partners, resolve their differences, and rebuild a relationship of trust. This result was needed for the continued growth of the business in Japan and for the opportunities that it would provide the people in their business. It was Pollard's job to do this as a leader, and it was something that he could not delegate to someone else. Pollard knew that Drucker was right. He obeyed Drucker's instructions. The trip was worthwhile, and he did not regret going. Moreover, he did not forget Drucker's lesson. Said Bill Pollard: "The leadership lesson was clear. My leadership responsibility was not about me or my feelings. It was about what should be done for our business and our people."[2]

Bill Pollard was not the only one to learn from Drucker. Some call Jack Welch the most acclaimed executive of the last decade—some say, of the last century. During his 20 years of leadership at General Electric (GE), Welch increased the value of his company from $13 billion to several hundred billion. Asked about his accomplishments, Welch gave significant credit to Drucker. We'll see exactly how and why in Chapter 14.

But not only business executives have admired, learned from, and applied Drucker's principles. Jim Collins, author of the 3 million copy bestseller *Good to Great*, told the faculty at Claremont Graduate University that his book could have been entitled *Drucker Was Right*. Minglo Shao, with Drucker's advice, built the Bright China Corporation. Among its developments are the Peter F. Drucker Academies of China and Hong Kong with more than 50,000 graduates and the new California Institute of Advanced Management of which I am honored to serve as president. Then, there is Rick Warren, who built the Saddle Back Church from nothing to thousands of members; and Frances Hesselbein, who as CEO reinvigorated the Girl Scouts of the U.S.A., won the Presidential Medal of Freedom, and is now chair of the Leader to Leader Institute in New York. This was recently renamed the Frances Hesselbein Leadership Institute in her honor. There are thousands of others of Drucker's "students" all over the world. All are happy to acknowledge Drucker as a prime instrument of their success. But I use the quotation marks because only a very few of us were lucky enough to have Peter as our professor in the classroom. Nevertheless, he treated us all the same. And I got my marching orders from Peter on occasion just as did Bill Pollard.

My Adventures as Drucker's Student, Formal and Informal

During the period that I was Drucker's formal student in the classroom from 1975 to 1979, we developed a friendship that continued after my graduation and the award of my doctorate and almost until his death. Peter knew that his time was valuable and limited. He was willing to give his time generously as an investment, but only if he thought that investment would have some value for the future, not for himself, but for others and mostly for society.

In the years after my graduation, I saw him infrequently, but we stayed in touch by telephone, and we had an occasional lunch for which he insisted on paying. This connection would have been even closer, but I well understood the giant he was, and frankly I was concerned about abusing his friendship and willingness to help. I taught several courses at my doctoral alma mater, and Drucker allowed me to use his office once when I taught during his sabbatical.

Two years after his death, I was invited to speak at the first Global Symposium of Drucker Societies. This was in 2007. Several hundred attendees from around the world were present. Dean Ira Jackson introduced me. Included in my introduction was the fact that I was not only the first graduate of the executive PhD program which Peter and then Dean Paul Albrecht had developed, but also that I had since become an Air Force general. Later at lunch, Doris Drucker, then 97 years old and still speaking around the world and promoting Drucker's concepts and values, approached me. She said, "You know Bill, I've known you for years, but until the dean introduced you as a general, I did not know who you really were. You were Peter's favorite student. He talked about you all the time." Such a tribute was unexpected and overwhelming, and with great emotion I placed my hand over my heart.

How and Why I Wrote This Book

In my first book about him, *A Class with Drucker* (AMACOM, 2008), I discussed this relationship and what I learned, and I covered important general management lessons that had not been given wide publicity, were misinterpreted, or were given a different emphasis from the one he gave in the classroom. In that book I covered all disciplines that he taught under the general label of "management." This did not leave much space to cover anything else. Yet there were two areas that Drucker emphasized heavily and continuously, although not always explicitly. The first was leadership, and I spent more than a year writing *Drucker on Leadership* (Jossey-Bass, 2010). After this work was published, I had intended to begin the research for a book that would organize Drucker's genius, insights, and principles about marketing. I had done my doctoral dissertation in the marketing area and had become very interested in it when it finally dawned on me that it was really the main component of any successful organizational strategy. Subsequently I spent more than 20 years in the classroom as a marketing professor even as I served part time in the Air Force. It soon became crystal clear why Drucker considered marketing, along with innovation, which he spoke of as a separate element, to be one of the two essential elements of any successful business. And here we should understand that he meant "business" writ large, since his insights applied equally to all organizations, from baseball teams and volunteer groups and to both profit and nonprofit organizations, and from huge organizations down to hospital operating teams and quartets playing classical music, and certainly the military, which he frequently used in his historical examples. Yet much of what Drucker taught ran counter to what is said about marketing even by many expert marketing practitioners and academics and what is written in many marketing textbooks.

Drucker Was Different

Drucker was no shrinking violet about what he believed about the subject of marketing. He was a different "violet" entirely. As I mentioned, Drucker wrote that business success rested primarily on innovation and marketing, thus positioning himself contrary to powerful experts in the academic and corporate worlds who favored their own approach or discipline. Although Drucker never wrote a book specifically about marketing, there is much he did write about it in comments and chapters scattered throughout his 39 or 40 books (depending on how you count them) and hundreds of articles and in important sections in his books. These "bits and pieces" about marketing are so potent that these sometimes unorganized scraps have in many cases had a major impact on management thinking and how business is conducted.

At the presentation of a top award to a marketing educator by one of the major marketing associations, the awardee named three marketing professors who most influenced his career. I was not surprised when he named Peter Drucker as one of these "marketing professors," although in 70 years as a professor at various institutions, Drucker never held or claimed such a title. But it was Drucker's powerful marketing insights, which predated much of the marketing research that followed, that caused a famous marketing researcher and thinker holding the earned title of the "father of marketing," such as Kotler, to refer to Drucker as "the grandfather of marketing."

However, most certainly Drucker was different. I have rarely seen marketing researchers claim the preeminence of marketing among the major business disciplines. Drucker, who was not a marketing researcher, did. Drucker was one of the first marketing thinkers to show us that business, product, or service divestment was as important as business, product, or service introduction. Many marketing and strategic gurus recommended business, product, or service introduction or acquisition, but said nothing of the need for abandoning existing products or businesses, much less if they were profitable. Drucker did. Almost all marketing educators explain sales and selling as an overall subset of marketing, just like advertising or marketing research. Drucker was not the only academic or general management writer who claimed that marketing and selling were not the same. Most people over the last 40 years or so have been saying that. But Drucker wrote that selling and marketing were not necessarily complementary and could even be adversarial! Yes, Drucker was different and frequently took an approach to marketing different from others.

What This Book Is About

It is with some pride that I write this volume regarding the principles and concepts that the "grandfather of marketing" uncovered, believed in, and recommended about marketing, which is a fundamental function of management and business. These principles have the potential to set marketing and its concepts in new directions and to reach new heights. But there is more to it than that. There is value to organizing Drucker's thoughts about marketing. The impression among some is that since he wrote so much about management, he wrote little about marketing. This is a mistaken notion. Moreover, what he did write was profound and of major impact. The need for his knowledge goes well beyond simply organizing Drucker's marketing thoughts. Drucker told us what to do. He rarely went further to tell us how to do it. Yet at times his ideas need this additional "how to" explanation. Change also demands more.

Several years ago, Henry To, president of the Peter F. Drucker Academies of China, was interviewed by the *Wall Street Journal*. Asked about how Drucker's U.S. examples from the 1940s and 1950s are accepted in China, To responded: "I tell students: 'The truth will not be outdated.'"[3]

But while basic truths do not change—and Drucker used examples throughout history going back to ancient times—there are changes as to what these truths mean to us today. He frequently spoke about how such changes were occurring more and more rapidly and wrote that even the near future would present us with "new institutions, theories, ideologies, and problems."[4] These would all require new ways of looking at not only our environment, but how we go about implementing "truths which will not be outdated." His academic colleague at Claremont Graduate School and coauthor of several of Drucker's books when it became difficult for Drucker to write, Professor Joseph Maciariello, confirms this through his work. I was amazed when Joe undertook to update Drucker's masterpiece *Management: Tasks, Responsibilities, Practices*. This was the "textbook" I was assigned for the majority of my work as Drucker's student when I became the first executive graduate of the PhD program that he and Dean Paul Albrecht had initiated in the mid-1970s. I was most impressed with what Joe had done. He updated the old examples and, more important, by using Drucker's own material from his later articles and speeches, updated his concepts according to his later analyses. In every way he helped ensure that Drucker's truths would not be outdated.

All this requires a reexamination of how we see and apply Drucker's genius. Thus as those who follow the theories and genius of Freud have reinterpreted and applied them differently as society has changed since he revealed them, so those who follow Drucker stand on his shoulders to further develop what he started. I read recently that even Einstein's theory needs some modifications. The content of this book contains what Drucker taught us, but in addition I have tried to add examples as to how he would have implemented and applied his concepts as well as how the interpretation of his contributions might change in application today and in the future.

If there are errors, you can bet they are mine, but the genius of the ideas, principles, and concepts—they are pure Peter.

Bill Cohen
Pasadena, California
2012

Part I
The Ascendancy of Marketing

Chapter 1

Two Different Views on the Development of Marketing

Traditionally marketing theorists have categorized marketing by different eras of marketing development. These eras are important to understand because they not only help to explain the development of marketing thought, but if we can understand why these eras occurred, they will help us in formulating marketing strategies in a variety of environments in both the present and the future. Drucker did not use this approach. Nevertheless, we need to understand this traditional approach before we look at Drucker's analysis of marketing development because the two differ conceptually, and these differences provide insights necessary to understand the basis of Drucker's thinking. While different writers and marketing researchers have given different titles to these eras of marketing development, they can be generalized as follows:

1. **Craftsmen and simple trade era.** The manufacturer, a craftsman, traded for what he made for something he wanted or needed. A caveman no longer able to actively participate in hunting, but with a developed skill in design and construction of weaponry, was still able to earn his keep and was considered valuable to the tribe through the production of hunting tools. This progressed through

other skilled craftsmen selling their services to obtain goods or services that they required.

2. **The production era.** The production era arrived as a result of the development of technology. This greatly enhanced our ability to produce formerly scarce goods. Once a worker struggled for months to meticulously produce a single book that few people could afford to buy. The invention of the printing press permitted satisfactory reproduction of thousands of copies of the same work over the same amount of time it took to produce a single copy in the past. This brought the cost down significantly, and now many people could afford the product. Previously the emphasis was simply on producing the product, since buyers who could afford the expense competed for the limited number of products available. Now the emphasis shifted to reducing the cost of production in order to further lower the price in order to win additional buyers.

3. **The selling era.** Those who were doing the selling, whether manufacturers or intermediaries who bought products from the manufacturer for resale or their agents who earned a percentage from all products sold, recognized that it was one thing to have competitive features, but in addition the prospective customer had to know about these features and to understand and be persuaded to purchase the product because of the benefits that resulted from these features. At the same time, since more advanced production methods had led to plenty of available product, the bigger challenge for producers and those getting the product out the door and to market shifted to getting customers to buy what had been produced. Thus sales departments and sales forces increased in size, number, and skill. But the emphasis was more on the product and convincing the customer to buy the product than on any notion of customer satisfaction except in a very basic sense.

4. **The marketing era.** Most industrialized countries had suffered in their ability to produce as a result of physical damage to industry during World War II. U.S. industry, untouched by the war directly, had greatly increased its capacity and ability to

manufacture goods during the war. This put the United States in a highly competitive position relative to other countries, but it also created a highly competitive environment within the country. At the same time sophisticated techniques of analysis that were developed during the war could be applied to analyzing potential customers and markets. Thus manufacturing opportunity and the ability to discover what the customer wanted before the product was developed came together to implement a conclusion about how to increase sales that was unexploited before the war. Simply said, more products could be sold if they were the right products for the right market. The know-how was now available to determine exactly what the "right products" should be. With the impetus of internal competition in the country, and the attraction of worldwide markets, the marketing era was born. Even today, some do not understand that marketing is not simply a sophisticated way of speaking about selling. Marketing is differentiated from selling in several important ways. Drucker led the way in deducing that selling was persuading someone to buy something that you had and wanted to sell while marketing was having something that a prospect already wanted to buy. Drucker concluded that if marketing were done perfectly, selling would be unnecessary, and he made the on-the-face-of-it outrageous statement (which we examine more closely in Chapter 15) that marketing and selling are not complementary and might even be adversarial.[1]

5. **The marketing company era.** Drucker's thinking is clearly closely intertwined in the idea of the marketing company, although he did not think of its onset as an era. He simply noted that all business depends on only two functions: marketing and innovation. We examine this principle in detail in Chapter 4. However, in passing, we should note that a closer examination including that of the "P" of product in Jerome McCarthy's four Ps of marketing must lead to the conclusion that this product innovation is itself an integral part of marketing.[2] However, Drucker meant innovation in a much broader sense.

The philosophy of bringing all departments together with the objective of satisfying their customers' needs was incorporated into the very heart of marketing in what has been termed "the marketing concept." What Drucker wrote is that marketing "is the whole business seen from the point of view of the final result, that is, from the customer's point of view. Concern and responsibility for marketing must therefore permeate all areas of the enterprise."[3] But Drucker did not claim this concept as an era. It seems somewhat presumptuous to claim it as such, when even today some companies do not have marketing departments, or if they do, they are sales departments misnamed.

6. **The societal marketing era.** Drucker would certainly agree with the notion that corporations should recognize societal benefit as an important goal for any organization and that they should not lie, cheat, or steal from society in the interest of selling a product. Drucker took this further and reasoned that it is creation of a customer and not profit that is the basic purpose of a business. However, he also noted that it would be disastrous to somehow overlook profit as a business necessity. Looking at the evidence of corporate scandal and lack of consideration of the potential harm to customers that exists today hardly supports the idea that we are in an *era* of societal marketing, although many companies, to their credit, do attempt to consider the impact of what is done in the name of marketing on society. Unfortunately it is doubtful that we are in an era in which companies routinely follow basic tenets that are not required of them by law, although we should be.

Drucker Saw Things Differently

While Drucker did not deny that marketing development could be categorized by eras, he did not do so. Rather, he looked at critical incidents of historic catalysts. He thought these incidents to be the crucial turning points in marketing development as he conceptualized marketing (along with innovation) as the two essential foundations of all business enterprise.

According to Drucker, modern marketing was invented in Japan in around 1650 by an unknown member of the Mitsui family who moved to Tokyo to take up retailing. Yes, this is the same family that founded the Mitsui Group and is today one of the largest corporate conglomerates (keiretsu) in Japan and one of the largest publicly traded companies in the world. This original Mitsui family member was a businessman with a difference. Previously, a merchant sold only the products that he had made himself, regardless of whether he was a caveman or Johannes Gutenberg, who invented the device and processes that allowed the mass production of printed books, most famously, the Bible.

The Mitsui family did something entirely different. Rather than focusing on a single line of products that they made or manufactured, they offered a large assortment of different types of products to their customers coming from many different manufacturers and sources. Mitsui wasn't just ahead of its time. It was a full 250 years ahead of some of the concepts and policies that Sears, Roebuck later incorporated into its business and used to lead the way in marketing in the United States beginning in the late 1890s and early 1900s.[4]

Drucker also gave credit to another American, Cyrus McCormick, but it was not for developing the mechanical harvester for which he is best known, but rather for a large number of the modern tools of marketing from marketing research to pricing policies, service salespeople, and installation credit. It took 50 years after McCormick did this for anyone to take notice and imitate his practices, even in the United States.[5]

Europe had greater difficulties with marketing resulting from prejudice against selling by the upper classes. It was undignified. So only until Marks and Spencer came along and became Europe's largest, fastest-growing, and most successful retailer in the 1920s did anyone even take selling seriously. It was not until much later that marketing practices such as those practiced by Marks and Spencer caught on.[6] In the United States Drucker saw the Cadillac as the first product that was truly marketed, and that did not happen until the 1940s.[7]

Drucker also noted that considerable success could be achieved by abandoning modern production methods to attain competitive marketing advantages over the competition. He pointed out that the founders of Rolls-Royce deliberately renounced the advantages of Ford's famous production line and the latest manufacturing methods to create hand-made vehicles that were individually machined and assembled and were promoted as "never wearing out." Originally the cars were designed to be driven only by chauffeurs who were especially trained by the Rolls-Royce company, which carefully selected its target market and priced the product accordingly.[8]

Why Drucker Didn't Follow the Era Theory

Drucker did not believe that there were eras in marketing because by implication each era occurred because of forces, be they economic or technological, beyond the marketer's control. Drucker believed strongly that a business enterprise is created and managed by people, and not controlled primarily by external forces. He took issue with the claim that the marketer's sole function in this respect was to adapt business to the forces of the market. He acknowledged that this was partially true. However, he believed that management not only had to find, identify, and market taking these forces into account, but to manipulate these forces as well. In this he was similar in his thinking to that of Carl and Valerie Zeithaml who discussed such an approach in an article in the *Journal of Marketing* at about the same time that Drucker wrote this for publication.[9] However, there was an important difference. The Zeithaml theme was that such forces, or environmental variables, could be controlled, just as more tactical variables pertaining to product, price, and so on had been the focus and been termed "controllable variables" previously. Drucker believed that management had to actually create these forces.[10]

In marketing development, he provided concrete examples that were different from those usually provided by people using the era approach to explain marketing development. He cited individuals and how they met marketing challenges. These individuals or organizations might come from any time, and they might be from the East as well as from the West. They were all innovators. They did not blindly follow a trend or think they were in an "era." This would limit their thinking. They tried out new ideas and new ways of doing things. They did not take advantage of an era. They took advantage of the situation they faced and what they had to work with, and they created forces to enable these advantages. Thus Gutenberg might take advantage of a technology, Mitsui of a new concept of marketing, Rolls-Royce of demands of a special market, and McCormick of better ways of doing things. Drucker even found the origins of societal marketing in the actions of Julius Rosenwald in the early days of Sears, Roebuck and Company.

This was central to Drucker's thinking about marketing—that the successful marketer did what was required to ethically supply society with what was wanted and needed. Drucker's conclusion came from a different approach to the development of marketing thought and might be summarized as follows:

- Marketing is the basis of all business and is therefore of critical importance to all aspects of it.
- The development of marketing thought did not necessarily originate in the West, and therefore important aspects could also be found elsewhere geographically, and Asia could not be ignored.
- Rather than categorize this development of marketing through eras, critical incidents by individuals or organizations in history provided the framework for analysis.
- Every marketing proposition had to be critically examined individually and the issue had to be thought through to provide the concepts of marketing as a body of knowledge.

The conclusions Drucker provided through this different approach make up the content of this book.

Chapter 2

The Purpose of Business Is Not to Make a Profit

I heard Peter say many strange things when I was his student, but his saying that the purpose of business is not to make a profit has got to be one of the most unusual. I think most of my Drucker classmates agreed with me. Indeed, until Drucker came along, most everyone believed the basic "fact" that the purpose of a business was to make money, in other words, to make a profit. This belief leads to a corollary, another myth, believed by all—that the goal of any business is profit maximization. Whatever your business, your goal should be to make as much profit as possible. If you accept making a profit as a business's purpose, the second part just follows naturally. This might even seem worthy to many. To quote Michael Douglas's famous (or infamous) statement in his role as Gordon Gekko in the 1987 movie *Wall Street*, "Greed is good." Even today many people "know" greed, or profit maximization, to be both the correct goal and the correct prescription for business success, even if amoral or wouldn't be "good" from a moral perspective. Thus we sometimes hear of the dichotomy between "business ethics" and "personal ethics," a dichotomy Drucker deplored.

Not so fast, Gordon. As Drucker so often said, "Whatever everyone knows is usually wrong," Hollywood films not exempted. Drucker told us first that profit is not the purpose of business and that the concept of profit maximization is not only meaningless but dangerous. However, he stated that it didn't make any difference if the board of directors was populated entirely by archangels—wings, harps, and all. Board members would still be challenged by the fact that they must ensure profitability, but not necessarily profit maximization.[1] This seeming contradiction between profit maximization and profitability needs to be understood by all marketers.

The Myth of Profit Maximization and Why Drucker Thought It Was a Dangerous Idea

Drucker explained that the source of the confusion was that many economists consider profit maximization a basic theorem. In its simplicity it is simply another way of saying that a business buys low and sells high, or rather, buys as low as possible and sells as high as possible. However, as Drucker was quick to explain, this simple prescription by itself hardly explains the success or failure of any business. If we look at the difficulties as many businesses struggle today, and the many failures that have already occurred, it is clear that buying low and selling high explain very little about why these businesses fail, just as buying low and selling high explain very little about those that are still successful, and even those that are accelerating their success despite the current economic challenges of a major recession with its attendant financial challenges.

Profit maximization implies that you might save any business from failure by simply raising prices and creating a greater differential between revenue and cost. Simply maintain (or increase) the profit margin. In fact, as costs for business rise, be it gasoline, material, or anything else, simply passing the costs on to consumers is the immediate and simplistic response of many businesses. Yet they still fail, or succeed, independent of the act of raising prices and passing any increases on to the ultimate consumer may not be the determining factor. Recently I was told that a local restaurant failed because of the rising cost of produce. Yet other restaurants in the same general area serving the same target market did not fail. In fact, some thrived and even increased sales amid the same rising costs of their basic raw materials.[2]

Problems with the Profit Motive

Drucker also called the profit motive into question. He claimed that there has never been any evidence for such a motive and that the theory was invented by classical economists to explain something their theory of economic equilibrium could not explain. In support of his contention, there is considerable evidence against the profit motive. So-called dollar a year men in the higher levels of government are examples that run contrary to the profit motive. But we don't need to look that far or that high up in management or idealism. A good deal of volunteerism in which individuals, some quite highly paid in other roles, work long, hard hours for the common good in the Boy Scouts and Girls Scouts, religious and community activities and services, and more. Moreover, they work and don't get paid a penny. In fact, few can doubt that many talented individuals knowingly choose occupations that are not especially financially rewarding because their personal interest or calling takes them somewhere else.

It's always fascinating that a class of workers exists that work very hard physically, including weekends, with few complaints, that these workers receive little compensation or material benefits for their services, that the work is dangerous and workers are frequently injured on the job, that the workers usually have very high morale, that the organization always has more workers than can be put to work, and that the workers are highly engaged and motivated to achieve the organization's goals. I'm speaking of course about a high school football team.

There's more. The profit motive, expressed as compensation, isn't necessarily the prime motivator for normal, not necessarily altruistic, employees. Social scientists study many industries to determine what factors employees consider most important in their jobs. My psychologist-wife tells me that over the years questionnaires have been given to hundreds of thousands of employees. The results have been known for some time. They are not secret. One study was done by the Public Agenda Foundation and noted by John Naisbitt and Patricia Aburdene in their book *Reinventing the Corporation*. This study involved ranking various factors in the order of importance *you* think your employees would put them. Here are the factors ranked in the order of importance that many *employees* put them:[3]

- Working with people who treat me with respect
- Interesting work
- Recognition for good work
- Chance to develop skills
- Working for people who listen if you have ideas about how to do things better
- A chance to think for myself rather than just carry out instructions
- Seeing the end results of my work
- Working for efficient managers
- A job that is not too easy
- Feeling well informed about what is going on
- Job security
- High pay
- Good benefits

Note that high pay is ranked next to last of 13 factors. Obvious economic and business conditions come into play here. For example, take job security during a recession. Job security is ranked number 11 here, but might easily rank number 1 with many employees during bad economic times. The point is, over time and in many industries, ranking job security first usually isn't true for individual employees; and according to Drucker, none of the last three on the list usually holds up much as the main purpose for a business.

From this we can conclude that while profit can be motivating, it is not necessarily the primary motivator and that the notion of maximizing profit as the goal for a business or the life purpose of an individual is at best overstated.

Profits Still a Necessity

Drucker didn't stop here. He stated that the danger is that we might think from the foregoing that the concept of profitability as a goal must be a myth, so why worry about it? It might even lead us to the mistaken belief that seeking profit in business or privately is not only a waste of time, but immoral. In fact, every time there is moral failure on the part of an Enron, or a business thief such as Bernard Madoff is exposed, we hear new cries to develop laws to protect us not just from illegal acts and lapses of morality, but from those who seek "excessive profits," and to punish and discourage perpetrators wherever possible. Thus the "occupy" movement sweeping the country, if not the world, started to supposedly punish Wall Street bankers for excessive profits. Some people question the basic principles of capitalism and whether profits are really necessary at all. Government managers occasionally fall into this trap. I've heard a few say, "We don't work for profit. Why should business or industry."

The net result is that the profit motive is worse than irrelevant. It does harm because it creates hostility to profits, a hostility that Drucker called "the most dangerous disease of an industrial society" causing some of the worst mistakes of public policy and the notion that there is an inherent contradiction between profit and an organization's ability to make a social contribution when actually a company's ability to make a social contribution is highly dependent on its being profitable.

Drucker said that considering profitability a myth is a great danger because profitability, far from being a myth, immoral, or unneeded, is crucial for the success of both individual businesses and for society. In fact, he considered a business making a profit (as opposed to profit maximization) even more important for society than for the individual business.

Why Profit but Not Profit Maximization Is Necessary

Profit and profitability are absolute requirements. That's why even nonprofit corporations must strive mightily for profitability. They cannot survive without it. Witness the current struggles of public universities and other public services. These problems do not mean that profit is the basic purpose of a business or a "nonprofit" public enterprise. Profitability really is an essential ingredient by itself which might be better spoken of in terms of an optimal, rather than a maximum, size. In support of this thesis, Drucker noted that the primary test of any business is not the maximization of profit but the achievement of sufficient profit to allow for the risks of the financial activity of the business, and thus to avoid catastrophic loss leading to failure. And we might add the goal would be to achieve the success that would benefit both the business and society. So profit is necessary, but not the purpose of business.

Why is profit so necessary? Because profit is like oxygen for the human body. Oxygen ensures that the body lives, survives, and grows. Without it, the body dies. The same is true of profit for a business whether a for-profit or a not-for-profit organization under the law. Oxygen supplies the body with needed energy. According to Drucker, profit supplies the business with energy by supporting its two basic functions: marketing and innovation. Only a business action can create a customer, and that means innovation, advertising, selling skill, strategy, service, you name it. These business actions cost money that comes from the difference between buying low and selling at a higher amount.

Some months ago a corporate CEO was attacked for the "unconscionable profits" made by his company. He pointed out that 90 percent of the so-called unconscionable profits were actually reinvested in the corporation in research and development and marketing. Assuming the accuracy of his estimates, Drucker would have probably agreed with the defense made by this executive.

It is the right amount of oxygen that the body needs. Too much oxygen can cause damage to cell membranes, the collapse of the alveoli in the lungs, retinal detachment, and seizures. Too much profit, that is profit maximization without consideration of other elements in the business's equation, like too much oxygen, can cause problems just as too little profit can. If the focus is solely on profit maximization, the customer can be ignored or given secondary consideration. This can lead to poor management decisions resulting in cutting corners on safety, service, or product performance. We have seen this recently in many industries, including pharmaceuticals, aviation, and automotive. In truth these bad decisions resulting from a profit maximization focus can and do occur in all industries.

If profit maximization drives the company's purpose, it can allow competitors with a better focus to win markets by providing greater value or charging less. Profit maximization can cause organizational toxicity in the same way that oxygen toxicity can damage the body. Starbucks made a major mistake in the last few years in making expansion a strategy aimed purely at profits. The coffee juggernaut actually set a goal of seven new stores opened every day. It reached this goal in 2008. It even had a bigger goal in mind: 30,000 stores worldwide. Along about store number 15,000 CEO Howard Schultz realized that something was wrong. Profits disappeared even before the recession came into full force. With profits falling rapidly, Starbucks closed almost 900 stores and eliminated more than 34,000 jobs before it got back on track.[4]

What Should the Purpose of a Business Be?

According to Drucker, there is only one valid purpose for a business, and that is to create a customer. This is because, as Drucker wrote, "The customer is the foundation of a business and keeps it in existence. He alone gives employment. To supply the wants and needs of a consumer, society entrusts wealth-producing resources to the business enterprise."[5]

What has this to do with you or me or marketing? Regardless of our organization, and whether it is a for-profit or not-for-profit, Drucker's truth holds. If we want our organization to be successful, we have to remember that while profit is essential to support innovation and marketing actions, profit maximization is not only not the primary purpose of a business, but it could be bad for society and hazardous to the organization's health.

Chapter 3

Any Organization Has Only Two Functions: One Concerns Marketing, and the Other Is Marketing

I n one of his earliest books focused entirely on management, Drucker wrote that because the purpose of business is to create a customer, the business enterprise has two—and only two—basic functions: marketing and innovation. Marketing and innovation produce results; all the rest are costs.[1] Almost 20 years later in 1974 he went further. He wrote: "Marketing and innovation are the foundation areas in objective setting. It is in these two areas that a business obtains its results. It is performance and contribution in these areas for which a consumer pays."[2] Was Drucker being overly simplistic? Overly enthusiastic about these two functions? Was he mistaken? Was he denying pundits who for years have said that a business existed to make a profit, its function being a duty or responsibility toward stockholders, customers, employees, and society? Moreover, what has this to do with you if you are not a senior manager or a top executive, but a professional or a first-line supervisor? Like much of what Drucker wrote, his concepts don't just apply to big business or higher management levels, but they can and should be applied to small businesses, start-ups, governments, nonprofit organizations, and individual professionals in whatever their line of work, not just marketing. And, more than anything, they underline the fact that marketing is of great importance, not only if we are directly engaged in it, but also if we are in any part of a business or organization. Perhaps all this isn't so obvious because sometimes Drucker's ideas seem about as clear as the prophesies of Michel de Nostredame, the sixteenth century seer we know as Nostradamus.

Drucker and Nostradamus

The problem with Nostradamus's predictions is that no matter how accurate they are or are not, they are definitely difficult to interpret. Detractors point out that since they are mostly interpreted after the fact of historic occurrences, people tend to analyze them in such a way as to confirm their accuracy. Not so with Drucker. Among his economic and business predictions, he foresaw the rise of healthcare, the future of online executive education, and 50 years ago warned us of the terrible price society would pay as a result of the greed of both management and labor.

Although hoping to become a professor at the University of Cologne, he escaped Germany not months or years but days after Hitler took power, clearly demonstrating his ability to accurately visualize and forecast the shape of things to come. Still there is sometimes a touch of Nostradamus in Drucker's observations which makes it difficult for those of us trying to apply or even understand Drucker's advice. As one of Drucker's consulting clients complained years ago, "It's not that Drucker isn't explicit; he is very explicit in everything he writes. The problem is, Drucker frequently tells us what to do, but not how to do it. He asks questions that we ourselves have to answer."

Investigating the Essentiality of Innovation and Marketing

While I was struggling with Drucker's recommendations on marketing, I decided to investigate what Drucker really meant about innovation and marketing being the two basic functions of any business. If you look *innovation* up in a dictionary, you'll find descriptive words like "improvement," "advancement," and "originality." The implication is that an innovation is the introduction of something new and better. Drucker also justified the need for "something new and better" in about as strong a way as he could put it. He said that if any business continued to do what made it successful in the past, it would ultimately fail. This is counter-intuitive. It seems logical that if you've been successful, you should keep doing what helped you to succeed. Yet as usual Drucker was right. There are countless examples to support his thesis.

There was a time, not so long ago, when every real engineer used a slide rule for mathematical calculations. In fact, an engineer either carried a miniature slide rule in a pocket or a full-sized device about a foot long in a holster attached to a belt much as some carried a holstered cell phone until its size shrunk so it would fit easily in a purse or pocket. The slide rule device originated in 1612 when a Scottish nobleman turned mathematician named John Napier discovered the logarithm. This made it possible to perform multiplications and divisions by addition and subtraction. This basic idea was refined by others into hardware that consisted of one or more sliding ruler–like bars held in place between other ruled bars encapsulated by a cursor. This constituted the slide rule.

By the late seventeenth century, the slide rule was a common instrument. Engineers for the next 300 years carried this around to perform calculations on the spot and without paper and pen. The user manipulated bars and cursor to obtain the solution to complicated mathematical calculations in minutes or even seconds. Of course errors could occur because of failing eyesight or cursors that were not perfectly aligned and perpendicular to the bars. But to a couple of decimal points, they were usually within acceptable limits of accuracy for most purposes, and no engineer was without one. The companies that manufactured them, K + E, Pickett, and others, were financially solid and profitable. Their products weren't discretionary for engineers. They were essential. You'd think that all they needed to do was to keep doing what made them successful in the past and that with improvements these slide rule companies would be successful for another 300 years. Not so. Within a few months in the early 1970s, these companies no longer could sell their products. Engineers wouldn't buy them. Why should they when the handheld electronic calculator was introduced, first as a mail order product by Joe Sugarman, the same entrepreneur who later sold the BluBlocker Sun Glasses on TV, and by Sears, Roebuck and soon just about everyone.

A strange, rare occurrence? Hardly. This sort of thing happens all the time. The vinyl record companies did hundreds of millions of dollars' worth of business, but they all disappeared within two years when CDs came on the scene. Like the slide rules, vinyl records weren't overcome by a better vinyl record, but by a totally new product based on a technology that made vinyl records obsolete. Are the iPod-like devices going to replace CDs? We'll see. These are technological innovations. But it isn't only technology that causes such sudden and rapid change.

Beethoven's Wig Was Very Big

No eighteenth century gentleman would dare be seen in public without a wig. This apparel accessory was not designed as a precursor to Rogaine or to mask a balding head of hair. The popularity of wigs grew in Western Europe to discourage head lice, a serious problem of the Age of Enlightenment. However, though head lice largely disappeared as sanitary practices improved, wigs eventually became a requirement—similar to the suit and tie for upscale professionals and gentlemen of a later era. They were invariably large and powdered to give them their mostly white appearance. As a result it was not until my late teens that I learned that George Washington actually had red and not white hair. But it was only the first five U.S. presidents who wore wigs. The wearing of wigs to denote a higher social status died out in the early 1800s. So wig manufacturers either innovated very rapidly, or they went out of business, not because of technology, not because of the complete annihilation of head lice, but because of cultural changes. Innovations, whether the introduction of wigs or their discontinuance, can be considered an advancement or improvement according to social notions of what is or is not acceptable or desirable at the time. Wearing the modern bikini would have resulted in the swimmer or sun bather's arrest only a few years before French engineer Louis Reard designed and popularized this garment shortly after World War II. Yet, this innovation not only rapidly gained social acceptance, but grew into what is today an $800 million a year industry that revolutionized swimming apparel for women. It should be noted that innovation is not only needed for an existing business, but for a start-up as well.

Going into Business Without Innovation

For many years I headed a program at a university sponsored by the U.S. Small Business Administration in which professors formed and led teams of business students to do various types of consulting for small local businesses without charge. I was amazed at the numbers of businesses whose owners went into business without understanding that the mere desire to open a retail store, laundry, restaurant, barbershop, or tofu manufacturing plant (yes, we really had some of these as clients) did not automatically mean customers and success. Innovation was always needed, just like marketing. A large number were having difficulties because they didn't consider the question as to why a prospect should buy from them rather than from an established enterprise that was already serving the market in their geographic area.

Drucker on Marketing (Again)

So innovation is always needed. But why did Drucker consider marketing such an important element? The answer to this question is bound up in both selling and marketing. If you still think that marketing and selling are pretty much the same, you are wrong because you have only part of the answer. Drucker knew that not only are selling and marketing not the same, but that good selling could actually be adversarial to good marketing. How can this be? You need to remember that selling has to do with persuading a prospect to buy something that you have. But marketing has to do with already having what prospects want. Having salespeople bust their chops to sell a barely profitable product is adversarial to marketing when a different product could be sold in greater quantities with a lot less effort. Making a decision concerning what innovation to invest your time, money, and effort in is part of marketing. You can see that marketing is much broader and more strategic. We look at this in more detail in Chapter 14.

Drucker liked to say that if marketing were done perfectly, selling would be unnecessary. Of course, marketing is not done perfectly, and selling is always a requirement. However, good selling of a product or service that you shouldn't be selling in the first place can encourage you to waste time, money, and effort when you should really move on and seek something more valued by your prospect, and then to sell easier, at lower cost, and in greater quantities than would be sold in the first instance.

Drucker's Analysis

No one doubted that every business (or human endeavor, for that matter) has a purpose. Unfortunately individuals engaged in the business or who are responsible for its operation frequently misidentify this purpose. Drucker used the example of a for-profit business. Executives may think that its purpose is to create a profit. Drucker said that this was inadequate. Profit was only a means to an end. Thus Drucker reasoned that the ultimate purpose of any business was to create a customer.

Many focus on profit as the business's ultimate objective because it is an easy measurement. However this focus can actually impede success. This is why even in a recession some businesses increase their quality, level of service, or advanced products and stand head and shoulders above their competitors who try to cut corners in order to stay profitable. Customers look around with certainty at a correctly focused business and know that such a business is not only going to survive and continue to be profitable, but it's going to emerge from the recession in a highly successful fashion. The future of other businesses that have cut services, quality, or development in order to stay profitable is certain only in that their likelihood of surviving difficult times is low.

Drucker recognized that profit was needed for business survival and growth. In fact, he speculated about replacing the word "profit" with the word "responsibility." He agreed that profit was not the whole responsibility of a business, but it was the first. This was true because it was needed to cover the cost of capital, innovation, and future risks. But he also concluded that the business's ultimate purpose was definitely not profit. Rather its purpose was to create a highly satisfied consumer or user of whatever the product or service is. Drucker saw that those businesses that prosper in this way maintain their focus on purpose and have the advantage.

Important Relationships

The word "business" is actually one synonym for "responsibility," which is probably why Drucker contemplated using this word. "Profit" also means "return." In other words, you invest money in something, and you get a return on that investment. In some business disciplines money has been invested in your responsibility for which you expect to receive a return or profit, but you are not directly connected with selling the product. How is that profit measured? Rarely by money. Rather it is measured by the effectiveness or efficiency of your output. Let's say you are responsible for recruiting. Your recruitment of qualified engineers, salespeople, or whatever specialty is needed for the appropriate department is the resulting return on investment. This return is actually evaluated by your "customer," which internally is the department you service by your recruitment. Success means satisfied users of what you supply, and that is the ultimate purpose of your business. This is true of any internal business or responsibility, from production to sales and beyond. Identifying and focusing on the real purpose of your business is necessary for success because:

- Regardless of the area of the company in which you work, you are involved in "a business."
- Your output must result in a profit or a return on the investment made.
- This profit is evaluated by your customer, the organization that your "business" supports.

This implies that both correct purpose and "profit" are needed at many levels within an organization and for many different departments in order to create satisfied users of the "product" of that department.

Again, the Two (and Only Two) Functions of Any Business for Success

Drucker's conclusions that the two basic functions of any business are marketing and innovation may lead you to the conclusion that he was talking about selling and a sales job. He wasn't. As we saw previously, Drucker noted not only that marketing and selling were not the same, but that the two might not even be complementary.

Drucker wrote that marketing begins with the question, "What does the other party want?" Then we need to know, "What does it value?" "What are its goals?" "What does it consider results?" Marketing not only determines who the other party is, but it may also determine which other party we plan to target. So marketing concerns the strategy of any human endeavor.

Anyone who has completed Marketing 101 will tell you that tactically, marketing is described by the "marketing mix" of the four Ps. These are product, price, promotion, and place (distribution). Promotion is further categorized into subsets, one of which is personal selling. This means that selling is part of marketing and supportive of it. The general assumption is that the better the sales job, the better the overall marketing (strategy) effort and that there is an obvious and automatic connection. I read once where a well-known Harvard professor wrote that good tactics in marketing could overcome a poor strategy. No it can't! Again, selling might not only not be congruent or complementary to marketing, but successful selling of the wrong product or the right product to the wrong market results in misallocation of scarce company resources, even if the selling is successful.

Is This True for All Human Endeavors?

If any enterprise has only these two basic functions, we would expect to see this as a part of virtually any human endeavor where the purpose was to create a customer. Today, logistics, training, research and development, and even some combat units in the military routinely use words like "customer," "service," and "price" as part of everyday vocabulary, whereas in the past the military spoke of "supported units" and "duty," and "price" referring only to casualties sustained and nothing else. For example, a training organization realizes that it has an important customer who is not the trainee. This customer is the combat organization that acquires these trained soldiers after the completion of basic training. Basic trainees are expected to possess essential military skills such as the ability to operate as a small unit team, rifle marksmanship, and field skills so that the trainees can be integrated into a combat-ready organization as fully functioning members. This training is price and time sensitive, and the level of service provided represents a cost that must be carefully considered. While the training organization may not be able to choose its target customer as part of its overall strategy, it is expected to innovate, make changes in training, and do everything else it can to provide the most highly trained and capable soldiers possible within the restrictions of time and budget. In short, its success is based on marketing and innovation.

Apply the Two Basic Functions to Your Organization

Let's apply these functions to a business or any other type of organization in which you may be involved. If an HR manager is tasked with furnishing a variety of qualified candidates for varying levels of positions in widely different organizations within the company, these different organizations are really customers. If success rests on only two functions: marketing and innovation, such a manager faces a number of problems. Economic conditions are such that budgets are severely restricted. This affects the numbers of individuals that can be hired by your "customers," compensation levels that can be paid, level of experience of new hires, money that can be allocated for advertising openings, and a lot more.

Let's look first at Drucker's recommendation to start with the question, "What does the other party want?" Well obviously in this instance the customer wants qualified people, but there is a lot more. What does the customer value? Different departments value different aspects of gaining qualified employees. One department may value the absolutely best people it can obtain. Another department may value speed of recruitment above all else. It needs people *now*. It wants competent people. It doesn't want a lot of time spent on trying to recruit candidates who are so highly qualified that they demand compensation that cannot be afforded or those whose education and experience are so rare that very few are available. Good marketing in this instance means understanding the department's goals both short and long term and what it would consider good results. For the customer focused on speed, you may recruit the top three candidates in the country for the position with the thought that after interviewing all three, your customer can pick the perfect employee. If the customer needs an immediate hire, he or she may want you to send the first candidate in today and forget about providing multiple choices. Ongoing economic and business conditions in your industry always mean additional tactical problems. If you no longer have the budget for extensive media advertising, you might need to use innovation and develop new methods of candidate acquisition or screening.

Of course this is only one example in one department with one kind of requirement. In all cases you must adapt Drucker's concept of the true purpose of business and the two essential functions of marketing and innovation to your responsibility. For top managers it means organizing and motivating the organization toward these two functions, marketing and innovation, regardless of their functional area or responsibilities.

Chapter 4

Drucker's Marketing View

*T*he *View* is the name of a popular television morning talk show on ABC. It features a group of five women of different backgrounds and experiences discussing and vigorously arguing their views of the events of the day. Drucker had a view, too, which preceded this show by many years. It never appeared on television, but he did argue his point of view over many years. And he called it "the marketing view." Much to his chagrin, it came to be called "The Total Marketing Approach." He did not like this term because he felt it was too fancy and frequently misrepresented an entity that is not really a total marketing approach or his marketing view at all. Regardless, the name persisted. No matter what you call it, the concept was and is immensely important to marketing thought.

In Chapter 3 we saw how Drucker concluded that business has but two basic functions, innovation and marketing, and that these two functions are also basic to setting performance objectives, and not just performance in sales. If marketing is basic to setting performance objectives of all types, then marketing is basic to all aspects of businesses and all businesses and even more. In a discussion with distinguished marketing professor Philip Kotler, published in 1990, Drucker said:

What you are saying is that marketing in an organization is everybody's business, certainly everybody who has anything to do with the customer. So you are talking not about a function—though there is specific work—you're talking of a basic commitment. In talking of marketing in the non-profit organization, you are talking of the basic action that results in an organization that is both dedicated and positioned to satisfy its basic purpose.[1]

And that is exactly how Drucker saw things. We may refer to marketing as a function, but he saw it as much broader than that—as a basic commitment or as a view. This was a theme that ran throughout Drucker's writings and his analyses and thinking about business from his earliest work. In the *Practice of Management,* his first book devoted specifically to the topic, he wrote about marketing, "It encompasses the entire business. It is the whole business seen from the point of view of its final result, that is, from the customer's point of view. Concern and responsibility for marketing must therefore permeate all areas of the enterprise."[2] This concept is confirmed again in Drucker's famous *The Five Most Important Questions You Will Ever Ask About Your Organization*[3]:

1. What is our mission?
2. Who is our customer?
3. What does our customer value?
4. What are our results?
5. What is our plan?

Every one of these five questions, either directly or indirectly, has to do with marketing.

So Drucker championed what has come to be called, like the term or not, "The Total Marketing Approach." However, as I said earlier, he didn't much like the name even though it was based largely on what at the time he had been writing about for the previous 10 years as he encouraged management to take what he termed "the marketing view." In 1964 he wrote:

For a decade now the "marketing view" has been widely publicized. It has even acquired a fancy name: The Total Marketing Approach. Not everything that goes by that name deserves it. "Marketing" has become a fashionable term. But a gravedigger remains a gravedigger even when called a "mortician"—only the cost of burial goes up. Many a sales manager has been renamed "marketing vice president"—and all that happened was that costs and salaries went up.[4]

Selling Is Not Part of the Marketing View

It may surprise some people, but Drucker not only distinguished between marketing and selling as separate activities, but, as we see in later chapters, he took on marketing orthodoxy by recommending that these two activities not necessarily be organizationally integrated and, as we've seen from the beginning, even that marketing and selling could be at odds with each other. Clearly Drucker meant something entirely different and pervasive by the term "marketing" in his marketing view.

Implementing Drucker's Marketing View

The implementation of Drucker's marketing view is based on four major instructions to marketing and other executives:

1. Market marketing to all internal organizations at all levels.
2. Understand the difference between sales and marketing.
3. Educate and lead.
4. Approach the business from the customer's point of view.

Market Marketing to All Internal Organizations at All Levels

Twenty years ago, total quality management (TQM) swept this country, and to some extent, the world. I was never a big fan of TQM for a variety of reasons. It struck me as a fad that claimed it couldn't work unless everybody believed in and practiced it. As a result, some organizations put the screws on, and if you were a nonbeliever, you needed to keep your mouth shut or you were punished. That pretty much eliminated naysayers, which is a clever and effective, if highly unethical, way of forcing adoption. Finally it downplayed the objective in favor of the process. In other words, pay no attention to the customer needs, values, or preferences. Focus instead on the process fulfilling them. I don't think Drucker would have ever bought that one, although he did say some nice words about the intent of TQM at one time. When I found a military manual on TQM listing me as a TQM guru, I lost all faith.

Moreover, there were (and are) a number of good things about TQM that I liked at that time and still do. I liked the concept of continuous improvement. I liked the concept of ownership. I liked the concept of involvement and participation in decision making. And who can argue with the maintenance and improvement of quality? However, in my mind it all boiled down to good leadership, which is ageless. I found myself frequently quoting Drucker that the first systematic book on leadership was written by Xenophon 2,000 years ago, and it was still the best. So it was no great surprise to me when shortly after The Wallace Company, a Houston oil supply company that won the prestigious Malcolm Baldrige National Quality Award, filed for protection under the Chapter 11 bankruptcy law[5] and that when *Fortune* magazine did studies on corporations before and after implementing TQM, it frequently found a negative rather than a positive impact.[6] Stifling dissent is never a good thing, and eventually TQM was reevaluated and made more reasonable.

However, TQM did have one very positive use even during the heyday of its popularity when speaking out against it could be hazardous to one's career. When I found myself getting bad service from government organizations, telephone companies, airlines, or whatever, I would say, "I guess TQM hasn't hit your organization yet." Of course it almost always had, and most organizational members had been extensively trained in it. I saw an instant change of attitude, and I received help that had previously been denied to me. I wish that magic sentence still worked, but the TQM myth doesn't have the clout it once had.

Marketing marketing is not as difficult as it may first seem. Since all performance objectives eventually relate to marketing, all you need to do is show how this is so. No one seems to argue with how sales performance relates, but consider other departments. For example, engineering's work on low production cost for a new product helps to determine the price and profitability of the product in the marketplace. Engineering's selection of the right materials affects durability, reliability, and replacement costs to the customer. Human resources' ability to develop policies that will retain the best people affects all departments including marketing's ability to develop strategy and people with the contacts for foreign programs and joint ventures. Accounting and finance performance factors again affect all departments which indirectly affect marketing, while impacting on marketing's ability to forecast costs accurately.

Of course there is more you can do with actual examples. The point is that if you want the marketing view to succeed in your organization, you need to start pervasive promoting of the marketing view as TQM was once promoted and taught. In that way, everyone understands it and why it is important and will try to implement it.

Once Again, Understand the Difference Between Sales and Marketing

The difference between sales and marketing is very simple, but oh so important. Years ago a company contacted me to interview for a job as project manager. It paid my expenses to fly to Los Angeles. As it happened, the company's business was developing radar systems. I had lots of experience in the Air Force and at a major aerospace company managing the development of aerospace equipment. So I was pretty confident in my ability to function in a similar role at that company, and I thought that the interview went pretty well. The president called me several days later. He told me that while the project manager's job was open if I wanted it, they needed a vice president of marketing badly and asked if I was interested. Although I had an MBA, I had never had a single course in marketing, and I had never been involved in sales since the time I had been a newspaper boy at age 11. I told him that I had no current sales experience and therefore that I wasn't interested. He responded that marketing isn't sales and that marketing was not a more sophisticated word for selling either. I doubted this although he made an attempt to explain. I thanked him, but turned the job down.

That was a major mistake and was entirely the result of my ignorance. However, managers with a lot more experience than I ever had in those days continue to make the same mistake today. No wonder Drucker used the example of the sales manager being made marketing vice president. Drucker said that the skills, experience, education, even the personalities of the two jobs differed. He criticized the marketing textbooks, which even today group sales management along with advertising and promotion and place the two functions together under one marketing executive. Using a typical Druckerism, he wrote, "The experience of large national manufacturers of branded and mass-marketed consumer goods has been, however, that this overall marketing job is impossible. Such a business needs both high effectiveness in field selling—that is, in moving goods—and high effectiveness in advertising and promotion—that is, in moving people."[7]

Since many top executives, and even sales and marketing executives, don't understand this, we need to make doubly certain that we understand it and that everyone in the organization understands these very basic but important facts and can distinguish between the two terms. Theodore Levitt, onetime professor of business administration at the Harvard Business School and author of "Marketing Myopia," one of the most famous articles ever written about marketing, confirmed Drucker's description of the difference between sales and marketing by stating that "selling focuses on the needs of the seller and the need to convert product to cash, while marketing focuses on the needs of the buyer and the need to satisfy the customer through the products produced."[8]

Another way of looking at this is that the salesperson influences the customer to buy what the organization has already produced. The marketer finds out what the customer wants and influences the organization to produce it.

In any case you don't need to look far to see that despite Drucker's repeated warnings and comments and those of others as well, many do not recognize that there really is a difference, and I suspect that this is especially true for those practicing specialties outside of marketing. So don't assume everybody knows this basic concept or doesn't gloss over this difference. Members of all departments of the corporation or organization must know and understand this basic difference. Ensure that they do.

Lead the Organization

Of course, it helps if you head up the entire organization. But it really doesn't matter if you are the marketing boss or no boss at all. Research on leadership demonstrates that you can lead from any level. Only the approach that you use may differ.

If you are the president of the entire organization, there is a lot you can do. You can mandate training from top to bottom. You can organize corporate resources around marketing objectives. You can create metrics supporting marketing activities in every department. You can publicize results. You can publicly give recognition for success. You have the authority to mandate and the resources to persuade. You can reorganize and restructure your organization to optimize the marketing view. You have the capability of creating the greatest changes toward the marketing view in the shortest amount of time.

If you are in charge of the marketing unit only, you can still do a lot, but you need to work more by persuasion. You need to convince your boss of what you want to do and develop a plan as to how to do it and measurements for quantifying outcomes. Your boss and others too will want to know exactly why you want to do these promotions and how you are going to do them. They definitely don't want you minimizing the contributions of other business specialties whose hardworking members are trying to do their best in their respective areas of responsibility. It is sometimes difficult to get the idea across without seeming to appear to be saying that you want to run everything. So your persuasion and your presentations may require some work. With approval of managers of other departments, you can send your minions out to convince others of what you are trying to do both one on one and through group presentations to other internal organizations. You can help other departments to develop and implement meaningful measurements of progress. You can analyze and promote the results you are attaining through the overall organization and solicit additional ideas through your marketing organization. Finally, you can make recommendations to other organizations and to executives in top management.

What if you are a sole marketer? Can you still do anything? Absolutely! Again, you need to persuade your boss, have a plan for implementation, and also have some tools for measuring results. However, being a sole practitioner has an additional advantage. It demonstrates your abilities while it allows you to showcase your ideas and show leadership outside your own area. A young woman who was my graduate student did this and, within nine months after being allowed to implement her ideas, was promoted to director level. So implementing Drucker's marketing view can have career advantages.

Approach the Business from the Customers' Point of View

The business involves everything. This includes products, strategy, personnel, policies, and more. The questions of who our customers are and what do they value sound basic. So do the questions: Where are they located? How much do they spend? What do they read and listen to? How can we best promote to them? How can we best distribute to them? What are their biases? Of course there are a lot more questions. The point is that we must examine these things from the customers' eyes, not our own. Even geniuses sometimes err. Steve Jobs once introduced the Lisa Computer which was designed to be so self-contained that an owner wouldn't need to work with its inner workings and hidden mechanisms. The customer didn't have a choice. But from the customers' viewpoint, being able to tinker was important, and so the product failed. Dell built its success by taking the opposite approach and letting customers design their own computer system.

Some businesses fail not because they have a poor product, but because the service is inadequate from the customers' point of view. The essentials of the University of Phoenix were proposed by John Sperling in the late 1960s when he was a professor at San Jose State University. He recognized that working students were treated as second-class citizens. They couldn't get the classes they wanted because of their jobs. As a result, it took additional years for them to graduate. Sperling presented the solutions to these and other problems to the administrators at his university for adoption. They didn't see the need. In their opinion students wanting an education needed to adapt to their model. So, beginning with eight students, Sperling started his own school. He recognized that students would pay a premium to get the product that they wanted. From those original eight, the University of Phoenix grew to one of the largest schools in the country with a half a million students. Other schools, including California public universities adopted many of Sperling's ideas, but it was a little too late.

It doesn't much matter whether you adopt Drucker's marketing view or the more sophisticated moniker, "The Total Marketing Approach." They are the same thing. What is important is that you adopt it.

Chapter 5

Marketing Is Leadership

One of Drucker's far-reaching and integrative ideas is little known. It is that good leadership is essentially marketing. He actually called leadership a "marketing job."[1] Unfortunately, many leadership scholars and practitioners ignore this concept or assume that it has to do entirely with selling and persuasion. While persuasion and making sales and marketing, too, are certainly a part of leadership, this idea is based on Drucker's view that all knowledge workers are partners in an organization. As partners, they cannot be simply ordered around or managed. They must be led, and this integrates persuasion with strategic thinking, segmentation, and many other elements of marketing. So the practice of leadership, Drucker concluded, is marketing. This conclusion can have far-reaching consequences for the practice of both business disciplines.

If Leadership Is Marketing, Then Marketing Is Leadership

If leadership is essentially marketing, than the reverse must also be true. This is important because just as leaders gain from applying research done in marketing, marketers gain from research done in leadership.

I was teaching and researching in both disciplines. I approached Drucker about a particular study I intended to undertake that was based on my own and observed experiences of leadership in battle, as well as the experiences of battle leaders who went on to successful civilian careers. Drucker encouraged me and shared his observation that, "In no other type of leadership must the leader make decisions based on less or less reliable information."[2] That's just for openers. Battle leadership probably represents the greatest leadership challenge for any leader. This is an environment in which conditions are always demanding and severe. There are terrible hazards. There are poor "working conditions." As noted by Drucker, there is probably greater uncertainty than in any other type of human activity. Although I appreciated the value of what I personally learned about leadership in battle, I wondered whether there were underlying principles or lessons in battle that were at the root of all leadership success. If the answer to this were known, leaders from all organizations could use these principles to dramatically increase productivity and the likelihood of success in any organization.

This research involved a survey sent to more than 200 former combat leaders and conversations with hundreds more. I especially sought those who had become successful in the corporate world or in other nonmilitary activities after their war experiences. Among the responses I received in the initial phase, 62 were from generals and admirals. However, I also received responses from younger men and women of all ranks and ages who had served in leadership roles. The research involved all military services. I asked these leaders what, if anything, they had learned from leadership in battle, and I asked about their success or lack of it in adapting these lessons to their civilian careers. I found that while there were successful leaders practicing many different styles, there were universal principles that successful leaders followed to dramatically boost productivity and achieve extraordinary success in all types of organizations.

Surprisingly, I discovered that 95 percent of the responses I received boiled down to only eight basic principles. Each of these battle leaders had one or more of these eight principles help them achieve extraordinary results in their civilian careers. More than a few wrote special notes or letters to express their support for my project. They knew its value, and they didn't want to see it wasted.

In a latter phase of my research, I interviewed other successful senior business leaders and reviewed dozens of corporate situations and the actions taken by these corporations' senior leaders. Some had combat experience; others did not. Some had developed their own lists of principles of leadership over the years. While their lists differed from each other, they invariably included the eight ideas in varied form that I had culled from my surveys. I also looked at 7,000 years of recorded history to confirm these concepts. There was an abundance of evidence to support these principles. Without argument there are hundreds of excellent techniques and rules that people may follow for leading others. But these eight universal principles always seem to be present, and my conclusion is that they are always essential. In sharing these results with Peter over lunch, he was in strong agreement with the results and gave me further encouragement on publishing and speaking about them, which I have done extensively to leadership audiences since 1998. However, this book is the first time that I have utilized Drucker's concept that marketing is leadership and explained it with examples.

You could violate many of these principles at times and still succeed because people can tolerate almost anything, but they will not tolerate a violation of the first principle: maintain absolute integrity. No one can guarantee success in every instance because there are other factors that might override anything a leader may be able to do or avoid doing. But there is no question that if you follow these principles, your chances of success are much increased. Following are the eight principles that I uncovered in my research. If you are a practicing leader or a leader researcher, you will probably recognize most:

1. Maintain absolute integrity.
2. Know your stuff.
3. Declare your expectations.
4. Show uncommon commitment.
5. Expect positive results.
6. Take care of your people.
7. Put duty before self.
8. Get out in front.

What do these principles of leadership, universal or not, have to do with marketing? It was during lunch with legendary direct marketer Bob Hemmings that I began to suspect that these universal leadership principles might also have significant value when applied to marketing.

Bob Hemmings had fought during World War II as a Marine Corps company commander, and later a Marine Corps aviator. After the war he entered the field of sales and marketing and began a career that continues today, more than 60 years later. During this period he built a major advertising agency and became a mainstay for teaching direct marketing for the Direct Marketing Association (DMA) all over the world. His influence has been such that he was inducted into the DMA's Hall of Fame. If there is a "grand old man" of direct marketing, Bob Hemmings fits the bill.

Recently Bob wrote a book for young entrants into the marketing field, *How to Jump-Start Your Career*. In it he relates how he interviewed a recent MBA graduate who was seeking a job.[3] Despite being educated at a leading university, this young man had failed to persuade Bob that he should be hired. In analyzing Bob's description of what had occurred, it was clear that the reason he failed to persuade Bob was that he ignored almost every one of these eight principles. Yet each represented an opportunity that could easily have led to his successfully reaching what was his marketing objective: selling himself to a potential employer. So let's look at each of these principles as being a principle of marketing rather than "the eight universal laws of leadership."

The First Principle of Marketing: Maintain Absolute Integrity

If you say something, make sure it is the truth. If you later realize that you have misspoken, correct yourself. If you say or promise you will do something, make certain you do it, no matter what.

Today Arby's is a highly successful fast food restaurant chain, with over 3,600 restaurants worldwide. However, Leonard Roberts became CEO at a time when the business was doing very poorly. He turned the corporation around when sales had been falling 10 to 15 percent a year. He did this by promising help, money, and additional support to Arby's franchisees. He delivered, and sales soared. Because of his success Roberts was appointed to the board of directors. The first meeting he attended lasted 15 minutes. Eager for more profits, Arby's owner declared that he was going to withdraw the help Roberts gave the franchisees. Even bonuses promised and earned by Roberts's staff would not be paid. Roberts resigned from the board, and the owner retaliated by firing Roberts as CEO.[4]

Unfortunately Roberts went directly into another situation that challenged his integrity. He became chairman and CEO of a chain of 2,000 restaurants headquartered in Nashville, Tennessee, called Shoney's, only to learn that Shoney's was the subject of the largest racial discrimination lawsuit in history. Unfortunately this was not some issue of a misunderstanding. The policy of the Shoney's chairman was to not hire African Americans. He enforced this policy by firing any restaurant manager who disobeyed these orders. "The settlement of that suit was the thing I am most proud of in my life," said Len Roberts. "The former chairman agreed to pay up and settle. This saved the company. But I had to agree to resign after he did so. This was my second time out of work in almost as many years. My stand on integrity was getting kind of hard on my wife and kids. However, I knew it had to be done."

Roberts became the CEO of Radio Shack after leaving Shoney's. A year after that, he took on the additional job as CEO of the entire Tandy Corporation. This began a 10-year career of success with many honors. *Brandweek* magazine named him Retail Marketer of the Year for his accomplishments. According to Roberts, "You cannot fake it—you must stand up for what is right regardless. You cannot maintain your integrity until it hurts your pocketbook or risks your job. You cannot maintain your integrity 90 percent and be a successful leader—it's got to be 100 percent."[5] Drucker clearly agreed. Roberts's success as a marketer was based firmly on this first principle.

The Second Principle of Marketing: Know Your Stuff

Bill Gates was the chairman of the Microsoft Corporation which he founded and built himself. His personal fortune has been estimated at $58 billion and possibly more. He achieved much of this success while he was still in his twenties. He became a billionaire when he was only 31. Was he just there at the right time and right place? Was Gates just lucky?

If you look at Gates's career, you can see that he took the time to know his stuff. His secret was not office politics, but knowledge and expertise. Gates learned how to program computers when he was barely a teenager. By the time he entered high school, he knew enough to lead a group of computer programmers, and he computerized his school's payroll system. He learned marketing by starting and running a company that sold traffic-counting systems to local governments. By the time he entered Harvard, he was already an acknowledged computer expert, knew sales, knew marketing, and knew management. He spent his freshman year at Harvard preparing the language for the world's first microcomputer. In his second year he dropped out of Harvard and eventually founded the Microsoft Corporation. The fact that he was still in his twenties and was not a college graduate was unimportant. That he knew how to create and market his creations was.

The Third Principle of Marketing: Declare Your Expectations

You declare your expectations in a number of ways. One of them is by setting your goals. From tactical selling to strategic marketing, this is essential. It was as a newspaper boy that I first learned the importance of "hitting my numbers" in signing up new customers. Goals like these must be declared at all levels, from the individual on up to the very top level of the organization. Let's call these expectations "visions." Almost invariably, compelling visions are the most important component of success.

All successful organizations, whether small businesses, Fortune 500 companies, athletic teams, combat units, or even countries must be built on clear and compelling expectations. This vision provides direction for everyone. It guides all action and tells everyone exactly where the organization is going. Properly involved in this vision, members of the organization willingly work toward it.

Barack Obama electrified the world by becoming, against all odds, the first African American president of the United States. He was an individual who but a few years previously was virtually unknown. He had been in the U.S. Senate less than two years. His primary opponent in his own party was Senator Hillary Clinton. Not only did Clinton have eight years in the Senate, but she was extremely well known as former President Bill Clinton's wife. She had many accomplishments to her credit and many political contacts. If Obama somehow succeeded in gaining the nomination of his party over Clinton, he would run against a popular war hero, another senator. Senator John McCain had even more years of experience in the Senate than Clinton and a long list of accomplishments. Yet Barack Obama won. How was this possible?

Of course there were many reasons including Obama's intelligence, charisma, and likability and the fact that he ran a nearly flawless campaign against an unpopular administration. Chuck Todd, who had been NBC News Political Director and was named NBC White House Correspondent after the election, wrote a book analyzing that 2008 presidential campaign titled *How Barack Obama Won* (Vintage, 2009). One of the interesting facts that he uncovered that he mentioned in a *Today Show* interview with Matt Lauer was that of the three leading candidates, Obama was the only candidate to state his expectations for the country, and of the three, he was the only one to make an announcement speech declaring both his candidacy and his vision.[6] You can't get "there" until you know where "there" is.

The Fourth Principle of Marketing: Show Uncommon Commitment

Only six months after its founding, the Dell Computer Corporation became the number one retailer on the Internet. Dell's sales grew at the rate of 20 percent each month. In one year, revenues exploded by 47 percent to $7.8 billion, and profit by 91 percent to $518 million. The secret was service and delivery as represented by speed. Founder and CEO Michael Dell said, "Speed is everything in this business. We're setting the pace for the industry."[7]

It was Michael Dell's absolute commitment to this concept that motivated his employees to an equal commitment to get the job done in a way that won the respect of customers and competitors alike.[8] By 2008, though Dell had faltered at times over the years, it claimed the position of number one PC provider in the United States and number two behind Hewlett-Packard worldwide.[9]

No one on your marketing team is going to be more committed than you. And that includes vendors and subcontractors as well. The fact that you are committed proves that what you want done is important and that you aren't going to quit. Does that sound a little like what we want from our salespeople?

The Fifth Principle of Marketing: Expect Positive Results

Expecting positive results can work miracles in any marketing campaign. However, the reverse is also true. Supercuts, Inc., was a revolutionary concept in the 1970s when it was introduced. It replaced the old barbershops and beauty shops with low-cost, no-nonsense, unisex hairstyling salons. It was instantly successful. It grew rapidly, and its franchises expanded across the country. Unfortunately at some point the organization began to doubt itself. As an organization, success no longer felt certain.

As sometimes happens when marketers are fearful, the company began to reduce advertising, and in the franchise business, it reduced support for franchisees. The franchisees formed an association to protect their interests. Corporate leaders attempted to stop them from doing this. The result was a class-action lawsuit against the corporation. Low sales, low morale, and all indicators were heading south. This continued until an investment company bought the company and brought in a new CEO by the name of Betsy Burton. Burton expected to win. She boosted advertising, actually helped the franchisees at corporate expense to form their association, and took other actions that confirmed her beliefs about Supercuts' positive future. Within 16 months, profits were up by 10 percent. Within three years, franchisees had double-digit sales increases. Revenue grew from $126 million to over $170 million. The corporation added more than 100 new franchisees.[10] Franchisees, employees, and management all expected positive results because Betsy Burton, a great leader and a great marketer, expected them first.

The Sixth Principle of Marketing: Take Care of Your People

"Your people" can be seen as either your employees or your customers or both. The two go together. That is, if you take care of your people (employees), they tend to pay more attention to taking care of your customers. I recently ate at a restaurant after an absence of more than a year. It no longer was the restaurant I once knew. Food quality had declined as had customer service. The serving staff was uniformly ill-humored. The owner, completely clueless, was actually heard to remark, "Well, if we had more customers, I could afford a better cook and pay for higher-quality ingredients and better waitresses. It's all due to the recession." He was blaming his prospects and customers for choosing not to eat at his restaurant. His response to his problems was to lower compensation, hire cheaper help, and cut service and quality of food in other ways. Shortly after my last visit he went out of business. New management bought the place and had an entirely different attitude. Managers took care of both customers and employees. I went back because I noticed that the restaurant was overflowing with customers, and I was curious about the reason. The servers were courteous and friendly. The service was superb, the food excellent, and the prices very reasonable. I think this is especially true in a recession, but taking care of your people is always a major principle of marketing.

The Seventh Principle of Marketing: Put Duty Before Self

Duty before self means that your customer and your employees should always come before your own wants and needs. Your employees and customers are rarely impressed by your compensation, the expensive car you drive, or the perks of your position. Let me put this another way. They may be impressed, but this doesn't help in your success at marketing your product or service. This is because the emphasis is on the advantages you receive and not the benefits for your employees and customers.

More than 2,000 years ago, the father of Cyrus the Great of Persia was trying to teach the young Cyrus how to gain the trust and loyalty of others. You can call them employees or customers. Cyrus thought that the best way was to reward those who obeyed his wishes and to punish those who didn't. His father agreed that this would work in many instances, but not all. He said that there was a much easier way of gaining trust and loyalty that would always work. And that was simply to look after the interests of others better than they would or could even look after them themselves. Cyrus followed this lesson throughout his lifetime, and he found that it always worked. In one instance, he conquered a neighboring kingdom. However, he treated the defeated king and his people so well that this king insisted on paying Cyrus twice the tribute required under the terms of the treaty. Political leaders as well as marketers would find far more success by implementing this single principle in their dealings with others.

The Eighth Principle of Marketing: Get Out in Front

I don't know where the idea came from that successful marketing is simply about having a great idea. The theory is that after you get the great idea, you turn the light switch on and begin the process of marketing it and work happily ever after. Yes, innovation and marketing are the basic elements, but successful marketers know that this is not how it works. There is more to it than that. If you want any marketing campaign to work, you need to be out in front during the implementation. There's no such thing as sitting in an air-conditioned office and simply thinking your way to success. You need to be where the action is, where you can see and be seen. Good marketers find ways of perpetuating this process and of constantly being out in front.

Beth Pritchard was the chief executive of the nation's leading bath shop chain, Bath & Body Works, which specializes in lotions, bath items, personal care items, and home fragrances. In addition to her corporate duties and responsibilities, she spent two days a month working "in the trenches," in an ordinary Bath & Body Works boutique. She didn't sit around observing or spending her time handing out advice to employees. She saw and was seen; she taught and she learned; but mostly she worked. She set up displays, stocked shelves, and arranged gift baskets. "Though," claims Beth Pritchard, "I'm not really good on the cash register." Whether she was good on the cash register or not seems not to have mattered. The power of getting out in front paid off. The cash registers in her stores were full. When she took over Bath & Body Works in 1991, it had 95 stores and sales of $20 million. Five years later, the number of stores had increased to a whopping 750, and sales hit $753 million.[11] Maybe this is why she went on to a number of other senior and top management positions in top companies.[12]

It is not surprising that if we accept Drucker's premise that leadership is marketing, it is equally true that marketing is leadership. If you apply the principles of one discipline, you will automatically apply the principles of the other for a supercharged benefit in marketing.

Part II
Innovation and Entrepreneurship

Chapter 6

Where the Best Innovations Come From: The Seven Mothers of Invention

I t seems like a thousand years ago that as a young man (really young) I was appointed director of research and development for a medium-sized company that developed most of the oxygen breathing masks for the aircrews of the U.S. armed forces, many foreign air forces, and the airlines. It also developed protective helmets used in military aircraft and tanks.

I did have some experience in leading small research and development projects in the Air Force and with large aircraft development projects abroad. However, it remained to be seen whether this experience plus my flying background would give me an advantage in selecting bright, new, innovative ideas having to do with aviation for a small company where every dollar spent was very limited and critical. Until then, I always thought that the big problem for all organizations was thinking up new ideas. In those days I hadn't heard of Drucker's claims for the importance of innovation, but it didn't take a lot of brains to see that staying ahead of the competition was critical for all organizations and that innovation was the key to success.

I Was Both Right and Wrong About My Preconceived Ideas

I was right about innovation being the key to success. However, I thought that my big challenge would be coming up with new product ideas to develop. I was wrong about that! I was on the job only three days before my budget would have been exceeded several times over with the number of bright, "breakthrough" ideas that kept coming across my desk for potential funding and development. I was leading a team of a half-dozen project engineers. Pretty small potatoes for a lot of organizations and a miniscule number considering the ideas that were soon directed my way. I could have easily put 10 times that number of development engineers to work if I had the budget to do so, which I didn't. Moreover, the ideas kept coming and coming and coming.

My boss was the company president. He had held my job some years earlier, and this should have helped, but it only added to my burden. He had a love of innovation which unfortunately was unrestrained by cost or limited resources. I think that he secretly wished that he still had my job. In the interim my job had defeated five managers, all far more talented than I in engineering expertise. One, as I recall, had even been president of a major national engineering association. My predecessors had all been fired or left the company of their own volition. I actually tracked one and questioned him. The reasons he gave for his dismissal were unclear. Everyone, including our customers, agreed that our research and development efforts were largely unsuccessful, but no one seemed to understand why. As a new hire from outside, I certainly didn't understand the problem, but I soon did. The problem was not too few but too many innovative ideas.

In addition to suggestions from other sources, every Monday I would be called to the president's office where he would strongly suggest that I pursue one of the new ideas that he had come up with over the weekend. At first, like my more brilliant predecessors, I actually tried to accommodate him. While I might ignore many of the suggestions from other sources, this was my boss, and I would need to find some way to stand up to him and refuse or I would soon join the ranks of my brilliant, but failed, predecessors. In self-defense, I eventually evolved a tactic that proved effective.

When I went to see him on a Monday morning, I would bring along my list of current projects and their cost and status and where each fit into my research and development budget. He would introduce his new idea, and we would agree that it was unique and had potential. Together, we would then estimate its cost and the time and manpower needed to develop it.

I would next show him my list of current projects under development and ask (innocently), "I know that you don't want to increase my budget. Which project should I drop so that we will have the money and manpower so I can proceed?" He would always struggle with himself over this question for a minute or two and finally begrudgingly manage to instruct me, "Well, get to it as soon as you can." To which, I would agree. Of course, if one of these ideas had exceptional potential, I would either recommend delaying one project with lower potential still on my list or recommend a temporary increase of my budget for that specific project. However this enabled me to keep budget, time, and results in balance and under control, and I managed to survive the job.

The Danger of the Bright Idea

Peter thought that the good idea was an excellent tactic. He told me that there would always be more good ideas than time, money, and engineers available to develop them. In addition, I learned that he well appreciated the danger of what he called "the bright idea," such as those that came along all too frequently from my boss. The "bright idea" was his term for an innovation that was vague and elusive and accepted for development without much real analysis. He did not disagree that one could "hit a home run" with a single bright idea, and he was happy to give me examples of bright ideas that had gone on to make millions of dollars for their originators including the zipper, the ballpoint pen, the aerosol spray can, and more. But he said that these were exceptions and should be ignored regarding how innovation should be approached and managed.

"The problem is," Drucker said, "that bright ideas are the riskiest and least successful source of innovative opportunities." He estimated that probably only 1 in 500 made any money above the investment costs, and he suggested that relying on the bright idea for innovation was akin to gambling at Las Vegas and was almost certain to lead to similar results. The solution, he maintained, was systematic analysis using seven precise sources of innovative ideas. This, he declared, was purposeful innovation, the kind that all of us must pursue regardless of our specialty, discipline, or functional area. He strongly recommended that we avoid the bright idea at all costs. Let's see what he did recommend.[1]

The First Source: The Unexpected

Drucker wrote that the unexpected was the richest source of opportunity for successful innovation, but one that was not only neglected but frequently actively rejected by managers of all disciplines.

At the Eastman Kodak Co. Engineer Harry Coover, Jr., asked a lab associate to try a cyanoacrylate as a heat resistant polymer for jet airplane canopies. The associate accidentally destroyed an expensive instrument when he brought two prisms in contact with each other while taking a reading. He thought he would be fired, but instead Coover tried sticking everything together using the polymer. He realized that through these unexpected results, they had stumbled on an extraordinarily strong adhesive. Eastman Kodak began marketing the powerful bonding agent now known worldwide as Super Glue®.[2]

The Second Source: The Incongruities

Incongruities are unexpected too, but in a different way. One expects a certain result, but instead the opposite occurs. Frequently, this has to do with economic results. In the 1950s someone found that companies that dominated markets were more profitable than those that did not dominate. This led to portfolio management and the well-known BCG matrix in which relative high market share was considered desirable and became either a cash cow or a shooting star. So if you could acquire a large share of the market, success and high profits were yours. The only problem was that it wasn't working. A little firm with 96 employees called ICS, Inc., looked at this incongruity and uncovered the secret. It depended on how you defined the market and how you focused on the customer.

If a larger company selected too broad a definition, a smaller company could beat a larger one in the market place. So at a time when mighty IBM dominated large computers, ICS, Inc., concentrated on computers for the educational market and dominated this niche from which mighty IBM withdrew.

In recent times, famous coffeemaker Starbucks fell into the trap by focusing on expansion instead of its customer. As CEO Howard Schultz said recently in an interview with Katie Couric, "We made expansion a strategy instead of an outcome of service."[3] The expansion led to great losses until Schultz spotted the incongruity and turned things around.

The Third Source: Process Need

Process need has to do with the old proverb that, "Necessity is the mother of invention." So this source is fairly straightforward. You need something done, and you simply work on this something until you figure out how to do it. The Wright Brothers, Orville and Wilbur, struggled to invent a workable engine-powered flying machine. They calculated that they would need an engine weighing less than 200 pounds which would generate eight horsepower. They searched and discovered that no such engine existed. All existing engines were either too heavy or too weak to meet these specifications. Finally they decided that they needed to have such an engine built themselves. They estimated that they would need one made of four cylinders with 4-inch bore and 4-inch stroke, weighing not over 200 pounds, including all accessories. They developed it. However, by itself, an engine was useless if it could not generate the thrust over the wings through artificial wind to create lift. Where to find a propeller to generate the wind for thrust? No data on air propellers existed, so the Wright brothers found themselves working in a theoretical vacuum. They concluded that a propeller was simply like a glider traveling in a spiral course. Because they could calculate the effect of a glider traveling in a straight course, their thought was that there was no reason that they could not calculate the effect of one traveling in a spiral course. At first glance this does not appear difficult, but it was hard to find even a point from which to start, for nothing about a propeller, or the medium in which it acts, remains stationary. The thrust depends upon the speed and the angle at which the blade strikes the air. The angle at which the blade strikes the air depends upon the speed at which the propeller is turning and the speed the machine is traveling forward. When any one of these changes, it changes all the rest because they are interdependent upon one another. Here was a task that would have challenged Sisyphus. Much of this was trial and error. Eventually they solved that problem, which led to yet another problem, which they eventually solved—their invention of three-axis control so the pilot could control his machine. Step-by-step they innovated as they solved problem after problem. Finally everything came together on December 17, 1903, with humanity's first powered flight.[4]

The Fourth Source: Industry and Market Structures

People tend to keep doing things the same way—forever—and this carries through to industries and markets. I heard a story once about a husband who asked his wife why she cut the ends off her roast before cooking it. Her answer: "That's the way it's done." The husband noticed that his wife's mother did the same thing. He asked his mother-in-law why she did that. Her response was the same: "That's the way you cook a roast." One day, he and his wife visited her grandmother. She prepared a roast, too. But she didn't cut the ends off. So the young husband asked her why she didn't. "Well, she said, for many years I did. But finally about the time our daughter left home and got married we bought a pan large enough to hold the roast without my having to cut off the ends."

Companies do the same things. What was magic about Henry Ford and his automobile company? Contrary to popular belief, Henry Ford did not invent the assembly line. Moreover, the assembly line wasn't even needed for great success and high profits. Rolls-Royce proved that. What Ford did was to observe that the market structure had changed such that the "horseless carriage" was no longer just a rich man's toy. So he designed an automobile that could be mass-produced at a relatively low cost and that could be driven and maintained by the owner. The assembly line was only part of this innovation. Ford changed the way both the industry and the market worked.

However, as Drucker pointed out, innovation could work equally well going another way, but still using existing industry and market structure in the same business as a source. About the same time that Ford was innovating, Rolls-Royce introduced its own innovations. It more than quadrupled its already high price, ignored the assembly line, and returned to manufacturing methods and materials that hadn't been used since the Middle Ages. Unlike Ford, Rolls-Royce guaranteed that its product would last forever. It made a vehicle that was not designed for the owner to drive or maintain. Rather than envision "everyman" as its future customer, it sought to restrict sales to royalty or those that had the financial resources similar to those of royalty. Rolls-Royce, too, achieved high success and profits.

The Fifth Source: Demographics

Demographics have to do with the characteristics of a human population. These may be characteristics of education, culture, income, and more. These characteristics are not static. They change over time. For example, people today live longer and tend to be in better health at older ages than people in generations past. They say that today's age demographic of the "eighties" were previously the "sixties" of times past. Can you see sources for innovation in this? These demographic changes have caused an explosion in the interest in and maintenance of health among seniors that has led to health maintenance organizations, health newsletters, vitamins, spas for seniors, and more.

About 15 years ago Drucker predicted that the future of executive education was online. His prediction was based partially on technology and convenience, but also on the fact that computer literacy and computer ownership was growing faster than the demand for executive education. Many traditional educators disparaged the idea of so-called distance learning. They said it had to be done in the classroom face-to-face as it had been done in ancient Greece. They said that discussions had to take place and that questions had to be asked and answered in this environment or it wouldn't be effective. Students might be exposed to information and ideas online, but they just wouldn't and couldn't learn this way. Drucker was right again. Research found that learning online was even faster and more effective than classroom learning in many instances, and today leading universities—Harvard, Stanford, and the like—all have online programs. Others such as Boston University even offer doctorate degrees entirely online.

The Sixth Source: Changes to Perception

How we look at things is critical. There is a very old example from psychology. When I first encountered it, I was amazed. It was an ambiguous picture that could be viewed as either a young, attractive woman or an old, ugly woman. Which image you saw depended on how you looked at the drawing. You could see either image depending on your perception at the moment. Later I discovered that you could control which picture viewers would see by the simple device of having them first view a picture of an image in which a few lines were redrawn so that viewers would see only the young woman or the old woman but not both in the same drawing.

Here's the way I used this in the classroom. I would put the doctored picture in which viewers could see only the young, attractive woman in one set of envelopes and the doctored picture in which viewers could see only the old, ugly woman in another set. I would distribute envelopes with the young woman to half of my class on the left side of the room and the envelopes with the old woman to half of my class on the right side of the room. I would then instruct everyone to open the envelope and look at the picture for 10 seconds and then return the picture to the envelope. I would next project the ambiguous picture in which either the young or the old woman could be perceived on a screen.

I would then ask innocently: "How many see a picture of a young, attractive woman?" The hands on the left side of the room would go up. Those on the right side of the room would look puzzled, and I would appear puzzled too. "How many see an old, unattractive woman?" I would ask. The arms on the right side of the room would be raised, and now those seated on the left side of the room would look puzzled.

Drucker employed a much easier example which required no props: Is the glass of water half full or half empty? It all depends on how you look at things. Moreover, your mood, values, beliefs, or what you see or "know" previously can all affect that perception. How can we take advantage of perception as a source of innovation? Once a rip in clothing was cause for the quality inspector to reject the product, and it was destroyed. If the tear was minor, the clothing might be sold at a significant discount. However, the 1960s began the onset of the hippie generation, with young people wearing clothing that was frequently intentionally ripped. Almost overnight, stressed, faded, frayed, and yes, even ripped jeans became status symbols that were desired by many young prospective buyers. In response to this new perception of what was considered desirable, jeans manufacturers began to manufacture clothing that was intentionally produced to resemble clothing that was once considered damaged and thrown away or donated to worthy organizations that could recycle the clothes.

The Seventh Source: New Knowledge

You might assume that new knowledge would immediately become the source of innovations and competitive advantages that would help to spirit companies to advanced positions in their industries while at the same time satisfying needs and wants, some of which were not even recognized until the innovations were introduced. Sad to say, this simply is not true. It frequently takes years, sometimes decades or longer, before new knowledge is applied in a way that results in innovations.

Alexander Fleming is generally credited with the discovery of penicillin in 1928. But the first documented cure with the use of the drug didn't occur until 1942. That would be 14 years later. However, the first published paper on the use of these fungi as a cure goes back to the 1870s, which would place the time between knowledge and innovation to be a considerable amount. Hold on. The blue mold of this antibiotic on bread was observed to help speed the cure of wounds of battle in the Middle Ages. So the amount of time between knowledge and innovation would more accurately be described as several hundred years in this case.

The knowledge needed to develop the Internet became available in the early 1960s. The knowledge for the Internet's close relation, the personal computer, has been around since 1962. Even ideas not requiring high technology take an amazing amount of time to generate innovation. Consider the marketing plan. Search for examples prior to World War II, and you will come up empty. Postwar articles in the *Journal of Marketing* began to tout the idea of a marketing plan similar to plans of strategy that became more familiar during the war. But it took 20 more years before most organizations began to innovate and adopt the process and produce the marketing plans resulting from it.

What this says is that there is "gold in them thar hills." That is, the knowledge uncovered and available today which is the source of innovations is not yet exploited for the future.

Drucker told us that we must innovate. However, he did not leave it there. He told us how we should approach innovation to build and maintain the success of our organizations with the best sources of new ideas.

Chapter 7

Demand-Side Innovation

D emand-side innovation involves purposefully working toward a pre-determined goal. Something demands a solution, and frequently this solution involves an innovation—something new and different, be it a product or a process to meet this demand. The goal results from a need evidenced by the situation. It could be a difficulty, a need in the market, a problem that requires solving, or something else. Drucker divided innovation goals for the typical business into five classes:

1. New products or services required to reach marketing objectives
2. New products or services needed because of technological developments making current products or services obsolete
3. Products improvements needed to reach marketing objectives or resulting from anticipated technological developments
4. New processes and improvements required in old processes to meet market goals
5. Innovation and improvements in all other supporting areas of business[1]

The Practice of Innovation

Reaching innovation goals requires a systematic routine. Drucker called this routine the practice of innovation, and he said that it involves analysis, system, and hard work. Moreover, he wrote that as in every other routine, the extraordinary performer in innovation could be effective only if he were grounded in the discipline such that the would-be innovator became master of the practice.[2] This hard work, going hand in hand with systematic methodology, is critical and more important than talent, ingenuity, and knowledge.[3]

The Many Techniques of Systematic Innovation

Drucker recognized that although innovation must be accomplished in a systematic fashion, there are many different ways to proceed. The old saying refers to the many ways of "skinning a cat." According to historians this rather morbid metaphor may have initially employed a dog as the foil, which to dog lovers is equally offensive, or it may even have referred to a cat*fish*.[4] In any case, the idea is the same. That is, there are many effective techniques for accomplishing systematic innovation, any of which might be termed "most effective" depending on the situation. Interestingly, when questioned in class regarding his ability to solve problems with innovative solutions, Drucker claimed that it was not his knowledge about a particular industry, but rather his ignorance that generally led to success. To prove his point, he told the following story.

The Ghost Fleet of the Hudson River

Years ago when I was a cadet at West Point, the Hudson River was packed with hundreds of immobilized, no-longer-used ships. Each looked the same, was about 400 to 500 feet long, and was clearly immobilized. The ships had the general appearance of sleeping giants. I was told that these were called Liberty Ships and had been built on an emergency basis during World War II. Drucker once told their story to illustrate his point.

After World War II broke out in 1939, the British were losing ships with thousands of tons of cargo to German submarines. They needed the supplies and munitions these ships brought to feed their population and to continue to fight the war. One response to their losses was the design of a relatively inexpensive cargo ship. These ships were so basic that they were barely expected to last to the war's end. Moreover they were slow, bulky, and inefficient. However they could be constructed much faster than any other cargo ship. It took only about eight months for each ship to be built from start to finish, a significant improvement over the time it took to build a cargo ship previously. The ship itself was a huge innovation, but not the innovation that Drucker wanted to talk about.

It still took skilled workers to build a ship, even one with a vastly simplified design like this one. Britain was fully engaged in all aspects of fighting the Germans. The manpower, shipyards, and production facilities to build the fleets of new cargo ships needed simply didn't exist. So the British looked to the United States, which was not yet in the war, to build their new cargo ships. Unfortunately the United States did not have an extensive record in merchant shipbuilding. In the previous decade only two ocean-going cargo ships had been built in the United States. However England was so desperate that it was willing to turn to the United States for help in this endeavor despite its lack of a track record. The hope was that with British help, it might take about a year to build each ship in the United States. In any case, with most of the developed world at war or in the enemy camp, there seemed little alternative.

Naturally in their search for potential U.S. manufacturers, the British couldn't and didn't limit themselves to shipbuilders. One of the promising individuals they contacted was industrialist Henry Kaiser. Kaiser knew very little about shipbuilding and was completely ignorant about cargo ships. However, he had a reputation for the ability to get things done. He examined the British design and moved forward, less with British help and expertise than with his own ignorance.

Since he didn't have experienced shipbuilding workers available, Kaiser asked himself how he could proceed. He came up with a unique American solution based on his ignorance. Kaiser redesigned the assembly process using prefabricated parts so that no worker had to know more than a small part of the job. Moreover, he introduced American assembly-line techniques. The British knew that for close tolerances in shipbuilding, special machinery was necessary to cut the metal accurately. Kaiser didn't know this, and anyway Kaiser didn't have the machinery. Again he came up with an innovation to get the job done without specialized machinery. He told his workers to cut the metal using oxyacetylene torches. This turned out to be cheaper and faster than the traditional British methods. In his ignorance, Kaiser replaced riveting with welding, also cheaper and faster. He started building his "Liberty Ships," and it didn't take him a year to build each ship. It didn't even take eight months. In Kaiser's ignorance he started building the British design from start to finish in about a month. This isn't a misprint. This ignorant American who had never built a ship started producing the British design in about 30 days! Eventually he got production time down to a couple weeks and for publicity purposes, he constructed one Liberty Ship in just four and a half days.

Ah, those crazy Yanks!

Approaching his problem out of his ignorance, Kaiser built almost 1,500 ships in much less time and at a quarter of the cost of other foreign shipyards previously. What an innovation! Other American shipbuilders immediately adopted his methods in building these ships. Interestingly, despite the fact that they were not built to last, a couple are still around and in use. Or at least they were in use back in 1975 when Drucker told us the story.

Drucker went on to emphasize that like Henry Kaiser, who knew nothing about building merchant ships and had approached the problem of building them out of his ignorance and not his knowledge in this area, he, too, looked at unfamiliar situations in which he had little background and of which he knew nothing. He asked questions stemming from his ignorance much as Kaiser was forced to ask himself and his staff questions out of his ignorance. Those whom Drucker consulted for and helped were frequently surprised that these questions led to effective solutions that helped them with their problems.

Of course Drucker recognized that there wasn't one single strategy leading to successful innovations. Though systematic methods are mandatory, Drucker knew that every situation that was faced by the innovator had to be thought through anew.[5] Let's look at some of the systematic methods of the kind that Drucker knew were necessary and Kaiser may have knowingly or unknowingly used.

The Left-Brain Solution

An effective left-brain methodology has been used for years in staff studies. It is also extremely effective not only in organizing and analyzing complex problems to reach innovative and logical solutions, but in presenting this information to others to convince them of the validity of the innovator's solution. I always understood that this was developed by a military staff college in the nineteenth century. However, I discovered that this method was also used and taught at Harvard University and that other professions such as attorneys and medical and other health practitioners use a very similar approach in analyzing and reaching logical conclusions when confronted with difficult and complex problems.

The left-brain approach involves defining the problem, deciding on the relevant information bearing on the situation, developing potential alternative solutions whether they involve an innovation or not, analyzing these alternatives, developing the best innovation or solution from this analysis, and finally making the decision to adopt the innovation or solution of choice. I've used it myself for organizational and business problem solving for years, even before I met Peter, though it clearly fit in with the way he thought and the systematic methods he sometimes unconsciously recommended. I say unconsciously because Peter thought that thinking the matter through was better than any methodology. Yet his thinking was systematic and sometimes could be made clearer by documenting it as a method. What follows is such a case.

Problem Definition

You can't get "there" until you know where "there" is. That's not one of Peter Drucker's injunctions; it's one of mine, and it will come up again when we look at Drucker's views on strategy in Chapter 11. That's my way of emphasizing that in order to solve any problem and come up with a left-brain innovation to solve it, you've got to first understand exactly what the problem is. That's the "there" in a problem situation. Drucker saw Kaiser's challenge as being how to build the British-designed ships given the constraints that he faced.

Relevant Factors

Kaiser's problem had a number of situational factors that were directly relevant to his problem. Therefore, he had to gather together all the information he needed. Kaiser knew what he didn't have. He needed to know what resources he did have or could have available. Kaiser looked into this, did his analysis, and decided to apply Henry Ford's assembly line methods to shipbuilding.

Alternative Courses of Action

In this part of the left-brain decision process, Kaiser had to decide on alternatives to solve the problem. One option might have been to develop new tactics. Maybe he could have started a worldwide search for expert shipbuilders in neutral countries and offered them high wages. Maybe he could have designed new metal cutting machinery and produced it quickly using his methods. At about the same time, experts in Asia who had other problems adopted a much different solution to build the 717-mile winding Burma Road through the mountainous terrain between Burma and China: 200,000 laborers working 24/7. Note that this method, which worked so well in building the Burma Road, wouldn't have stood a chance in the United States where laborers in these numbers were unavailable. Different advantages and disadvantages in different situations lead to different alternatives.

All alternatives have both advantages and disadvantages. Kaiser took an enormous risk with his solution. He had millions of dollars invested in it before he built his first ship. Many of the methods that he used had never been employed previously, and many were themselves extremely innovative to say the least. It was reported that because it took years and extensive training to enable novice fitters to tightrope across the high structures of a ship as it was completed, Kaiser hired ballet dancers as fitters for this task.[6]

Analysis, Conclusions, and Decision

During the analysis, the innovator essentially compares the relative importance of each alternative's advantages and disadvantages. Some alternatives have few disadvantages, but no great advantage either. In any case, the innovator needs to think it through and document his or her thinking. This helps this left-brain method be really effective in explaining the decision to others after the decision is made.

I'm sure Henry Kaiser went through this process in detail in explaining to his managers, his workers, and his board of directors what he wanted to do. He would have left nothing out, concluding that despite the risks, the best way to achieve the desired results was to implement the building of the British design in the way he outlined it.

The Right-Brain Solution

The right-brain approach to problem solving still works by starting out with an assumption of ignorance, and it is still systematic. However, unlike the very structured procedure that is part of the left-brain approach, the right-brain method uses no conscious, fixed sequence of logical steps to arrive at a solution. One of the best examples of its use in American business was by the famous inventor Thomas Edison. It is important to recall that while Edison had no formal education past high school, he was the inventor of numerous "high tech" devices, from the lightbulb to practical motion pictures and recorded sound. He held no less than 1,093 U.S. patents and a slew of foreign patents as well. His right-brain approach, according to his assistants, was to go into a dark room and sit there—sometimes for hours—until a solution to his problem presented itself. In the room his systematic approach was simply to give his imagination free rein. It rarely failed him.

A Ride on a Beam of Light

Another example of the use of this right-brain method of innovation was Albert Einstein's description of how he formulated the theory of relativity. One would think that anything as quantitatively complex or as mathematical as the development of this theory would require scores of white-coated scientists working months either at blackboards covered with hundreds of chalk-smeared formulas and equations or performing advanced work on complicated computer programs or in laboratory experimentation. Even if today's technology were available to Einstein, these scientists would have used up an awful lot of computer time. Yet Einstein explained that he thought the whole concept up by himself by the innovative methodology of simply closing his eyes and imagining himself riding on a beam of light and what would transpire as to time on earth during his speed of light trip. Systematic, but also simple!

Cannibals and Spears with Holes in the Wrong End

Dreaming can also be effective as a catalyst for the right-brain solution. In the 1840s Elias Howe knew nothing about sewing or the struggles of his predecessors for over 100 years in trying to invent a machine that could sew as effectively, but much faster, than a human seamstress or tailor. In fact, Howe was a young man still in his twenties. However, Howe was fascinated by the use of machines to increase the speed in repetitious patterns of handiwork. Somehow he became interested in applying machinery to the task of sewing.

He had an idea that such a machine would work if he used thread from two different sources. The problem was that a standard needle threaded through a hole at the back of the needle, as worked by hand, would not work at all with a machine. After struggling with this problem for some time, one night he went to sleep and had a strange dream that he recalled in the morning. He was on a desert island and attacked by cannibals. The cannibals were armed with strange looking spears. Each spear was attached to a rope, not from its shaft as one might expect in a whaling harpoon, but from a hole threaded through the spearhead. When Howe awoke and remembered his dream, he grasped this as the solution for his sewing machine needle. It was now possible in his machine for the needle to be pushed through the cloth. This created a loop on the other side; a shuttle on a track then slipped the second thread through the loop, creating what is now called a lockstitch. Presto, an innovation that changed sewing forever.

The Dos and Don'ts of Systematic Innovation

There are rules for systematic innovation regardless of whether the right- or left-brain approach is used. Drucker had five "do" rules and three "don't" rules. His "do" rules were:

1. Begin this process by an analysis of your opportunities; don't dwell on your limitations.
2. Look, ask, and listen. Regardless of whether you use a right- or left-brain approach, you are going to use both hemispheres of your brain. So look at numbers, but also at people. Follow this by asking questions and listening.
3. Keep it simple. Your innovation should overcome only one challenge at a time. Otherwise things get confusing.
4. Start small, not big. Think little money, few people, and a limited market.
5. Aim at leadership. No one can foretell whether your innovation will be modest or conquer the world. But if it doesn't aim at leadership from the start, it is unlikely to go anywhere.

Now for Drucker's "don't" rules:

1. Don't be clever. By this Drucker meant, "Keep it simple, stupid." I am constantly reminded of this rule when I attempt to decipher the instructions for using the latest high-tech gadgetry. Many times the writer makes things so complex that the instructions are almost impossible to understand. Note that Drucker also spoke of simplicity as a "do" rule.
2. Don't try to come up with too many innovations at once. Henry Kaiser came up with quite a few in solving his overall problem, but he tried to tackle each issue individually and sequentially to avoid confusion.
3. Don't try to innovate for the future. Innovate for the present. Fruition and ultimate advantage may be a long time coming. Your innovation must have some sort of advantage from the beginning.[7]

If you want to be a Henry Kaiser, or even an Albert Einstein as a marketing practitioner, just follow Drucker's advice. The practice of demand-side innovation requires analysis, a system, and hard work. By following the rules, many marketers have been highly successful with the process. This is demand-side innovation. However, as we will see in the next chapter, there is also supply-side innovation based on capability and also requiring analysis, system, and hard work. And it, too, has led to significant marketing success for innovators.

Chapter 8

Supply-Side Innovation

During World War II the main source of rubber came from trees grown in the Southwest Pacific and was under Japanese control. In response to this dilemma, the United States searched desperately for a synthetic rubber or rubber substitute. In 1943, General Electric engineer James Wright was attempting to create a new synthetic rubber by mixing boric acid and silicone oil. He came up with a product that had some very unusual properties. When dropped from someone's hand, the material bounced to a higher height than when it was released. It was impervious to rot. It was also soft and malleable. It could be stretched many times its length without tearing. Finally, it could copy the image of any printed material with which it came in contact and to which pressure was applied. The only trouble was, with all of these properties, one thing it was not. It was not a good substitute for rubber.

Wright went on to other engineering challenges, but General Electric was intrigued with this strange material with its unusual properties yet didn't apply supply-side innovation principles to result in a product that was marketable. General Electric had a fine product, but without a practical use. Fortunately, no one threw it away.

A few years later, a very unlikely innovator stumbled on the product. By varying accounts he was an unemployed marketing consultant, an unemployed advertising executive, or an itinerant salesman. In any case, what is known for sure is that his name was Peter Hodgson. Hodgson went to a party at which this material was the entertainment of the evening. Hodgson saw what many GE scientists missed. He witnessed adults playing with and enjoying the product for its properties. He was pretty sure that children would have even more fun playing with it. He visualized a much larger market as a child's toy, or perhaps something that captured the interest of children "from nine to ninety." Hodgson discovered where the product originated and who owned the rights. General Electric sold Hodgson the rights, but it was Hodgson who named it: Silly Putty.

Some millions of sales and 50 years later, I was in China teaching some MBA students something about marketing as conducted in the United States. None spoke English. I took some Silly Putty with me to impress my students with American marketing acumen. I took the sample from my briefcase. Before I could speak and my interpreter could translate, there was a universal shout in unison of the words: "Silly Putty." There could be no finer testimonial to Peter Hodgson, unemployed or not, who used the principles of supply-side innovation to find a use for a great product that had no purpose.[1]

The Two General Types of Innovation

There are two types of innovation: demand side as discussed in Chapter 7 and supply side discussed in this one. This has resulted in two views on how innovation might be controlled and encouraged. Both types are appropriate in different situations, but different principles are more important in their development. Drucker recognized that development of both types of innovation share the common demands of organized, systematic, and rational work.[2]

My definition of supply-side innovation is innovation based primarily on capability in which the originally intended objective becomes secondary to actual, and usually unexpected, results. The story of Silly Putty demonstrates examples of both demand- and supply-side innovation, even though the demand-side type didn't result in a successful product in this instance. In the first instance, James Wright had a precisely defined goal. He was attempting to create a new synthetic rubber. In this he failed, but with his background and experience, he had the capability of looking at the unexpected results he had achieved and still coming up with an innovation, not necessarily a child's toy and not necessarily Silly Putty. Because of the focused demands of the war and of his assignment, and after the war because of lack of rigorous logical analysis, no successful innovation resulted from this product at GE. However, it might have. In recent years the stuff Silly Putty is made of has become a grip strengthener, and it even went into space in this capacity on Apollo 8.[3]

Our second innovator, Peter Hodgson, was simply at a party. As a former advertising man with a background in sales, Hodgson also had the capability through work and experience to capitalize on the unusual performance capabilities demonstrated by the product used during the evening's entertainment. What Hodgson did was to grasp the potential and create the concept of Silly Putty. I doubt seriously whether he expected such a thing to occur when he went to the party. I doubt that he went to the party to witness a demonstration of the product's capabilities or that he knew the product existed before seeing it. He did not decide instantly that he would create what would become a profitable and internationally famous toy. But over time he did apply the principles of supply-side innovation to the situation which resulted in the successful innovation.

New Knowledge Is Not the Most Reliable or Predictable Source

A company whose products largely involved plastics started a new research division. To run it, the company hired a scientist who was considered number one in his field. He had many inventions and discoveries to his credit. One of these had propelled him to an award and designation as "plastics man of the year." He was adequately funded and given a small staff and laboratory. He was not assigned specific goals other than to explore whatever interested him in the company's area of interest. It was thought that one or more of his projects would automatically generate innovations that would give the company a competitive advantage and lead to the company's future products. This was an example of the company engaging in supply-side innovation since no specific goal was intended. However, after five years, the department was shut down, and the scientist was discharged. It wasn't that the innovations generated weren't important or that their numbers were insufficient to demonstrate a profit potential. Although the potential certainly existed, in five years not a single successful innovation had come from this department.

Drucker's findings supported what had occurred. Drucker found that new knowledge, and especially science-based innovation, was not the most reliable or even the most predictable source of successful innovation. This is not to say that demand-side innovation wasn't valid or that it should be ignored. It suggests that there was evidence of successful innovation based primarily on supply-side innovation and the capability and awareness of the innovator and that the potential might even be greater than innovation based on demand if done in the right way. This is especially true when unexpected results, both good and bad, occur. Unfortunately, in many instances, marketing decision makers ignore these unexpected results and actually abandon or miss capitalizing on potential innovations that could lead to great success. Though more forgivable than in most instances, with the Silly Putty innovation, GE executives did not apply the principles of supply-side innovation probably because their focus was on developing artificial rubber and the ongoing demands of World War II. At least GE didn't destroy the product and did get money through selling the rights to Hodgson. Others have abandoned potential innovations outright and all but given the innovation to a competitor on a platter.

R.H. Macy's War on Appliance Sales

After World War II, appliance sales at R.H. Macy's suddenly and mysteriously began to increase dramatically. Not only did sales increase, but profit margins were significantly higher on appliances than on fashion goods, Macy's flagship product line. Unlike fashion goods, there were almost no returns and no pilferage. Moreover, customers who came in the store to buy appliances frequently stayed to buy fashion goods and other classes of Macy's product line as well. We might expect Macy's to celebrate and exploit this unexpected windfall. Yet this experienced retailer, the biggest department store around, not only failed to take advantage of this potential innovation, but it did everything possible to make these unexpected results go away.

When fashion goods failed to increase as a percentage of total sales after Macy's tried everything in its bag of tricks to make this happen, Macy's actually began a campaign to intentionally restrict appliance sales. The obvious thing to have done on getting these unexpected results was to have taken the idea and run with it. Although just as heavy into fashion goods as Macy's, Bloomingdale's did just that. Bloomingdale's not only built on its appliance sales, but it built a whole new market around a new housewares department. It didn't stop there. Next Bloomingdale's examined the customer that represented the symptom behind the increasing demand for appliances and sought other product lines to satisfy this new customer and the demand. Bloomingdale's had been a weak number four in the marketplace previously. Its successful innovation based on these unexpected results soon enabled it to become a very strong number two.

Things didn't improve at Macy's until new management took over the reins 20 years later. But what caused Macy's to reject the clear signals for innovation in the first place? Simple. Everyone in the industry knew that in a well-run department store, fashion should produce 70 percent of total sales. But those errant appliance sales were providing three-fifths of total Macy's revenue! This had to be stopped! The chairman of Macy's came to the conclusion that if fashion sales couldn't be increased, appliance sales would have to be reduced.[4] And so he set out to do just that. Good thinking, Mr. Chairman!

What to Do About Unexpected Results

In order to determine what to do about unexpected results, Drucker recommended that management look at every unexpected success and ask four questions:

1. **What would it mean to us if we exploited it?** That is, what are the short-term costs and benefits of developing this unexpected result into an opportunity?
2. **Where could it lead us?** The man who thought up the sprinkler system based on simply making holes in a plastic hose found an unexpected increase in orders from poultry farms rather than households or gardeners. He enquired and found that these poultry farms were using the hose sprinklers as inexpensive air conditioners for their chicken pens. He did not refuse to sell to them. This opened up a new market that he quickly exploited.
3. **What would we have to do to convert it to an opportunity?** In other words, what would be the general way that the unexpected results could be converted into a profitable product or system for the company?
4. **How can we do it?** What would be the plan for doing this? What resources would be needed? What would it cost? What would the timing look like? What would be the approximate quantified results of the investment?

What to Do About Unexpected Failure

Unexpected failure can be just as useful as unexpected success. It's not that the questions are so different, but that many, perhaps most, marketing executives fail to examine and investigate the real reasons for the unexpected results. Very frequently they blame "the irrational customer." Drucker pointed out that Ford recovered from an incredible failure in the Ford Edsel, a car that was based on extensive marketing research and "correct" marketing socioeconomic segmentation indicated by the well-known low, lower-middle, upper-middle, and upper income groups and their subsets developed by William Lloyd Warner in the 1940s.[5] Ford's investigation into its flop uncovered the fact that other segmentation could be even more important. It then developed the Thunderbird, the most successful car for Ford since the Model T had been introduced.[6]

But that's not all. Ford repeated the same innovation strategy to turn another failure into an innovation lesson for success only a few years later. In response to the growing entry of small, more economical foreign cars into the American market in the late 1950s, Ford, Plymouth, and Chevrolet all introduced American versions of economical cars: the Ford Falcon, Plymouth Valiant, and Chevrolet Corvair. Although at first they were moderately successful, sales began to wane. Ford again investigated and discovered that while Falcon sales were declining, consumer demand for certain options were on the increase. These included bucket seats, padded dash, and other sports car features. Exploiting this finding, Ford again capitalized on these unexpected results based on an investigation of declining sales and introduced the Ford Mustang.

In addition to the four questions for unexpected success, Drucker didn't like the word "analysis." He said that large companies tended to do too much of that when they were faced with an unexpected failure. Instead he recommended the term "investigation." He recommended asking questions and really listening to the responses. He urged market-ers not to depend on what "everyone knew," that is, established facts such as what constituted a well-run retail store as at Macy's or the proper market segmentation for the automobile that resulted in the Ford Edsel.

The Unexpected Outside Event

Drucker also saw that innovations could come from unexpected outside events. Entrepreneur E. Joseph "Joe" Cossman, who built his fortune by introducing many "new products," was an innovator who took failed product after failed product and made each successful. Each product always seemed new and cutting edge. In almost every case he sought innovations from the unexpected outside events.

His first highly successful product was the "Cossman Ant Farm." No one had ever heard of an "Ant Farm" until Cossman came along. How-ever the product had existed since the turn of the century. The manufac-turer constructed an ant cage through the use of wood and glass. Mostly classroom teachers were provided with instructions on how to select the soil and ants to build an ant colony which could be observed through the glass. The ant colony was not really a toy. It was more of an educational product or tool for the classroom. Since the product was made partially of glass, it was potentially dangerous and thus adults, again mostly teachers, were advised to supervise children interacting with the ant colony. A few thousand of these containers for ant colonies were sold every year.

Cossman looked at this educational tool and realized that construction materials had changed dramatically since the product was first introduced. If the colony's cage could be constructed of clear plastic, the dangers of unsupervised observation by children would be completely altered. The ant colony would no longer be just an educational tool, but an educational toy that every child could own and enjoy. Substituting the new plastic materials for the old wood and glass structures constituted innovation based on capability and the unexpected results based on this substitution. Cossman innovated and did the following in addition to substituting the materials of which the ant colony was constructed:

- Renamed the product an "ant farm"
- Lowered the price based on cheaper plastic materials and simpler manufacturing methods
- Provided a "stock certificate" with each unit sold that would be sent to Cossman who in return would guarantee the live delivery of 25 ants to start the farm so buyers no longer needed to supply their own ants
- Repositioned the product as an educational but personal toy
- Sought new channels of distribution

The results of this innovation were nothing short of spectacular, and in short order Cossman sold over 1 million ant farms. He was propelled into national fame. He even sold one ant farm to the White House for Caroline Kennedy. He followed this up time and time again using the same procedures with other innovations based on outside happenings.

One year there was an unexpected glut of potatoes. Cossman had bought the rights and machinery to manufacture a toy gun that shot potatoes. He had paid $500 for the rights and the machinery. The original inventor had manufactured 100,000 potato guns but had sold only 10,000. Promising potato growers that he would get them out of the economic problems caused by the glut of potatoes, he gained their support and five tons of potatoes which were used in effective promotions. The *Los Angeles Times* claimed that he sold 2 million spud guns in six months. [7]

However, Cossman, with whom I had a friendship and who once wrote a book, told me that the actual number was 850,000. Still, that's a respectable number for a company that never had more than a dozen employees.

Once Cossman bought 10,000 pieces of costume jewelry in a closeout. Each piece consisted of a bracelet with seven imitation gemstones. It looked very pretty, but he was stuck. He couldn't sell them. About this time, a young woman under hypnosis was regressed to an early age. Then the hypnotist did a strange thing. He asked the young woman to remember a previous lifetime. And she did! This American woman remembered a life in Ireland during the previous century as "Bridey Murphy," a young Irish girl. Interest in hypnotism swept the country.

Always interested in new ideas, Cossman took a course in hypnosis. He heard the instructor say, "To induce a subject to enter a hypnotic trance, you need a point of fixation. This can be anything on which the subject can focus all of his attention."

"How about an imitation gemstone?" asked Cossman. "Sure," answered the instructor. "Suddenly," Cossman said, "I realized I had 70,000 points of fixation." Cossman made a deal with the hypnotist to record a hypnotic induction and other information on a vinyl record as they didn't have audiotapes in those days. Together with some printed instructions, and using a free "hypnotic gem" as inducement to buy, Cossman sold tens of thousands of units and made more than a million dollars by turning a disadvantage into an advantage. As a teenager, I was one of Joe's customers.[8]

One final example will show how effectively Cossman employed the principles of supply-side innovation. A firm manufacturing diving equipment decided to manufacture and sell a diving toy as a sideline. A human figure in a diving helmet was connected to a plastic bulb with a hose. The figure was weighted, and it sank when placed in a tub of water. A child would squeeze the plastic bulb which sent air into the diving helmet, and the helmet and figure would rise to the surface. The problem was that plastic was the wrong material for the bulb that pumped the air. About 10 squeezes was all it would take before the bulb cracked and ruined the toy.

Cossman got the rights and manufacturing machinery for a few hundred dollars. Many marketers would just replace the bulb with a rubber bulb and that would be it. That's no innovation, just a problem correction. But Cossman figured that the toy already had a bad name that would negatively affect sales. So he went to a local university and asked a chemistry professor if there was a common and harmless chemical he could use to make the figure move underwater. "Sure," was the answer, "baking soda pellets." Cossman threw away the diving helmet, hose, and bulb, added rubber flippers to the diving figure's feet, and where the hose had been attached, he inserted a baking powder pellet. His new product "swam" underwater realistically, and he called it "Flippy the Frogman." He sold several hundred thousand. But then he noted some additional outside unexpected results: the frogman figure moving underwater attracted fish. Presto, he had an additional product that he sold internationally, "Fisherman Joe's Fishing Lure."

Success in Innovation

Like demand-side innovation, success comes when it's done right. Although most times we put a definition first, knowing Drucker's definition of innovation now helps us to understand what Drucker was talking about and the importance of his stressing system, analysis (or sometimes investigation), and hard work. At the same time, we can understand his recommendations better. Drucker defined innovation as "the design and development of something new, as yet unknown, and not in existence, which will establish a new economic configuration of the old, known existing elements."[9] He summarized by suggesting that it was the missing link between a number of disconnected elements, each marginally effective, and an integrated system of great power. Thus innovators have a major characteristic that differentiates them from noninnovators: the ability to envision as a system what to others appear as unrelated, separate elements.

To develop areas in which innovation would create maximum opportunities, he recommended three questions for the would-be innovator to ask:

1. What is lacking to make effective what is already possible?
2. What one small step would transform our economic results?
3. What small change would alter the capacity of the whole of our resources?[10]

In Chapter 7 we discuss that Kaiser found his important change in the use of applying automotive assembly techniques to shipbuilding. Elias Howe found his small change in where to put the hole in threading a needle. Earlier in this chapter we discuss that Ford found change in the use of a different segmentation based on lifestyle with both the Thunderbird and the Mustang, and that Cossman found it was the use of different materials with his ant farms. With his Spud Gun it was the ammunition and where it came from that was the crucial innovative factor. His cheap jewelry was turned into points of fixation to enable a hypnotic trance. With Flippy the Frogman, it was not discarding or replacing the plastic bulb as one might expect, but in the use of a common household pellet. In all cases, innovators looked for small, easy solutions.

As Drucker wrote, the basis of all business is marketing and innovation. Innovation is the critical part of marketing that all who claim to be marketers must master.

Chapter 9

Drucker's Entrepreneurial Marketing

Entrepreneurship concerns transferring innovations into economic goods and services. It is not difficult to see its close relationship with marketing. Drucker not only identified this relationship but even wrote an entire book tying the two activities together. Moreover he not only recognized that entrepreneurship and the specialized marketing principles it required could be identified and structured, but that these needed to be organized for systematic application.[1] His work in this specialized field of marketing began more than 60 years ago when a small group of executives met under his leadership at the Graduate Business School of New York University once a week for ongoing seminars on this topic. This group of practitioners provided a laboratory for testing the initial concepts he developed. Even then, major corporations like GE and IBM were involved, and also major banks, book publishers, pharmaceuticals, and even the Catholic Archdiocese of New York took part. Afterward, he confirmed the principles of marketing entrepreneurship in his consulting practice over the years, not only in corporations and start-up businesses but also in labor unions, Rick Warren's Saddleback Church, and the Girl Scouts of the U.S.A.

Drucker's Systematic Marketing Strategies for Entrepreneurship

Drucker organized his systematic entrepreneurial marketing strategies into four general approaches. He indicated that while they were not mutually exclusive, they each have their own prerequisites and each best fit certain conditions. Here are the four:[2]

1. Dominance of a new market or industry
2. Development of a currently unserved market
3. Finding and occupying a specialized "ecological niche"
4. Changing the economic characteristics of a product, a market, or an industry

Dominance of a New Market or Industry

Drucker rather imaginatively titled dominance of a new market or industry as "fustest with the mostest," which he, like most, attributed to a Confederate cavalry general during the U.S. Civil War. The general was Nathan Bedford Forrest, one of the most gifted and controversial commanders in the Confederacy. Prior to the war, Forrest had amassed a fortune as a planter and slave dealer and was known as one of the wealthiest men in the South. Despite his wealth and the fact that planters were excused from military service by the Confederate government, Forrest enlisted in the Southern army as a private. Though lacking a military or even a college education, he was soon commissioned as an officer and within a year rose through the ranks to become a lieutenant colonel, colonel, and finally a brigadier general. He finished the war as a lieutenant general, a very high-ranking officer, and the only one who began the war as a private. However, he never uttered the words "fustest with the mostest," which were attributed to him. Queried by two other Confederate generals during the war as to how he attained his almost inevitable success in battle, he stated that he just got there first with the most men. Years later, someone thought Forrest should have a "cracker" accent and corrupted Forrest's original words.[3] Forrest had learned the secret that all strategy was concentrating superior combat power at the decisive point of battle. One way of accomplishing this was getting to that decisive point with this superior combat power before an adversary could do so. In general strategy terms in marketing, this has to do with concentrating superior resources to dominate a decisive point. In entrepreneurial marketing, this strategy aims at creating a new industry or a new market.[4]

How Apple Did It

Before Apple came along, there was no personal computer market. The IBM 5100, the Wang 2200, the Hewlett-Packard 9830 series, and the Datapoint 2200 dominated professional/business computers. These products were priced from $5,000 to $20,000. Large companies with lots of resources manufactured these products with IBM controlling 70 percent of the overall market. IBM not only had the resources and marketing clout, but the undisputed best research and development team around. There was also a home market for computers, but this was mostly for video games. Commodore, Radio Shack, and National Semiconductor all sold products priced from $500 to $1,000 through computer stores, electronics shops, and department stores. These were not, however, programmable personal computers.

Neither Steve Jobs nor Steve Wozniak, Apple's cofounders, had the money, the technical know-how, the marketing background or experience, a development team, production facilities to build anything, or a distribution system. Neither individual was even a college graduate. However, the two entrepreneurs did recognize the need for personal computers that were relatively inexpensive and could be used by anyone at home or in a business. They realized that such a market did not exist. However, if the two could gather the superior resources necessary to develop a successful personal computer, they could both create and dominate this market before anyone could challenge them.

They named their new first product Apple II. Apple I hadn't really been a personal computer, only a motherboard for other companies' computers. After introduction of Apple II, sales reached $200,000, and they expanded by hiring marketing talent in the person of Mike Markkula who had been marketing manager at Intel.

By 1979, Apple had 500 retailers selling its computers in the United States. However, as a result of its success, more than 30 companies were planning on entering the personal computer field. Many analysts thought that Apple would limit itself to the relatively small niche it had carved out. But remember, the whole point of this "fustest with the mostest" as conceived by Drucker is not to dominate a niche, but to dominate an entirely new market, and Apple was already there, "fustest with the mostest."

Apple added 100,000 square feet of manufacturing capacity to the 22,000 square feet it already had. It expanded its distribution through five independent distributors to reach a greatly increased number of retail outlets. Less than four years after beginning operations, the year Apple Computer went public, sales hit $200 million with a $12 million net profit. A year after that, it became the undisputed number one in its primary market and drove most of its emerging competitors out of business. Apple has had many ups and downs since that time, but no one can deny the successful application of the strategy being of the fustest with the mostest to both create and dominate a market.

How to Implement the Strategy of Dominating a Market or Industry

By Drucker's reasoning implementing the strategy of dominating a market or industry—the riskiest of entrepreneurial strategies—can succeed only under the following conditions:[5]

- It has to fulfill the objective of dominating the industry or market, or it fails altogether.
- It needs to be based on a thorough and careful analysis and estimate of the situation, or it can't possibly succeed.
- After the basic idea has become a success, substantial and continuing efforts must be made to retain a leadership position; otherwise the only thing that has been accomplished is to create a market for a competitor. Apple almost faltered in this several times, but with both ups and downs managed to retain control until IBM entered the fray, and IBM used another of Drucker's

entrepreneurial approaches to do this called "creative imitation," which we will look at shortly.

- The marketing strategist has to be the one to systematically cut his or her own prices before a competitor does so.

Create a New Market by Supplying the Missing Ingredient

Drucker gave the approach of creating a new market by supplying the missing ingredient a colorful name too: "Hit Them Where They Ain't." These words did not, however, originate from a general in the Civil War or any other war. Instead it came from baseball Hall of Famer Wee Willie Keeler. At 5 feet 4 inches Keeler was one of the shortest players ever to play for a major league team. Despite his short stature, his .385 career batting average after the 1898 (yes, that's 1898, not 1998) season is the highest average in history at season's end for a player with more than 1,000 hits.[6] His strategy was simple: hit the ball to parts of the field not well covered by opposing players. Every batter tried for success by hitting the thrown pitch of a ball with his bat. Wee Willie added that a batter should strive to hit the ball to areas of the outfield that were ill-protected.

Drucker thought that there were two basic ways to supply the missing ingredient in this strategy of "hitting them where they ain't." The first was to imitate an established success, but to do so in a creative way that fulfilled the missing ingredient. He borrowed a term originated by Harvard marketing professor Theodore Levitt to describe this substrategy: "creative imitation." The other substrategy was to leverage a product that was existing, but unsuccessful, or at least undeveloped. He called the latter substrategy "entrepreneurial judo." In other words, one substrategy targeted a successful product, while the other strategy targeted one that was not yet successful.[7]

Marketing guru Mike Brown suggested that marketers ask themselves the following questions in implementing this strategy:

- What are things that customers have been requesting that we've yet to deliver?

- What are the most frequent customer-precipitated exceptions to our product or service?
- What are the most frequent employee-created exceptions to our product or service?
- What are the best, most successful companies (regardless of industry) doing to grow customer relationships with their brands? How can we emulate them?[8]

How IBM Used Creative Imitation

Let's return to IBM. IBM struck back against Apple in the same market that Apple had created and dominated for personal computers only a few years after Apple's incredible success. It did this by immediately going to work on a computer operating system and computer that became the standard in the field. However, the ingredient IBM added was not technical superiority. Apple held that edge for years. What IBM did was create a reliable machine that worked well, capitalize on its name and distribution system, and, most important, allow anyone to write software for its system, a capability Apple didn't have for its computers. With this marketing strategy, IBM took over leadership of the market within two years.

Why Entrepreneurial Judo Works Again and Again[9]

Drucker thought that entrepreneurial judo was a particularly low-risk strategy because innovators frequently tend to repeat mistakes with the products that they originally introduced. So it is sometimes relatively easy to take a market away from them. Understand that in the martial art of judo, the secret is to use your opponent's own strength against him. Innovators may ignore a product they invented. The Japanese picked up the transistor this way. It was invented by Bell Labs in the United States but was ignored because it was felt that the technology needed to bring the product to fruition was far in the future. It wasn't. Or innovators may feel that they exercise so much control over their innovation that they can maintain a premium price almost indefinitely. This error, as Drucker noted, is certain to attract competitors.

Or innovators may be wrong about what constitutes value and quality for the buyer. It is always the buyer who determines what is or is not value, not the supplier. Or the buyer may try to maximize profits rather than optimize the product. That's what Henry Ford did after successfully innovating and producing the Model T and famously maintaining that buyers could have any color they desired so long as it was black. That rather arrogant notion cost Ford leadership of everyman's car for more than 40 years as GM introduced both many colors and options that were unavailable in the Model T.

Finding and Occupying a Specialized "Ecological Niche"

The third of Drucker's entrepreneurial marketing approaches comes very close to Phil Kotler's strategy of niche marketing. An ecological niche is the place or function of a given organism within its ecosystem.[10] Drucker differentiates this approach from the two previous approaches by contrasting it as one primarily emphasizing positional occupation and control rather than the grappling with competition. According to Drucker, occupying an ecological niche can make a marketer immune to competition altogether because the whole point is to be inconspicuous or to be in a market of what appears to be limited potential, despite the product's being essential, so that no one else is likely to compete until it's too late. The marketer places his offering or company in the optimum niche for it, in its very own ecosystem. I again refer to that little company, ICS, Inc., which once took on mighty IBM in the teaching computer business early in the computer wars and forced IBM to withdraw because it appeared that competing wasn't worth the effort.

Drucker saw three distinct ways of implementing this approach. First, he suggested gaining a toll-gate position. In other words, you control an essential piece of something else needed by competitors so that would-be competitors cannot do business without what you supply. Sierra Engineering Company got itself into this position by being the only company that could manufacture a unique valve for oxygen breathing masks for aviators. If you wanted to sell oxygen breathing masks, you needed that valve.

The other two ways to occupy a specialized ecological niche was to either have a specialty skill or to work in a specialty market. Life is so specialized today that it is not all that difficult to acquire a specialty in which few can compete in a specific market. At one time, a chiropractor was a chiropractor, just as a doctor of medicine was a doctor of medicine. This is no longer an accurate description of either of these professions. For example if you want a board certified upper cervical chiropractor, there are less than 50 in all of the United States. One man I know drives several hundred miles each way between two major cities several times a year to get these services. If you needed this specialized work, you would probably do the same. ICS, Inc., is as good an example as any of the specialized market. Sure IBM could have forced ICS, Inc., out had it wanted to, but it had other fish to fry and left the market at the time without protest.[11]

Changing the Economic Characteristics of a Product, a Market, or an Industry

Drucker's final entrepreneurial marketing approach is the only one that does not require the introduction of an innovation. In this approach, the strategy is the innovation. These innovation strategies were of four different types, all having the ultimate objective of creating a customer, something Drucker had been maintaining since his first explorations into the practice of management.[12] Drucker's four different strategy innovations involve:

- Creating utility
- Pricing in accordance with the customer's needs
- Adapting to the customer's social and economic reality
- Delivering what represents true value to the customer[13]

Creating Utils

Years ago when I studied economics at the University of Chicago, I learned that utils was shorthand for utility, and that utility in turn was actually a measurement of relative customer satisfaction. So Drucker's first strategy with this approach involves changing the product or service to increase customer satisfaction. The ice cream cone might fall into this category. Although stories abound as to who came up with the idea first, the first patent was issued in 1903 to an Italian immigrant by the name of Italo Marciony. He had come up with the idea as early as 1896 to solve the problem of his customers' breaking or walking off accidently with the glassware that he had used to serve his ice cream. He increased their utils by enabling them to eat what they had formerly broken or wandered off with.[14] In this case, the marketer increased his own utils as well by saving the cost of glassware he'd previously had to replace. The number of ways to increase utils is infinite. A manufacturer of exercise equipment added additional exercises available online to his buyers. A restaurant added a free glass of wine with each meal, making the experience far more enjoyable and romantic. The U.S. Postal Service made it easier to ship packages by providing free boxes of various sizes for priority shipping and charging a flat rate according to box size instead of by weight. Its utils, dramatized by the slogan, "If it fits, it ships," significantly increased sales.

Creating utils is easy. All you need to do is to ask yourself what would truly make things easier or better for your customers from the customers' point of view.

Changing How a Product or Service Is Priced

Pricing has long been a tactic used by smart marketers. However, Drucker went further in entrepreneurial marketing. He said that pricing should be done in accordance with the needs of the customer and what the customer buys, not what the supplier sells. We'll see a lot more of Drucker's emphasis on the customer and pricing in Chapters 20 and 21. The personal photographic industry provides all sorts of good examples. Who would have thought that cameras would essentially be given to the customer along with the film. After all, neither is what a customer really wants. He or she really wants the photos. And so customers today can buy a throwaway camera, film, and developed photos at an economical price. Other companies will mail you free film. You shoot the film and mail the exposed rolls to the developer in protective envelopes along with a check covering the number and types of photos you want. When your order is fulfilled, you'll find two more rolls of free film. Of course, you needn't buy photo glossies. You can also get your pictures on CDs. With the advent of such technology as digital cameras, along with cameras built into our cell phones, the need now may have become primarily that of photo storage. Not to worry. Companies will store your digital photos and in many cases won't charge you anything. They even facilitate your building your own photo albums and e-mailing these albums to friends and family. Of course, pricing is provided so that glossies, CDs, or imprints of your photos on cards, coffee mugs, or other items can all be accomplished, and that's where these companies profit. Notice how the pricing has changed from what the seller provides—camera, film, developing, and so on—to what the buyer really wants. That's the key to this strategy.

Adapting to the Customer's Social and Economic Reality

Many marketers speak of the "irrational customer." Drucker said that there was no such thing. He stated that the marketer must assume that the customer is always rational, even though this reality may be far different from the marketer's. Mary Kay Ash, the famed CEO of Mary Kay Ash Cosmetics, once told the story about saving money to buy her first new car on her birthday. She did the financial analyses, looked at the various models from the various manufacturers, checked all the sticker prices, and selected the car she wanted. Believe it or not, she even had the money in cash in her purse! However, in those days women didn't buy many cars, and she was ignored by the only salesman present. Finally, she got his attention, but he was so condescending in his attitude that she asked to speak to the manager. She was told he was out to lunch for an hour. Having an hour to kill, she went to the showroom of a competitor nearby. Here the salesman treated her so well, even though "she was just looking" that she bought the car he showed her and didn't return to talk with the manager at the first dealership. Irrational? Maybe, but not in her reality.

Similarly, when considering tactical pricing, consider this. If you don't know which is the best from among three products and you need to make an immediate purchase, how do you know the highest quality product of the three? Most potential customers go for the most expensive. Irrational? Not in their reality. Remember, it is the customer's reality that counts.

Delivering What Represents True Value to the Customer

True value, like quality, is up to the customer, not the marketer. This is critical because customers, or organizational buyers, don't purchase a product or service. They purchase satisfaction of a want or need. This means they purchase value.[15]

Some companies spend millions providing additions to their products. They think that these additions represent more value to and are appreciated by the customer. Unfortunately, the customer doesn't believe that these additions represent value. To a teenage girl, value might be defined primarily by fashion; that is, the fashion of what the teenage set wears in that geographical area at that particular time. Even comfort might come in a poor second. To the same teenage girl's mother, value may be represented by durability. To her father, it might be price. That's why it's important to do the research to find out who is using the product or service, who might influence the purchase decision, and who is actually putting out the money. It's what the customer and who might influence the customer directly or indirectly consider value, not what the supplier or marketer considers value. Some marketers consider this irrational too. However, value is part of the customer's reality.

If in reading this chapter you are thinking, "Wait a minute. Drucker's entrepreneurial marketing is applicable to many different marketing situations," you would be correct. The marketing gems that Drucker placed in entrepreneurial terms should be considered in large corporations as well as in start-ups. All innovations need to be transformed into economic goods, and that's part of the marketer's job in any organization.

Part III
Drucker's Marketing Strategy

Chapter 10

The Best Way to Predict the Future Is to Create It

World leaders, politicians, corporate heads, and, yes, marketers would love to be able to predict the future accurately. For a marketer, to be able to know the technology of the future; to understand future business, economic, and political climates and when they will be present; to forecast accurate demands for future but unknown wants and needs in the marketplace—all of this is a marketer's dream, and hundreds of millions of dollars are spent every year in attempting to fulfill this dream. Science fiction frequently attempts to fill the gap between these dreams and reality. There are numerous tales of travel to the future and then return to the present enabling time travelers to make a fortune based on their knowledge of what is to come. Obviously being able to know the future would be a tremendous competitive advantage. With Drucker, it was no dream. He found a way to do this. Or rather, he found two ways. But he started from two assumptions that seem to be the exact opposite of what he eventually recommended. Drucker stated that we know only two things about the future:

1. The future cannot be known.
2. The future will be different both from what exists now and from what we expect.

These two basic assumptions led to the two ways he recommended for predicting the future. First, he reasoned that any attempt to base today's decisions on unknown future events was doomed to fail since future events could not be known and would be different from what we expect. However, one could predict future *effects* of events that have already occurred. In other words, he clearly distinguished between future events and the *effects* of events that have already occurred and are therefore known. This distinction is critical to understanding his methodology. Next he reasoned that while relying on being able to make the future happen is risky, and in many cases difficult, it was at least a rational activity and certainly less risky than doing nothing.[1]

We shouldn't be too surprised to learn that while we can understand Drucker's statement, the best way to predict the future is to create it. This creation may require some prediction along the way. The necessity of prediction in this sense might be seen as akin to the ancient riddle of which came first, the chicken or the egg. The best way to predict might be to create, but to create might also require some prediction. Fortunately, Drucker provided us with guidance as to how to solve this conundrum. His guidance is not quite as easy as simply suggesting that we create the future ourselves, but it is still good, intelligent and original Drucker direction.

How Drucker Did It

As a self-proclaimed social ecologist and not a practicing manager, Drucker was not in a position to create the future of large organizations, events in society, products, new businesses, or anything else. Yet without creating many futures, Drucker frequently and accurately predicted them. He did it just as he said:

> In human affairs, political, social, economic, and business, it is pointless to try to predict the future, let alone attempt to look ahead 75 years. But it is possible and fruitful to identify major events that have already happened, irrevocably, and that therefore will have predictable effects in the next decade or two. It is possible, in other words, to identify and prepare for the future that has already happened.[2]

In this way Drucker predicted the rise of the healthcare industry and the birth and preeminence of the knowledge worker. He also predicted that greed on the part of both top management and labor would eventually lead to the major economic problems that we began to see in 2007. He made this latter prediction more than 40 years ago and repeatedly warned us that it would eventually happen.

In the classroom he was once asked about his ability to predict the future so accurately. With his wry sense of humor Drucker answered, "It's easy. I listen." After a dramatic pause he added, "to myself." After the laughter died down, he explained: "I simply look out the window and report what I see and what events that have already occurred mean for the future. This simple step of describing the obvious result of previous occurrences gives some the impression that I am predicting the future. The reality is that I am merely stating the obvious. Most never even look out the window to see what has occurred, or if they do, they don't invest the time to think much about the obvious outcome of these events."

Following Drucker's method, we can also "predict the future." We can look out our windows and then predict the future accurately by simply thinking through what these events, which have already occurred, mean for us and our products, services, and businesses in the future. What a great marketing advantage!

How to Use Drucker's Looking Through the Window Technique

Drucker's solution of looking out the window was not a careless metaphor. He recognized that analyzing only internal information: hiring and firing, turnover, productivity, competency, resource allocation, and so on were of limited help unless one knew what was going on in the world outside the window. Drucker knew that a full prediction of any sort had to be based on information about "markets, customers and noncustomers; about technology in one's own industry and others; about worldwide business conditions; and about the changing world economy."[3] All these things are external and can be seen only by looking through the window, outside ourselves, outside our department, outside our company, and outside our industry. He knew that a major recession was inevitable when he considered the unbelievably high salaries executives began to pay themselves on one hand with the continually increased benefits and compensation unions demanded and received at every contract negotiation on the other hand. And neither side was paying any attention to the need for increasing productivity in the process.

A Presidential Example

In the 2008 U.S. presidential campaign, two major candidates ran for the nomination of the Democratic Party. Hillary Clinton, wife of former President Bill Clinton, had years of experience in the Senate and was considered smart and highly competent. Moreover, Bill Clinton was a strong friend of the African American community. Many African Americans who might have normally supported the rising political candidacy of Barack Obama were supporting Hillary.

In the summer of 2007, I found myself on the presidential yacht *Sequoia* in a nonpolitical event celebrating Claremont Graduate University and especially Drucker's legacy. In conversation with a well-known, high-level Democratic African American politician, I was told: "This just isn't Barack's year. He is smart and very charismatic. But this is Hillary's year. Barack will become president some day, but it won't be in 2008. This isn't his time." Later as the Obama political steamroller rocketed on and began to look unstoppable, many pundits predicted that it might be close, but that ultimately Hillary would prevail. Of course, it was Obama who did the prevailing.

In the national election, some predicted a white backlash or a backlash by women because of Hillary Clinton's defeat in the Democratic primary. After all, even with his charisma, likeability, and popular message, Obama's record of political experience and accomplishment was pretty thin if not nonexistent. As his rival Hillary Clinton had frequently claimed in the primary, the only national political exposure Obama had was a speech he had made at the 2004 Democratic presidential convention. "If president, what would he do if there were a national crisis in the middle of the night? Say that I have this great speech?" she challenged. There was plenty of room for sore losers or biased voters to vote for a candidate other than Obama.

No African American had ever been so serious a presidential hopeful. Moreover, John McCain was a war hero with many years in the U.S. Senate. Though his party was unpopular, McCain himself was considered a maverick and not afraid to buck powerful interests, including his own party, and he had proved himself many times politically over the years. He was generally popular with the American electorate. Moreover, he was white. Might not whites say they were going to vote for Obama, but in the secrecy of the voting booth vote for McCain?

What Would We Have Seen Had We Looked Through the Window?

Drucker would have said, "Look out the window and tell me what you see and what it means." For the previous 30 years, Americans had elected increasing numbers of African Americans to top posts in all levels of government. We had elected African American mayors, governors, representatives, and senators across the country. Others had been appointed to high office in growing numbers. President George W. Bush had appointed two secretaries of state during his tenure. Both were African Americans. Neither appointment had to do with affirmative action.

Before becoming secretary of state, General Colin Powell had been promoted to the highest ranking military office in the United States as chairman of the Joint Chiefs of Staff. He was not an affirmative action success story. Affirmative action didn't exist when he was commissioned and for most of the years as he was promoted to increasingly higher rank in the Army. So what looking through the window should have told us is that while prejudice might still exist, it could no longer stop any minority American citizen from reaching the top in a position of high national responsibility.

At the same time we saw that our economy was heading for the worst times since the Great Depression of 1929, and Americans knew it. Rightly or wrongly many blamed this, the war in Iraq and Afghanistan, and a good deal more on President George W. Bush and the Republican Party. Obama's message was: *change you can believe in.* Even Clinton's and McCain's longtime service in Washington worked against them since it implied that they were Washington insiders and unlikely to bring the change that the American people wanted. At a time when the American people demanded change, Obama was the only candidate who promised it. I think Peter would have easily predicted this election. All you needed to do was look out the window and ask yourself what you saw in events that had already occurred and what they meant for the future.

Creating the Future Is Not Necessarily Easy

There is clearly a big difference between predicting the future and making things happen. As Drucker said, making things happen is risky. It is most certainly difficult, and no one can anticipate all the obstacles that might have to be overcome along the way. Obama ran a terrific campaign to make his election happen. It can truly be said that he "predicted" his election to the presidency of the United States by making it happen. It certainly wasn't easy. However, he found the next step of creating the change for which he campaigned to be even more challenging, even with the Democratic Party in control of Congress. Yet, other challenges in many different environments have been met successfully. So that's not to say that a future can't be created just as Drucker suggests, only that it is not automatic and certainly not necessarily easy. Yet it is possible.

Creating the Future

World War II brought the end of the prewar automobile industry in Japan. Automobiles were not available, and individual transportation, except by foot or bicycle, was nonexistent. One man, thrown out of work by the war but with experience in manufacturing machinery on the production line, got the idea of fabricating and attaching a small engine to a bicycle for transportation. Lacking money, he wrote to 18,000 bicycle manufacturers in Japan and asked for their financial assistance to help rebuild the country. Five thousand people responded with real monetary aid.[4] Unfortunately there was a gasoline shortage too. In an era before the high-tech advances of battery operation today, he still didn't let this shortage in Japan stop him. This man configured his initial models to burn pine fuel instead of gasoline.[5] His engines were a little off-beat, but they worked, were needed, and people bought them. This man, Soichiro Honda, built his bicycle engine company into the largest motorcycle company in the world. Then he turned to making Honda automobiles, which for years have sold well worldwide. He didn't predict this future. He created it.

I knew an economist once who graduated with a PhD from a first-rate university, but because of the business conditions at that time, he could not find a permanent job in a university where most doctoral-qualified economists looked. Finally he found a university that agreed to hire him on a one-year contract, with the promise of hiring him the following year for a permanent position. A year later, the university broke its promise and hired someone else whom it considered to be a better catch. It gave this professor another one-year contract and promised it would hire him following the next year. The following year, the same thing happened.

I advised my economist friend to leave the university. But the members of the economics department put it in writing that the following year they would definitely recommend him for hiring. And they did. The problem was that they made three recommendations that year and that he was listed as number three. Higher administration approved only two positions. So this finally forced my friend to face facts—leave the university, and go elsewhere.

At this point he looked out the window about the direction of his future career. PhD economists were mostly heading for universities. As a result, there was an oversupply. However, the aerospace industry was beginning to realize that economists with doctoral degrees could be very useful. A high demand was building. He completely altered his aspirations and sought a position in aerospace. Within three months a major aerospace corporation had hired him as an economist at a much higher salary than the university would have paid him as a tenured professor. Six months later, he became a department head in that company. Six months after that, still in his early thirties, he was promoted to vice president. Looking out the window, drawing conclusions from what you see, and taking action has its rewards, even on a personal basis.

Even Drucker Had to Create His Own Future

Peter Drucker never intended to become "the father of modern management." Nor did he intend originally to become a consultant. His doctorate from the University of Frankfurt was in international law. He had planned on becoming a professor and had already written his uncle at the University of Cologne asking for help in securing a position. When Hitler came to power in Germany, however, Drucker fled to England and got what work he could from a bank and an insurance company. Emigrating to the United States in 1937, he found a job teaching various undergraduate subjects, none of which had anything to do with business or management. Mobilized for World War II, he was made a consultant to the military. When he started, he had no idea what a management consultant was or did. However, he found out, and his work led to consulting work for General Motors after the war and eventually to a book, first about General Motors, and then about management in general. The rest, as they say, is history. But once the predictions are done, how can futures be created?

How Drucker Did It

In practice, Peter first looked at a company's overall objectives and whether they matched the results of his injunction to determine what business the company was in, what the business should be, who the customer was, what the customer wanted, and what the customer termed successful in fulfilling this want. Then he looked at the events that had happened and what they actually meant. Drucker called the results of this analysis "certainties." Pleasant or unpleasant, the certainties had to be faced squarely. In other words he started with an analysis of the situation in the marketplace and identified those certainties that would have to be faced.

Once he knew the certainties, he brought together the resources that would be required to reach the objectives and the most effective strategies. This resulted in a plan. He also looked at risk and investigated four basic questions.

What to Do About Risk

Drucker knew that risk could not be avoided. In fact, he believed that some risk was a requirement for success. Little or no risk meant that the aim was not high enough. The future was always unknown, and unknowns always mean risk. He felt that the risks from unknowns could best be dealt with by taking the initiative to create one's own future. Therefore, a marketer had to take the actions to achieve the goals he or she had established. Of course major threats had to be identified along with alternative courses of action should these threats become realities.

Four Questions That Must Be Answered

Drucker recognized that any company's plan for creating the future had to incorporate the answers to four questions:

1. What opportunities does the company want to pursue, and what risks is it willing and able to accept?
2. What are the scope and structure of the organization's strategy, including the right balance among such aspects as specialization, diversification, and integration?
3. What are considered acceptable trade-offs for a company between time and money and between in-house execution and using a merger, acquisition, joint venture, or some external means to reach its objectives and attain its goals?
4. What is the organizational structure appropriate to the company's economic realities, the opportunities, and it performance expectations?[6]

Above all, Drucker was not just a thinker, but a genius of action. So he decided on the action steps needed to implement the plan that evolved, and then he took action. Did he predict his success, or did he create it? On the face of it, it was mostly the latter. However, an observer would have to say that there was a good dose of the former as well.

Chapter 11

The Fundamental Marketing Decision

arly nineteenth century author Henry David Thoreau wrote, "It is not enough to be busy . . . the question is: What are we busy about?" Peter Drucker placed enormous emphasis on the answer to this question of what are we, or should we, be busy about. He framed this answer as determining the real business of an organization, "To think through and define the *specific purpose* and mission of the institution, whether business enterprise, hospital, or university."[1]

Drucker saw this as a basic responsibility of any manager of any business. It doesn't take much imagination to realize that it is also the basic marketing decision. It was one of the first lessons I learned from Drucker, and I learned this lesson even before I met him and became his student. In those days, I was a young manager, but one who knew very little about business management.

Shortly before meeting Drucker, I became director of research and development for a small company producing life support equipment for military aviators and the airlines. My job included marketing responsibilities. The company was continually plagued with an ongoing problem resulting from the U.S. government's purchasing policies which were dependent on its cyclical fiscal year approval of funds for the coming year. Since the government received this approval for funds expenditure only once a year, we would contract for goods and services at about the same time every year. When the work was complete and the product delivered, we had to wait until the end of the government's fiscal year for the next year's contracts. As a result, the production schedule was a continuous cycle of peaks and valleys, and we always seemed to have too many or too few production workers.

In our production, most of our costs were for governmental work. We had no products for consumers. We did some work for the airlines, but it was miniscule in comparison to what we did for Uncle Sam. Even though we did some exporting of our products to friendly foreign countries, most of this work was funneled through U.S. aid programs and thus through U.S. government contracts as well.

Every five years or so the president of our company would look at this problem and initiate a project aimed at producing and marketing a consumer product to smooth out the peaks and valleys of manufacture. We chose a product similar to our regular product line and used the same machinery, workers, and materials to produce the consumer product. This minimized the investment. However, the result was always the same. At project initiation there was much enthusiasm and high hopes followed by an investment and a concentration of resources for the new venture. Then ultimately there was failure. Each time the failure was apparently the result of a different reason, and no one ever stopped to consider that maybe a larger issue was involved that was causing things to go awry and lead to failure.

One year we had the annual sales meeting, and it was decided that the company would present a copy of Drucker's book *Management: Tasks, Responsibilities, Practices* to each attendee. In the book Drucker exhorted managers to determine what business they were engaged in as their first responsibility. This subject was number one on the agenda for our meeting, and a lengthy discussion followed its introduction.

It soon became obvious why our efforts at getting into one consumer market or another always failed. The consumer market had nothing to do with our business of providing life support protection for aviators. For example, several years before my arrival, the company had decided to enter the commercial market with motorcycle helmets, about which it knew nothing.

Sure the company knew how to produce a protective helmet. It was doing that for aviators. But motorcycle helmets were different. What was considered of primary value to the consumer was different. The consumer valued light weight, comfort, and then price. For the military, it was protection first and then comfort. Price was secondary. The company didn't even know how to reach the consumer to sell the motorcycle helmet product. The end result was that the company invested a million dollars, produced a heavy, overly protective, relatively uncomfortable, high-priced motorcycle helmet that no one wanted and few would wear by choice. That's a major marketing blunder.

Your First Responsibility Is Deciding What Your Business Is

Deciding on what your business is doesn't just apply to products; it is critical to all elements of a marketing organization as well as the organization itself. It doesn't even need to be a business. It could be a nonprofit organization. I remember a couple of years back when parents of Little League baseball players got into a fistfight over a particular baseball game, and there were some serious injuries. As officials of Little League pointed out, these parents had lost sight of what the whole Little League concept was about—teaching sporting behavior and other desirable qualities to the kids plus having fun, not primarily winning baseball games.

Determining what business you are in is the top rung in creating a marketing organization's future. Once you determine this one aspect about your practice of marketing, a lot of other aspects fall into place. Accurately defining your business will automatically save time, money, and resources on aspects that might detract rather than add value to what you are doing. At the same time it will help you to focus on those opportunities and possibilities that are important for success. Until you decide what business you are in, your organization will drift, no matter how effective or imaginative a marketer you are. Moreover, resources of any kind are always limited. No marketer ever has sufficient resources to pursue every opportunity. Therefore, you must pick and choose and concentrate these always limited resources on where they will do the most good. This can be accomplished only after you decide what you are really about: what business you are in.

Without this important definition, members of the organization may be striving to support a direction, product, or a way of operating that will hurt rather than help even if successful, since it diverts resources from the main purpose simply because no one has a clear understanding of the real objective of the organization. Deciding on your organization's business is the first step in obtaining commitment and engagement of your organization to achieve the maximum results in the business you've defined.

The Magic of Commitment Follows Business Definition

Several years ago I did the research that resulted in the book *The Stuff of Heroes: The Eight Universal Laws of Leadership* (Longstreet Press, 1998), which I mention in Chapter 5.

You may recall that one of these eight laws of leadership is to show uncommon commitment. What's so special about showing uncommon commitment? Why do others follow a leader who demonstrates this quality both on and off the battlefield? Psychologists have identified two main reasons why showing uncommon commitment yields such dramatic results:

- It proves that the goal is worthwhile and really important.
- It proves that the leader isn't going to quit.

My research involved those in all kinds of work in addition to marketing and sales. However, there is no question that this is applied to Drucker's thoughts on marketing, and I was able to review the results of this research with him. Here's what he said specifically about uncommon commitment: "The failure of many is because they show no commitment, or commitment to the wrong goals. . . . Commitment comes from a worthy mission and then strong commitment."

Drucker wrote (referring to The Ford Motor Company's disastrous Edsel project in 1958): "And so when it got into trouble, nobody supported the child. I'm not saying it could have been a success. But without that personal commitment it certainly never could be."[2]

We Go All Out Only for Important, Challenging Goals

People don't generally exert themselves very much for small, unimportant goals, especially those that may be too easy. We work hard, take great risks, and let nothing stop us only when a big, important goal is involved. That's why marketing leaders who try to play down the difficulty of a task or marketing or sales campaign make a big mistake. It is far better to be up-front than to blow a lot of hot air about how easy things are going to be. It is much better to tell things exactly as they are even if the situation is serious or difficult and will require significant effort. This doesn't mean that you should be discouraging or say something to indicate that things can't be done. Only that the goal or goals are going to be tough but that they are important and doable. Do this, and you are far more likely to encourage a maximum effort.

Others Follow If They Know You Won't Quit

Others won't follow you if they think that your commitment is temporary or that you may quit the goal short of attainment. Why should they? Why should they invest their time, money, lives, or fortune for something if you aren't going to be there yourself and are not willing to share the pain? Others will follow only when they are convinced that you won't quit no matter how difficult the task looks or no matter what obstacles you encounter along the way.

The Three Forces on Which Commitment Is Built

British Major General J. F. C. Fuller was not a marketer. However, he wrote many books on strategy based on his personal observations and analyses beginning with his firsthand participation in the fighting during

World War I. He articulated the concept of a foundation, consisting of the three aspects of physical, mental, and moral forces on which both strategists and marketers should proceed. The physical force he described has to do with actual physical strength defined by resources; the mental force with knowledge or intelligence; and the moral force with attitudinal or spiritual values. According to Fuller, "Mental force does not win a war; moral force does not win a war; physical force does not win a war; but what *does* win a war is the highest combination of these three forces acting as *one* force."[3] When we analyze any successful strategy after a marketing campaign, we will invariably find that the basis of success is the commitment based on these three forces. They go hand in hand with the commitment beginning with Drucker's fundamental business or marketing decision.

Applying Commitment to Marketing

Any marketer can apply the principle of commitment to both the planning and execution of a marketing campaign by first following Drucker's injunction to determine, "What business am I in?" and then considering Fuller's three forces: physical, mental, and moral. Here are five proven techniques that will help you apply commitment to marketing:

1. Think through your goals until they are clear and definite.
2. Make a public commitment.
3. Promote your goals and objectives.
4. Expect and deal with the dragons.
5. Adjust your marketing strategy and tactics but not your objectives.

1. Think Through Your Goals Until They Are Clear and Definite

Commitment must start with defining your goals clearly. Only in this way can you proceed to strengthening this commitment, publicly committing to reaching your goals, and then promoting your goals to others. You can't make some public commitment to go somewhere until you know where this "somewhere" is. Once you have clearly defined your goals and objectives, you can proceed to make a public commitment to reach them. That's the whole basis of first determining what business you are in.

2. Make a Public Commitment

Some marketers are afraid to make a public commitment to the objective or goal they select. They are afraid that they will appear foolish or incompetent if they don't reach the objective or objectives to which they have publicly committed. But you can't gain commitment unless you have the courage to say what you intend and then go out and do what you say.

3. Promote Your Goals and Objectives

Promoting your goals and objectives doesn't start with a single public commitment. You must promote continually every chance you get. Amilya Antonetti started Soapworks to help those who were allergic to chemical soap products, including her own infant son. With her savings she hired a team of top formulators and worked with them to design a line of natural soap-based household cleaners for those who suffer from allergies, asthma, and chemical sensitivities—and for those who want the safest products and the cleanest clean for their families at the best price. She had made a public commitment to break into the $4.7 billion soap industry despite the odds and the giant corporations that dominated her potential markets. She promoted constantly to family, friends, employees, bankers, vendors, and potential customers. Eventually this resulted in shelf space in 3,000 stores and annual revenues in excess of $10 million in three years despite giant competitors that were already in her market.[4]

4. Expect and Deal with the Dragons

Once you've committed to a clearly defined objective, you can focus on what you want to accomplish—your mission. But getting from "here to there" often is not easy. There will invariably be obstacles—"dragons"—that appear along the way. Many of them will be unexpected. You must deal with them while keeping your eye on your goals and objectives and continuing toward them. In my studies of strategy and marketing operations, I've found that there are two actions you can take that will help you to maintain your resolve when the going gets rough and dragons appear, as they invariably will, to thwart you on your way toward your goals.

First, during your planning, think ahead and anticipate what obstacles, problems, or threats are likely to appear. Anticipating such obstacles allows you to think them through and come up with potential solutions before they appear. Moreover, the more difficulties you can anticipate, the fewer that will crop up unexpectedly for which you may be unprepared, forcing you to come up with ad hoc solutions under the pressure of time or competition.

The Emperor Napoleon, one of history's great strategists, wrote, "If I always appear prepared, it is because before entering an undertaking, I have meditated for long and have foreseen what may occur. It is not genius which reveals to me suddenly and secretly what I should do in circumstances unexpected by others. It is thought and meditation."[5]

The second action you can take is also during the planning stage when you define your objective. Write down each and every benefit you will achieve when you attain your objective. Review these benefits frequently, especially when obstacles appear. Keeping the benefits of gaining your goals in front of you—especially when you must deal with difficult problems—will help you to persist during those periods of stress when you may ask yourself, "Is it really worth the effort?"

5. Adjust Your Strategy and Tactics, but Not Your Overall Objectives

Irwin Jacobs, chairman of Qualcomm, Inc., was forced to adjust his strategy on several significant occasions. Because his ultimate goals remained basically unchanged until he achieved them, Jacobs's story is the essence of sticking to a defined objective no matter what has to be done along the way.

Jacobs, a former engineering professor, cofounded Qualcomm to develop digital wireless technology in 1985. The U.S. wireless industry had previously adopted a system known as time-division multiple access (TDMA) as its digital standard. TDMA had greater reliability than other systems, and this was considered its most important factor.

Jacobs stubbornly developed his products using a far less popular system called code-division multiple access (CDMA) based on compression technology. Jacobs was convinced his system had far greater potential because of its increased access capacity.

It took Jacobs four long years before he got compression technology working reliably. At that point, he approached the Cellular Telephone Industries Association (CTIA) to present his concepts. However, his timing could hardly have been worse. The CTIA had just completed its own internal fight over standards and technologies. The main competitor to TDMA was the general standard for mobile communications (GSM), the European standard. The fight had been bitter, but TDMA had finally prevailed. That's when Jacobs wandered in with his proposal that the organization now consider CDMA again. According to Jacobs, "They threw us out on our ears."[6]

Jacobs stayed focused on his objective. He didn't quit. He knew his compression technology would increase networks' capacity by many times that of competing systems. He didn't abandon his objective, but he realized that he had to change his strategy to reach it. Instead of trying to directly convince the CTIA, he decided to persuade a single corporation to try his system. He reasoned that if he could prove the advantages he claimed in actual practice, he would influence the CTIA indirectly to adopt CDMA as a standard.

After two more years of struggle, he convinced the wireless division of Pacific Telesis to put up $2 million to build a trial network in San Diego. The results of the trial convinced the CTIA to do something it had once hoped to avoid—it reopened the standards debate. Two years later, CTIA approved Jacobs's proposed CDMA as a second standard.

Just when it seemed like Jacobs was on the verge of achieving his objective, another dragon appeared. Several corporations had already sunk millions in TDMA. They attacked CDMA as too expensive, too complicated, and susceptible to jamming, and they attacked Jacobs as a fraud.

Jacobs once again adjusted his strategy. He sought new adoptions from any source. After considerable effort, two large companies, Northern Telecom Ltd. and Motorola agreed to limited licensing of Qualcomm's CDMA technology. Jacobs also went to Asia to look for more business. Meanwhile his detractors tried everything to prevent additional Qualcomm sales. Fortunately for Jacobs, objective testing began to support his claims. Then came a huge sales breakthrough. Major carriers of digital wireless, including PrimeCo and Sprint PCS, signed on to use CDMA technology.

Unfortunately, no one made CDMA handsets, and Sprint and PrimeCo needed tens of thousands. Yet another dragon had reared its head.

Jacobs didn't falter in his commitment to his objective. Where earlier he had decided not to consider making ancillary equipment such as phones, now Jacobs adjusted his strategy again. He convinced Sony to put up 49 percent in a joint phone-making venture. Qualcomm was now in the cellular phone-making business with a hefty multi-million-dollar order for Qualcomm phones, a product Jacobs hadn't even previously considered.

This led to the next dragon. A Qualcomm shipment of thousands of phones was halfway across the country by truck as Jacobs tried desperately to meet a delivery deadline for Sprint. Suddenly and unexpectedly it was discovered that each and every phone had a defective menu screen. Fortunately, Qualcomm managed to catch the truck and get it turned around. It rushed back to Qualcomm's plant in San Diego and the shipment of phones was given speedy reprogramming. Think Qualcomm's problems were at last over? Think again.

Ten days before PrimeCo's national rollout of the phones, someone tried one of the buttons on a Qualcomm phone. An ear-piercing screech nearly deafened him. A second and third phone was tried with the same results. Testing uncovered the problem. It was in the software, so every single phone was affected. With 40,000 phones already shipped, it was too late to ship them back to San Diego. Engineers flew out to PrimeCo's Florida warehouse with a just-in-time fix. Over four days all 40,000 phones were reprogrammed with help from every set of hands they could find to turn screws, open up the phones, and make changes. Again, Qualcomm managed to just barely make the deadline.

How many times along the way did Jacobs have to change is strategy or tactics in order to continue pursuing his objective? Who cares! Irwin

Jacobs's commitment to an objective had its rewards. Over the years most of the new generation wireless systems are built used Jacobs's CDMA technology. *Industry Week* named Qualcomm one of the 100 best managed companies, and *Fortune* magazine named Qualcomm one of the 100 best companies in America to work for. Although the company has gone through numerous sales and acquisitions of businesses in its general line, revenue recently was $10.99 billion and net income $3.25 billion (both "billion" with a "B").[7] Not a bad testimonial for marketing based on commitment to a fully defined business and an objective in which the strategy was adjusted, but the objective never was.

When Should You Ask the Question?

Most marketers don't ask the question of what business they are in at all, or if they do, it is usually only when they get into trouble, and then it is too late. A smart marketer will keep asking this question when the business is formed and then periodically and not wait until dragons appear. Waiting too long is somewhat like a patient going to a doctor only when it is too late for a cure. In order that trends are spotted and addressed before it becomes too late to take advantage of opportunities or avoid threats, it is wise to ask this formally on an annual basis, and even more frequently informally, and on your own at closer intervals.

The Fundamental Marketing Decision Leads to Success

The answer to the fundamental marketing decision, from Drucker's basic question that all managers must first ask about what they are engaged in, leads to:

- Focus and concentration of resources for the correct target market for that particular organization
- Commitment and engagement of the organization's members
- Your ability to proceed toward goal attainment despite inevitable dragons that appear

Above all, Drucker taught that it was the customer who ultimately determined this fundamental marketing decision. "It is the customer who determines what a business is," he wrote. "For it is the customer, and he alone, who through being willing to pay for a good or for a service, converts economic resources into wealth, things into goods. What the business thinks it produces is not of first importance—especially not to the future of the business and to its success. What the customer thinks he is buying, what he considers 'value,' is decisive—it determines what a business is, what it produces and whether it will prosper."[8]

Chapter 12

Drucker's New Certainties for Formulating Marketing Strategy

T he word *strategy* comes from the ancient Greek, and it means "the art of the general." So when you are developing marketing strategy, you are literally practicing the art of the marketing general. Drucker wrote that the purpose of strategy is to enable an organization to achieve its desired results in an unpredictable environment. This is contrary to what many believe, but Drucker was dead right. Marketing strategy is not about achieving results in a known and foreseeable environment, but an environment that is unknown and unforeseeable. In Drucker's own words, it allows an organization to be purposefully opportunistic.[1] One can make an excellent case that strategy is all about marketing. But even if this were not so, marketing is the one essential, crucial ingredient. As Drucker so forthrightly stated: "The fact remains that so far, anyone who is willing to use marketing as the basis for strategy is likely to acquire leadership in an industry or a market fast, and almost without risk."[2]

Marketing Theory and the Strategic and Environmental Variables

Traditional marketing visualizes two sets of variables in the development of strategy. These are frequently termed the strategic or tactical variables, or "four Ps" of product, price, promotion, and place, and the environmental or situational variables such as conditions of business and the economy, technological developments, consumer or cultural behavior, politics, laws and government regulations, competitors, and more. Strategic variables can be selected, varied, and applied as desired by the marketing strategist and are made possible by the resources available. Environmental or situational variables are assumed fixed and relatively uncontrollable. As we've seen in Chapter 1, this isn't true in actuality, since with more time and effort one can work with them, and Drucker recommended it. However, environmental variables are more difficult to manipulate over a shorter period of time and usually require more effort on the part of the marketer.

For example, a marketer might change laws through lobbyists, but this is usually very difficult to accomplish, and it may take a relatively long time and require a disproportional amount of resources. The manipulation of any or all of the so-called four Ps is more under the marketer's control and in most cases results in achieving the objectives intended at less cost and in a shorter period of time.

Where Drucker Differed: The Five Certainties

For strategic analysis to have an impact on a business, Drucker knew that its purpose wasn't to predict the future. The assumptions about the future are just by-products. Their purpose is to give the business direction and help the strategist determine the goals and strategy needed to attain these goals.[3] In thinking through the challenges of such an analysis, Drucker was never afraid to propose ideas that others may never have even considered or thought possible. This was certainly the case with the five environmental variables that he felt were phenomena so unique that they could safely be considered certainties for the foreseeable future. Moreover, he believed that they were different from anything current strategies considered because they were not essentially economic; they were primarily social and political. These were derived based on his notion that future certainties could be accurately predicted based on events that had already occurred.

The five certainties he felt that strategists must consider for developing marketing strategy are:

1. The collapsing birthrate in the developed world
2. Shifts in the distribution of disposable income
3. New definitions of performance in an organization
4. Global competitiveness
5. The growing incongruence between economic globalization and political splintering[4]

Drucker noted that the certainties don't tell a strategist what to do. And of course, Drucker rarely wrote how to do things. But in typical Drucker fashion, his five certainties raised important questions that every marketing strategist should consider in the development of marketing strategy.[5] Let's look at each of these certainties in detail.

The Collapsing Birthrate in the Developed World

Drucker found the falling birthrate in the developed world to be a phenomenon unique in history, with dramatic and important collateral effects. Perhaps the most obvious is the very old and comforting assumption that markets would continue to grow as a population increased at normal rates. How many times have we heard that markets are bound to enlarge because of the automatic increase in birthrate and more prospects? But Drucker looked at the facts and found that birthrates were no longer steadily increasing for populations in the developed world. Note that he referred to the *developed world,* and note also that he did not limit his prediction to just the United States. The biggest decline may actually be in Japan.[6] Of course, the decline in birthrate anywhere could be somewhat offset, delayed, or hidden by immigration. But even this would result in dramatic changes and would also cause turmoil as other populations with different customs, religions, and even languages were attracted to countries of diminished numbers of younger workers.

We are already seeing this as increasing controversy over immigration causes turbulence in the United States today, a country built by, and with a long history of, receiving and absorbing immigrants. Drucker described this immigration pressure as both controversial and inevitable. More important, the United States with its diverse population and past history of immigration is well positioned to cope with it. In Japan immigration is bound to cause major upheavals since this is not only a country with no history of immigration, but one that historically has actually forbidden it.

Drucker found that a dominant issue in all developed countries is an increasing gap between a steadily shrinking number of younger workers and a steadily growing number of people capable of working who are living past traditional retirement age.[7] This aging of the population would cause even more problems and opportunities, and this too is an issue that we can observe today.

So our Social Security system is in trouble? What a surprise! In 1936 when the system was adopted in the United States, the retirement age was 65 and this was viewed as pretty much a maximum age for productive work. But Drucker's calculation was that in the developed countries, retirement age would be moving up to about age 79 in the very near future. With a lower birthrate to support a much larger and older population, it is no wonder that Social Security is in trouble. Of course, there is always opportunity in change, and we can all look out the window and see some of these opportunities in anti-aging products, healthcare, and adult recreational industries, as well as what many do after official retirements by starting second careers. We examine this phenomenon shortly.

Drucker saw several important secondary effects resulting from the collapsing birthrate. He said that for the immediate future demographics would dominate the politics in developed countries, shunted aside only temporarily by wars and economic conditions. In any case the result would be that government instability in developed countries would likely soon become the norm. The definition of the concept of retirement would be certain to change. While early "retirement" will continue, it will no longer mean a return to childhood in some kind of golden year's playground as envisioned by many socialists only a few years back. Rather it may mean extended employment with one's former employer, but under different conditions.

It has long been recognized that an experienced employee paid as an outside consultant could save the corporation a lot of money. I recall a book for prospective independent consultants that recommended that the new consultant's first and best prospective client should be the former employer. For others, "retirement" may mean an entirely different second career. For years it was assumed that one was restricted to one single profession per lifetime. Today we've seen former successes from one industry, or even profession, retire and start anew in a completely different profession, with many becoming more successful in that second career.

Drucker noted that older workers, especially the knowledge workers who worked primarily with their minds and not their hands, would be increasingly productive. He speculated that firms that first discovered how best to utilize this experienced talent in a new type of relationship, since the old model of increasing responsibility in business as a motivator would not hold for this group of older knowledge workers, would acquire a significant competitive advantage. Perhaps of even more direct importance to the marketing strategist would be the effect on potential markets. The youth and younger markets will inevitably decline, and the senior markets will increase. But the increase in potential will not be a result of only numbers of potential older consumers, but the individual purchasing power of those who retired from a first career and went on to a second.

Forty years ago during a minor recession, the local government in the Los Angeles area hired retired elders to go on the radio waves and plead with listeners to save for their future retirement. "I'm not doing this commercial only for your good," explained one retired actor in his commercial. "I'm doing it because I need the money." Congress passed laws allowing taxable income earned to be deferred until retirement when the tax was predicted to be lower because of a lower tax bracket based on reduced income. However, with the opportunity for increased work after retirement combined with retirement pay offered by many organizations, this isn't happening. Rather than the lower pay anticipated, the total pay received in many cases is actually increasing.[8] And though many nonretirees are out of work and seeking employment, many retirees are making high compensation even during the current recession. As one retiree told me happily recently, "My total compensation has increased by 20 percent since I retired!" A recent article in the *Los Angeles Times* reported that some retired government employees hired recently as consultants to the California government were making a six-figure income, and in one case $300,000 year, despite cutbacks in California government resulting from the recession.

Shifts in the Distribution of Disposable Income

Drucker found that the truly important statistic that most companies overlook completely is the share of disposable income that is being spent on the products or services that they provide. Drucker believed that this figure was the most reliable as input in formulating strategy because the statistic changed very little over long periods while trends of disposable income, if they occurred, are even more crucial to a firm's strategy. He categorized these trends into four areas: government, healthcare, education, and leisure. Drucker predicted that all four were certain to change significantly in the coming decades and not necessarily in the way that you might expect. This is happening right before our eyes.

First, Drucker asserted that government control over disposable income is growing. This has little to do with the present national administration. Recall that Drucker died in 2005, and his assertion was made in 1999. So for those who want to blame this all on either Presidents Obama or Bush, this prediction preceded them both.

Consider regulations over the environment and how a business can function in society and in a competitive environment. Whether you agree or not, society now expects government to at least try to control what it approves or disapproves or what it thinks right or wrong. As a result it is illegal to import or sell certain animal furs or skins. It is against the law to own certain exotic animals outside of a licensed zoo. And while many consider the sale of firearms to be largely unregulated, the fact is that many firearms controls in place today would shock citizens of only 50 years ago, when only fully automatic machine guns and heavy weapons of war were restricted and all other guns could be bought freely in most cities and most states or through mail order, and they were not otherwise restricted.

New York City was the sole exception by the way. It has had the Sullivan Law since 1911, authored by Timothy Sullivan, a notoriously corrupt Tammany Hall politician. His law required licensing of handguns small enough to be concealed as well as knives, brass knuckles, and razors. Italian immigration had increased from a reported 4,000 in 1850 to nearly a half a million by 1900. The law was passed during a wave of anti-Italian prejudice and was specifically intended to disarm Italians who those in power in New York at the time deemed to be the trouble makers.[9]

Whether you agree or disagree with the changes in healthcare, they too constitute considerable additional control. I'm not saying that all these changes by government are necessarily a bad thing. Only that government has come to be a major factor in the formulation of strategy for any organization, and its significance is growing.

In contrast, and contrary to general opinion, the leisure sector may be declining. Recall the concept of the product life cycle. It also can apply to an industry. The stages of the life cycle are introduction, growth, maturity, and decline. Drucker's definitions were a little different from that of products. A growth industry meant one in which demand for its products grows faster than national income and either population or personal income, or both. If a comparison showed both to be equal, the industry was mature, and if it was not growing as quickly, the industry was in decline.

Drucker thought that at the very least, leisure was in the mature stage. As evidence, he cited increased competition, declining profit margins, and lowered product differentiation. Although many competitors may remain in the growth stage, they are now competing for smaller and smaller market shares. As a result the competition heats up and shake-outs of less effective companies begin to occur. Less efficient competitors go under or withdraw from the market. Buyers who have been purchasing the product or service exhibit repeat buying, and although sales continue to increase, profits begin to fall. Manufacturing costs are much lower than previously, but the increased competition for a smaller market share ultimately forces prices down. This encourages a strategy of entrenchment, yet a search for new markets is still possible. Typical tactics include reducing some channels to improve profit margins, lowering price as a tactic against weaker competitors, and increasing emphasis on promotion.

Drucker found that healthcare and education were both going to continue to be major growth sectors, although there would be shifts within them. An example is education shifting from an emphasis on educating the young college student to educating already career-engaged adult knowledge workers. This was probably one reason why Drucker felt that the future of adult education was largely online rather than in the "brick and mortar" traditional classroom, since online education causes a minimum disruption of family and regular work.

Drucker concluded that utilizing this certainty required both quantitative information and qualitative analysis. Thus this is another example of looking at data but deciding what the data meant rather than primarily crunching numbers.[10] Most try to quantify the information and the analysis. The "tyranny of numbers" rather than human thinking becomes the governing factor, and Drucker tried to avoid this.

Defining Performance

According to Drucker, the traditional view of performance in many countries outside the United States was that the corporation was run for the interest of the manual worker. This included Japan, Germany, Scandinavian countries, and others. Of course, in the United States and Great Britain, the interests have been defined somewhat differently, at least since the late 1920s. Though not clearly defined, business is supposed to be run for an ill-defined conglomeration of interests including customers, employees, shareholders, and society. The only big question is whether this should be short-term interests for gain in stock price or longer term for future growth. Drucker notes that even "long term" isn't necessarily all that long since the average span of a "successful" enterprise is less than 30 years.[11]

However, a fixed certainty is that all these traditional views will need to be revised and thus the definition of performance, in marketing or in a marketing support function, will need to be revised as well. All this is the result of the new demographics and longer life spans in developed countries. And this is also the result of the investments made by these groups; these seniors now own a considerable portion of all publically listed corporations. Drucker put the numbers of this considerable portion at between 40 and 60 percent of corporations in the United States.[12]

Drucker did not attempt to come up with these new definitions of performance except to state that there would be new definitions that would have a clear impact on strategy, that they would be based on longer-term estimates and less and less on "social harmony," and that performance would need to be defined nonfinancially with a nonfinancial "value" return.[13] Only in this way would this be meaningful to knowledge workers and generate the commitment that today is frequently termed "engagement."

Global Competitiveness

Global competitiveness relates to the competiveness of nations. Each year the *World Economic Forum* compiles a weighted average of many different components measured by publically available data and surveys of a country's relative competitiveness globally. That's not what Drucker was talking about with this certainty.[14]

Consider this. A little more than 30 years ago I recall an entrepreneur with worldwide interests telling me that many fellow entrepreneurs he spoke with regarded world trade as if it were business done with Mars and that only about 7 percent of small-business people he had talked with did business on a global basis when the markets were wide open and hungrily waiting for these companies' products and services. What a dramatic change in such a relatively short time span! Partly because of technology and the Internet, no small business, giant corporation, hospital, university, you name it can ignore institutions outside of its own national boundaries. Drucker said more. No entity can either succeed or even survive without measuring up to standards set by the leaders in its industry anywhere on the planet. This would be of considerable benefit if our political, corporate, and labor leaders would simply integrate the knowledge into their strategies. It is Drucker's contention that traditional means of protection of home industries no longer protects, "no matter how high the customs duties nor how low the import quotas."[15] Drucker easily predicted the struggles now occurring for increased protectionism, and one can easily see that this in the failure of the G20 summit.[16] Drucker maintained that the net result of protectionism would not solve a nation's problems, or a particular institution's, but only make individual companies even more vulnerable. The only solution was for the organization to find a way to compete considering the standards set by the best organizations in every area of management and essentially to consider such issues as government subsidies of global competitors as environmental variables that must be overcome by superior strategies, not by similar protection strategies of its own government.

The Growing Incongruence Between Economic Globalization and Political Splintering

Drucker's first book, *The End of Economic Man*, took on the historic notion that people behaved rationally in response to economics. According to Drucker, the rise of Nazism confirmed the disproval of that theory. Sixty years later Drucker revisited his earlier work in a management context and strategy development. His conclusion, even within transnational economic units, was that national politics will overrule economic rationality.[17] His certainties concerned four implications that strategists should consider. Two of them they should avoid; two they should embrace.

First, the strategist shouldn't be seduced into subordinating economic decisions to local politics. That is, the marketer shouldn't be making economic decisions based on political "bribes," be they government subsidies, exemption from taxes, or a guaranteed monopoly. Drucker flatly stated that if the strategy didn't make sense economically without the bribe, it was pointless to take it, no matter how attractive. But Drucker went further. He wrote that even if it did make economic sense without the bribe, one shouldn't get into a situation where bribes are involved. The reason was simple. Taking a decision motivated by these bribes always turned sour aside from issues of ethics or integrity, which may be important for other reasons. As evidence, Drucker pointed out that every U.S. company that built a manufacturing plant in a small Latin American country in the 1960s and 1970s because of the promise of a monopoly ended up dealing with a disaster.

He also cautioned against expanding globally by going into business unless it fit into the company's theory of business and customary strategy. He restated what most marketers already know—that products behave differently in different countries. How else could it be explained that Coca-Cola did far better selling fruit juice than Coke in France?

For his two "dos," the first has to do with foreign expansion based on alliances, partnerships, and joint ventures. The expansion should be structured on economic and not independent legal entities.[18] For his final certainty in this category, he suggested that managing currency through fluctuations must be made a part of strategy, since no organization has been or will be immune to this factor.

In Drucker's view, incorporating these certainties was more important than incorporating the usual environmental variables that strategists, and especially marketing strategists, routinely consider. Marketers ignore Drucker's certainties at their own peril.

Chapter 13

Success by Abandonment of Profitable Products

In 1981, Jack Welch began his 20-year tenure as CEO of General Electric and his legend as one of the leading CEOs of the twentieth century. He was also the youngest CEO in GE's history and the greatest sales and profit increases came under his leadership. When he became CEO, the company's market value was about $12 billion. When he left, it was worth more than 25 times that figure. According to Welch, two simple questions from Drucker helped propel GE to these amazing accomplishments. The first question was, "If GE wasn't already in a particular business, would you enter it today?" Then Drucker asked a follow-up question, "If the answer is no, what are you going to do about it?" According to Welch, Drucker's questions led him to shed profitable but underperforming businesses; this streamlined GE into its extraordinary success. Welch mandated that any GE business that was neither number one nor runner-up in its market would be sold or liquidated.[1, 2] These two questions are examples of Drucker's theory of abandonment, which he discussed first in his book *Managing by Results* in 1964 almost 20 years earlier. They also provide us with a powerful example of Welch's successful application of Drucker's theory.[3]

The Twentieth Century's Most Influential Car Should Have Been Abandoned

Henry Ford's Model T was named the world's most influential car of the twentieth century. The actual title of the award was "The Car of the Century," and this was an international award resulting from an election process overseen by the Global Automotive Election Foundation in 1999. No doubt the award was well deserved since no less than 15 million Model Ts were built between 1908 and1927. Although there were minor changes over this 19-year period, the Model T was primarily characterized by a stubborn lack of change and maintenance of design. This was exemplified by Ford's well-known instructions to his staff that Ford's customers could have any color they wanted as long as it was black. Challenged by rival GM which had begun to provide a variety of designs and options, Henry Ford replied that the Model T design "was already correct" and therefore would not be altered. Barely profitable at the end of its career, the Model T could no longer compete with more modern offerings. Ford's failure to abandon this successful product much earlier cost his company's leadership to General Motors for 40 years, early confirmation of Drucker's claim that abandonment of a successful product at the right time is a necessity whether the product was "already correct" or not.[4, 5]

The Systematic Process of Abandonment

Drucker's concept of abandonment comes from the dynamics of knowledge advancement and requires a single imperative for every organization: management of change has to be instilled at the cellular level, that is, in the organization's very structure. He saw that logically this meant that an organization must be prepared to abandon everything it does at the same time that it must devote itself to creating the new, so abandonment must simultaneously be executed along with continuous improvement, exploitation of past successes, and innovation.[6] In fact, he recommended that a proposal for a major new effort must always spell out what old effort must be abandoned.[7] This is something I found out from necessity early in my career as director of research and development, when one boss I had insisted on initiating products for development without simultaneously increasing my overall budget.

Drucker saw that all these processes must be systematic, but he emphasized that abandonment especially was not to be done in a haphazard fashion and must be subjected to a systematic process. The process begins with rethinking. It progresses to deciding on the criterion of abandonment. Then it requires an abandonment plan and implementation of that plan.

Rethinking the Preamble to Abandonment

In an essay on his thoughts on "re-thinking re-inventing government," Drucker considered rethinking as a preamble to abandonment. The notion of rethinking is easily applied to reinventing anything, including a company's products or ways of marketing. Drucker said that rethinking should result in a long list of activities, programs, or products to examine and to be ranked by their success. Those at the top of the list should be strengthened; that is, they should be given even more resources to exploit their success. They would roughly correspond to GE's businesses which were both profitable and the leaders in their markets. Those at the bottom of the rethinking list should be dumped. Those in between should be refocused. That is, some thinking should occur as to what to do. Drucker noted that conventional policy making ranked programs and activities according to good intentions. This was probably true for GE's businesses when Welch became CEO at GE and Drucker asked his now famous questions. The same can be said for retention of the "already correct" Model T when technology had changed significantly over time. But rather than good intentions, correct rethinking ranks all on the list according to performance.[8]

How Often to Rethink

Drucker was specific regarding how often to rethink things and wrote:

> Every three years, an organization should challenge every product, every service, every policy, every distribution channel with the question, if we were not in it already, would we be doing it now?[9]

The question assumes that conditions have changed and that perhaps even more importantly that the organization has learned something new since the original action was initiated or in the interim. Drucker emphasized that if the answer to the above question was no, the reaction must never be for additional study, but always "what are we to do now?" That is, there must be action taken.[10]

Why Abandonment Is Not Only a Necessity, but an Opportunity

During rethinking, the marketer conducts categorization which will identify opportunity. Like the "sorting hat" in the Harry Potter books which automatically categorizes new wizard students and sends them to different academic houses of magic in the fictitious Hogwarts School of Witchcraft and Wizardry, the rethink list categorizes products (or businesses, or anything else) into three categories:

1. A high-priority ongoing group in which there is a significant opportunity to achieve extraordinary results
2. A high-priority group in which the opportunity is in abandonment
3. A large group of mediocre items in which efforts to exploit or abandon are likely to lead to significant results[11]

You already know that resources are always limited and that no one ever has all the resources that they'd like to have to run a marketing campaign or develop a new product. So if something is abandoned, this frees up resources: money, personnel, facilities, equipment, and time for necessary resources for new opportunities or to take advantage of older ones with higher potential. Drucker called this sorting into areas of higher priority "push priorities." He said that they were easy to identify. Push priorities are opportunities where the results, if successful, earn back what they cost many times over.[12]

In addition there are other advantages to abandonment. Psychologically, it stimulates the search for a replacement for an old successful product that is no longer present. According to Drucker, abandonment is also necessary to render an "existing business entrepreneurial"; that is, "to work *today* on the products, services, processes, and technologies that will make a difference tomorrow."[13] Finally, abandonment even facilitates change management since the most effective way to manage change is to create it yourself.[14]

When to Abandon

Most marketers are familiar with the product life cycle concept in which products (or businesses) proceed over the life of a product through the stages of introduction, growth, maturity, and then decline. In the maturity stages a phenomenon occurs in which profits begin to decline even while sales continue to increase. This is the result of increased competition and other factors. It is then that marketing executives need to think seriously about abandoning a formerly successful product. Yes, there may be reasons to refocus and to initiate a product extension strategy to extend the life of the product. However, the fact that the product is still profitable is no excuse for inaction.

Moreover, Drucker maintained that the real opportunities were not in product extension, but in cutting loose completely and declaring obsolete your own successful product. This would lead to the advantages noted previously. So Henry Ford might have made major changes to update the Model T and still continued with the basic design. This however would not have been as successful as abandoning it completely and creating a new car design concept that fit the changing market more perfectly and took full advantage of developing technology. Similarly, Welch might have executed an extension strategy for GE's second tier businesses instead of abandoning them. No doubt they would have been more successful and more profitable than previously. However, the truly incredible results achieved in using the resources saved by abandonment to create entirely new and even more successful businesses would not have been achieved. Drucker was absolutely convinced that abandonment was a far better strategy than extension.

Candidates for Priority Help or Abandonment

Any rethinking list or more extensive analysis in a systematic abandonment review process will result in certain areas that deserve priority for our attention. These are the push priorities we spoke of earlier. They include:

- Tomorrow's "breadwinners" and "sleepers." Breadwinners are those candidates that routinely produce positive results. Sleepers, which Drucker also termed "Cinderellas," are those that have hidden potential and might succeed if given a chance.
- Development efforts to replace tomorrow's breadwinners the day after tomorrow.
- Important new knowledge and distribution channels.
- Reducing high support costs, high control costs, and waste.

The candidates for help are obvious—they need resources to pay for the potential that clearly exists. Those would be Welch's profitable businesses that were market leaders. The candidates for abandonment are equally obvious including where the investment is primarily managerial ego, unjustified specialties, unnecessary support activities, waste that can be almost effortlessly dispensed with, and of course yesterday's breadwinner. Finally Drucker noted that whenever the cost of incremental acquisition is more than one-half the probable return, abandonment should be seriously considered.[15]

Toward the end of his career, Drucker summarized a lifetime of observation of the abandonment concept by stating three cases where he could barely contain himself and boldly stated that "the right action is always outright abandonment":

1. If a product, service, process, and so on still has "a few good years left"
2. If the only argument for keeping it is that it is "fully written off"
3. If a new candidate is being stunted or neglected because an old, declining product, or whatever, is being maintained

Drucker wrote that case 3 was the most important reason for abandonment.[16]

Why Marketers Frequently Dislike Abandonment

With the importance of abandonment, one would have thought that managers, especially marketers, would be eager to adopt the concept of abandonment and would be looked to for leadership in this endeavor.

Alas, this is not so. Drucker found that the most frequent argument to justify retention of the old way was something along the line of, "We must grow; we cannot afford to shrink."[17] In other words, those favoring abandonment were accused of wanting to shrink the business. Let's face it. Everyone is uncomfortable with change. Those who are currently successful got that way on the basis of mastering the ways and requirements of the old product, service, or business. Dealing with the new, especially with potentially unproven ways where much is unknown, is risky and will at minimum require effort that is not currently demanded. Who needs it?

This is true in just about everything historical or that I've experienced myself. No surprise that the Wright Brothers first flew a powered aircraft in 1903, but couldn't convince a hidebound U.S. Army to buy one for test until four years later and the dynamic duo had already sold planes to several European powers. "I can see no possible use for a flying machine in battle," one experienced officer proclaimed. Respected professors at our best universities predicted that for a human to fly was impossible—even after it happened!

However, don't think this was unique and applicable only to those thinking about manned flight and could not see future potential when it was right before their eyes. Even today I've seen incredible opposition from forward-thinking, top researchers when a new idea comes on the scene. Drucker wrote years ago that education on the Internet was the future of executive education, predicting that it could well become our greatest growth industry.[18] But what did he know? Intelligent, highly regarded educators tell me today, in all sincerity, that there is no way that online education can ever replace that of the traditional face-to-face method of classroom teaching used for the last 2,000 years. They say this even as education online increases at 15 to 20 percent a year and in the face of research showing online education as being superior to classroom learning. Yet mostly these professors have no direct experience with online education. But what can we expect? They have gained fame and tenure the old-fashioned way by lecturing in the classroom. They are comfortable with this old model. The Internet represents the unknown. It represents risk. It represents learning an entirely new way of imparting knowledge. This is what abandonment is up against.

The Criteria for Abandonment

Drucker provided no specific criteria for abandonment. This is because the potential items that might usefully be abandoned and the criteria for their selection are almost unlimited. However, he did provide clues. For example in decision making he recommended looking at what he called "boundary conditions." These are specifications regarding intended objectives, minimal attainment goals, and other conditions that must be satisfied. He felt that clear thinking regarding the boundary conditions was needed to know when something must be abandoned, and by inference their being understood was also necessary for development of criteria for abandonment.[19] He also commented that budgeting, the most widely used tool of management, provided a forum for evaluating and analyzing the existing situation. Other measurements and controls as well as organized information needed to be reviewed as candidates for abandonment.[20] It follows that quantitative criteria for deciding what should be eliminated and what should remain could be determined.

The Abandonment Plan and Its Implementation

Once the candidate for abandonment has been identified and criteria for specific abandonment have been established, this is followed by organizing everything with a plan complete with specific objectives, numbers of people of various capabilities needed, and the tools, money, information, and other resources necessary for completion of the abandonment along with unambiguous deadlines.[21] Drucker noted that the "how" of abandonment was no less important than the "what," or abandonment would be postponed because abandonment policies are never popular.[22] This is confirmed by the fact that the abandonment at GE, which led to GE's incredible success, involved the displacement of more than 100,000 employees during the first years of Welch's tenure as he discarded underperforming businesses and acquired new ones. It was also the source of the disparaging nickname given him of "Neutron Jack."[23] However, supporters argue that not only did this boost GE to the heights it ascended, but ultimately benefited employees as well as stockholders. Regardless, without this final systematic step of planning, all this is just good intentions, which Drucker added should rarely include the adjective "good."

Chapter 14

Marketing and Selling Are Not Complementary and May Be Adversarial

One evening in class, Drucker made a rather startling claim: "Everyone knows that marketing and selling are not identical," he said. "But few understand that marketing and selling are not necessarily complementary and may even be adversarial."

"Another astonishing Drucker pronouncement," I thought. I had only recently completed a graduate course in marketing taught by another professor. He had carefully explained the idea that marketing and selling were not identical, something known by any business undergraduate today, but not necessarily in my era when many companies still lacked marketing departments and others dealing with the government avoided even awarding a sales or marketing title to its executives so as not to give the impression they were trying to sell anyone anything. Sales managers in such companies carried titles such as "program development manager" or some such. Of course this polite disguise in title is still in use in many organizations. Only companies that actually had sales departments and wanted to sound sophisticated called their sales departments "marketing departments," but everybody knew the department was really supposed to sell something. So while not cutting-edge material, the difference between the concept of marketing and the concept of selling was worthwhile explaining, even to (or maybe especially to) seasoned executives who had decided to return to school to pursue business knowledge at the doctoral level.

The Structure of the Marketing Concept Explained

My professor had also explained the organization of the marketing concept and where this other concept, selling, fit in. This had only recently been conceptualized by Professor E. Jerome McCarthy at Michigan State. Marketing was at the top of the model. Below marketing sat the "four Ps" described as: product, price, promotion, and place. These were usually called "strategic variables," but I think someone gave them that name not knowing what strategy really entailed, since the way they are used is generally tactical, not strategic.

What was meant by product and price was fairly self-evident, even to the uninitiated. However the second two Ps required a little more explanation. Place referred to physical distribution (by land, sea, or air) or distribution channels such as wholesale, retail, agent, and so on. Promotion included subsets all emphasizing communication of one kind or another. These were advertising, publicity, sales promotion, and personal selling. Let's look only at personal selling. One might quibble regarding the differences between personal selling and selling. The American Marketing Association today says that personal selling is, "Selling that involves a face-to-face interaction with the customer." Whereas just plain old selling is defined as, "The personal or impersonal process whereby the salesperson ascertains, activates, and satisfies the needs of the buyer to the mutual, continuous benefit of both buyer and seller."[1] I'm pretty sure that Drucker was not trying to distinguish whether the selling process was done either personally or impersonally. The point was that selling was considered a subset of promotion by marketing orthodoxy then, and it still is. Clearly the idea was that all these variables, both within promotion and as part of the overall four Ps, known as the marketing mix were intended to be complementary. By which I mean they satisfied mutual needs or helped to offset mutual deficiencies within the overall purview of marketing.

It Ain't Necessarily So

Here was Drucker saying that this was not necessarily true—that not only were marketing and selling not complementary, but that they might actually be adversarial. That was not the point of Drucker's lecture that night and embarrassing as it is to relate, I did not challenge him, and no one else did either. I do not know why. I don't recall whether he moved on to another subject, or whether we were inured to his statements having heard so many previously, such as "What everyone knows is usually wrong," or "Most of what we call management consists of making it difficult for people to get their work done," or "The most important thing in communication is hearing what isn't said," or "When a subject becomes totally obsolete, we make it a required course." We learned to accept these Drucker insights not with a grain of salt, but as an uncontested, but sometimes unexplained, fact. Accordingly, it was left for me to discover on my own why he said this and what he meant by it.

My Son, the Musician

Some years later, my old friend and wizard marketer Joe Cossman was telling me about the time he had such high sales that it almost put him out of business. With sudden insight I finally understood what Drucker was telling his executive PhD students that night in Claremont.

Cossman had gotten control of an unusual product called "My Son, the Musician." The inventor had told Cossman that it was guaranteed to end parental problems of helping to potty train an infant son to go to the bathroom when he or she was supposed to and to use the toilet bowl properly when doing so. The device consisted of a bowl containing a sensing device connected to a music box. When the bowl sensed a liquid such as urine, it would immediately begin to play a nursery tune popular with children of this age. Cossman tested it with his own offspring and it worked beautifully, 100 times out of 100.

With considerable enthusiasm, Cossman rushed the item into production, wrote advertising copy, engaged salespeople, and began to promote the product. There was tremendous interest, and the number of products ordered by intermediaries prior to actual production was one of the largest of any of his products. Cossman thought that sales of My Son, the Musician might rival that of products that had sold as many as 1 million units in the past.

Then one day his enthusiasm came to a dead end when a child psychologist who had seen a unit in a local store called to tell him the bad news. My Son, the Musician worked all right. The problem was it worked too well. It would absolutely encourage the child to go to the bathroom when he heard the music he could create by using the toilet bowl properly. In short, the act of urinating became associated with the music. These associations are extremely powerful. You've probably heard of the Russian scientist Dr. Ivan Pavlov's experiments with dogs. Every time he fed his dog, Pavlov would ring a bell. The dog would salivate. Before long, the dog would salivate when he heard the bell, whether Pavlov fed him or not. A strong association had been created between the sound of ringing the bell and the involuntary physiological act of salivation.

It doesn't take much imagination to understand the consequences of the music being played long after the child had stopped using My Son, the Musician as a learning device and even after he had grown to adulthood. Cossman confirmed all this with other psychologists. The selling had been a great success, but it if continued, lawsuits from parents or former users of My Son, the Musician would probably have put him out of business. The more sales and the more successful the selling was, the greater the likelihood of this happening.

Strategy Is More Important Than Tactics

Cossman's problem with My Son, the Musician was one consequence of Drucker's beliefs that selling was not complementary and possibly even adversarial to marketing, and it relates to the fact that the strategy of marketing is employed at a higher level and must be more important than the tactics of selling. The strategy used in My Son, the Musician was based on a flawed concept, flawed not because the idea that the link between use of music when the device was used wouldn't encourage usage that would become habitual, but flawed because of the unintended consequences of the music causing a physiological reaction that might be undesirable at a later date. My Son, the Musician is but a single example of something that is actually true in many situations. Robert E. Wood, who was chief executive officer of Sears, Roebuck and Company during its years of greatest growth and was also a retired army general, stated, "Business is like war in one respect—if its grand strategy is correct, any number of tactical errors can be made, and yet the enterprise proves successful."[2] Unfortunately, the reverse is not true. If the tactics are correct, they can't make an erroneous strategy successful.

The Mistaken Notion That Good Selling Can Overcome Poor Marketing

Because without sales there is no business and thus the importance of sales is undeniable, some have the simplistic notion that effective selling automatically can overcome a poor marketing strategy. I recall some years ago that a professor at one of our top universities wrote exactly that in a journal article. There is absolutely no way that this can happen. If the selling is good enough, it *can* result in high sales, even with a bad strategy. However, this is misleading, and the high sales may conceal a major problem that could result in disaster in the future as was the case with My Son, The Musician, or it could cause the marketer to misallocate resources to a strategy that is inefficient in creating customers or to a business that should never have been entered.

Adversarial Relationships Cause a Misallocation of Resources

Consider the target market at the strategic level. There is an old adage that so-and-so is such a good salesman that he could sell anything to anyone. The line I've heard most refers to selling an icebox to an Eskimo. Let's say that you have a team of super salespeople and it can perform the impossible in selling to a target market, pork to Jews and Muslims, or iceboxes to Eskimos. You name it. The success of our super salespeople may lead us to believe that our overall strategy is just fine, when actually these super salespeople could sell twice as much to a different target market with less effort and resources. Now we begin to understand Drucker's point in declaring selling and marketing to be not complementary and possibly adversarial.

If Drucker Is Right, What Are You Going to Do About It?

Drucker's point is no small thing for marketing managers; it has serious implications. First, it applies to any of the tactical variables. Outstanding advertising, sales promotions such as discounts or special sales, pricing, or selection of channels or means of physical distribution can all get you in the same trouble. They are not necessarily complementary to strategy, and they may be adversarial. So what are you going to do about it? Following the direction in which Drucker pointed, it is most critical that we consider three points:

1. Strategy first.
2. Strategy determines tactics.
3. Good tactics are not only complementary to each other but they are also synergistic.

Strategy First

Drucker wrote, "First decide what business you are in," and then he went on to say that the purpose of this, or any, business is to create a customer. This was Drucker's rationale for stating that marketing is the distinguishing basic function of business. In this sense strategy or marketing is the means used to create a customer. Some call this the "business model." The only problem with this label is that it is too easily expanded to cover everything including tactics, and that's where things begin to go wrong. A marketer whose strategy is actually a tactic is at great risk. Should that tactic fail, he soon finds himself in deep trouble. This is what happened to the company that has become the poster child for wrong government investment, Solyndra.

Solyndra was founded in 2005. It designed, manufactured, and sold solar photovoltaic (PV) systems—in simple words, solar panels. However, they were not conventional flat solar panels. They were cylindrical in shape, and in their most efficient configurations, mounted horizontally and packed closely together. Solyndra claimed that in this way they covered significantly more of the typically available roof area and they produced more electricity per rooftop on an annual basis than a conventional panel installation. There were other technical advantages. Because of their shape, they could capture more solar power than conventional panels, and they could do so without moving.

The company was attractive at a number of other levels. First there was the "green" aspect of the electricity produced. Then there was the hiring of over 1,000 employees during a recession when jobs were scarce and layoffs plentiful. The problem was that the strategy was a tactic—low pricing resulting from materials, design, and technology. Indeed the price of Solyndra's cylindrical solar panels was low compared to conventional solar panels when Solyndra was founded. However, as the years went by, the price of conventional solar panels plummeted because of a combination of subsidies to Chinese manufacturers by the Chinese government and economies of scale as more and more conventional solar panels were sold. In the end, Solyndra's panels were not only far more expensive than the old flat panels, but even the total system was more expensive over time. Solyndra panels were still novel and technologically more sophisticated, but there was no immediate competitive advantage, and the company could no longer compete.

Previously, even President Obama posed at the plant for photographs at Solyndra headquarters shortly after the government's decision to guarantee loans to Solyndra to the tune of over a half billion dollars in 2009. This was against the advice of administration experts including both Lawrence Summers who was director of the White House United States National Economic Council at the time and Treasury secretary Timothy Geithner, both of whom recognized that Solyndra's strategy was faulty and was unlikely to succeed.

In July 2011 company executives were all smiles and announced that sales were doubling. Two months later Solyndra declared bankruptcy. The U.S. taxpayer was the biggest loser when the company filed for bankruptcy on August 31, 2011. Company officers shrugged their collective shoulders and claimed market conditions: "It's not our fault. It's the market. Price of the old style solar panels went way down."[3, 4]

Solyndra's marketing was a tactic based on price. Even a cursory look would have shown how vulnerable Solyndra was from the beginning. If the price of the standard solar panel came down, a virtual certainty as worldwide sales increased, even without Chinese subsides, it should have been obvious that Solyndra could not succeed despite its good intentions and potentially technologically superior product.

Strategy Determines Tactics

Marketers must first have their strategy firmly thought through. Then they are in a position to develop tactics to support that strategy. During the Great Depression, Procter & Gamble's president Richard Deupree realized that consumers were still buying essential household products and that competitors were cutting back on advertising. His strategy was to introduce a phalanx of new, innovative products and to significantly increase advertising as competitors reduced theirs.

This was a strategy he initiated against significant pressure from his own team. At a time when his shareholders were demanding that he cut advertising budgets and reduce other expenses, Deupree went the other way and increased acquisitions, research and development, and advertising. Moreover, just as President Obama took advantage of new technology in the 2008 election by using the cell phone and tweeting to get his messages out to millions of potential voters, P&G looked at the radio as the new vehicle of advertising choice. In addition, P&G capitalized on radio in a highly creative way. Each product sponsored specific programming. So in 1933, P&G began advertising Oxydol, a laundry soap it had acquired several years earlier. It did so by sponsoring the radio show *Ma Perkins*. The announcer's introduction to each episode became a part of the permanent American scene. "Oxydol's own *Ma Perkins*," a booming voice would intone at the start of every show. This sponsorship was so successful that six years later P&G was sponsoring 21 radio shows like *Ma Perkins*, all associated with specific products. P&G not only significantly increased its sales, but it doubled its radio advertising budget every two years during the Depression and virtually built the daytime radio industry by itself. It even gave a new terminology to the English lexicon: "the soap opera."[5, 6, 7]

Good Tactics Are Not Only Complementary to Each Other; They Are Synergistic

Selling and marketing may not be complementary, but tactics should not only be complementary with each other, but synergistic as well. This means that the whole should be greater than the sum of the individual parts or tactics. During the Great Depression P&G emphasized product and advertising. Both worked together. Oxydol really was better than competitive products at the time. It really did make clothes come out four or five times whiter, and it saved the long suffering housewife of the day 25 minutes of pounding wet clothes against washing boards assisted by suds from other brands in attempts to get clothes clean.

In a different generation with origins in a different part of the world, under different economic conditions, Swatch watches present another example of how this synergism of tactics supporting a workable strategy should be applied effectively. Swiss watches, once the gold standard in entry level watches, had been under attack by Japanese companies like Citizen and Seiko for years. This became acute in the 1960s and 1970s as the Japanese launched the digital watch. The price advantage these watches represented was irresistible, and it seemed that there was little the Swiss watchmakers could do.

Then in 1983, through a conglomerate that became the Swatch Group, the Swiss struck back. Through manufacturing improvements and design, the Swatch Group almost halved the number of working parts, brought the price down by 80 percent, and reintroduced the analog watch at the entry level for watch buyers. With other tactics, they did even more. The Swatch Group also made it a fashion watch with bold new styling and design. Inasmuch as fashion watches are usually highly jeweled and expensive; this was a very gutsy thing to do. It also did the right promotion to promote these innovations, and distribution was limited to fashion outlets. Then it introduced the watch concentrating first on the home market where it became an instant success and sold 1 million units the first year, and more than doubled sales the year after[8, 9]

Drucker's genius for marketing was sometimes counterintuitive, but his clarity of thought that selling and marketing were not complementary and might even be adversarial was right on the money.

Part IV
New Product and Service Introduction

Chapter 15

How to Do Marketing Research the Drucker Way

D rucker investigated and confirmed that marketing research was essential. However he also discovered that too few marketers understood how to do it correctly and that this led to poor results and major problems. Of course, "the correct way" was the Drucker way. It's a fact that IBM, the leading manufacturer of corporate computers, researched the market for personal computers before it put up a penny for development. The IBM people did a thorough study too, and their investigation cost a lot of money. The researchers concluded, with little margin for error, that if IBM invested the millions necessary to develop a personal computer for home use, the total market was no more than 1,000 units a year. So overwhelming and convincing was the data that the marketing researchers were able to dissuade their management from this terrible waste of money and resources, and IBM dropped the whole personal computer idea.

This left the door open for a couple of computer geeks who had never graduated from college to work in their garage and develop the computer called Apple. They did no market research of the type done by IBM, and what they did didn't cost them anything. But Steve Jobs and Steve Wozniak not only founded a company, but they founded a billion-dollar industry and changed the world. Steve Jobs later said, "A lot of times people don't know what they want until you show it to them."[1] As we will see, Drucker was a proponent of demonstrating what you have in mind to the customer, with great attention to understanding the customer first. He favored this over an overemphasis on quantitative analysis in marketing research. Drucker was not against quantitative analysis, only that it must not substitute for thinking, gut feel, and the marketers making the final decision rather than a computer doing this.

Many large companies have erred in research, and governments have too. It sometimes seems that the more sophisticated the math, the more in error the results can be. IBM's marketing research erred because of a single critical assumption—that the personal computers envisioned would be used only by those involved with quantitative analysis. They didn't envision anyone using a personal computer to replace a typewriter or any of the thousands of other uses we have found for personal computers today. Drucker thought marketing researchers should emphasize use of the best computer available—the human brain.

Why Drucker Preferred Thinking to Number Crunching

Robert McNamara was one of smartest Secretaries of Defense the United States has ever had. He made his reputation on his ability to analyze quantitative research, and he was the greatest proponent of what was called systems analysis in which everything was analyzed as a system with all factors quantified and therefore measurable. At times it was difficult to challenge any decision he made because there was so much numerical analysis of so many factors that the uninitiated couldn't understand exactly how this came together to result in the final decision.

At the time of McNamara's tenure as Secretary of Defense, I was a young Air Force officer and was sent to the University of Chicago to earn an advanced degree and to gain some understanding of this systems analysis that Secretary McNamara was using with devastating effectiveness to overrule every major decision made by the U.S. Joint Chiefs of Staff. Receiving talks from some of the experts who supported McNamara during my degree program, some problems soon became clear. One was erroneous basic assumptions. For example, at the time we were at war in

Vietnam and there was a pilot shortage. The Air Force wanted to increase the output of pilots, but the secretary said no because he had done the analysis and there was no pilot shortage. Yet even the most junior Air Force flier knew there was a real shortage because he had to put in the additional flying time and combat tours in Vietnam to make up the difference. The error was so simple that it was almost laughable. When an officer completed the required basic flying training, he was rated as a pilot. So long as he continued to maintain his flying proficiency and remained medically qualified, he was carried on the list of "rated pilots" by the Air Force.

McNamara had asked the Air Force for the number of its rated pilots. I don't know the number or kinds of analyses that were performed on these data. However, at the end, McNamara had a number. He also knew the number of rated pilots that the Air Force said it needed. His analysis proved irrefutably that there were sufficient pilots available for the Air Force's needs. Why weren't there? Senior commanders who commanded organizations that contained airplanes, right on up to the Chief of Staff of the Air Force, were also rated pilots and were counted as such. But they obviously couldn't fly in the squadrons as junior lieutenants. Other positions such as a Director of Maintenance were also required to be a rated pilot. However, this person had other duties and couldn't fly in a regular aircrew role. Probably half of the rated pilots couldn't serve in active crew positions while simultaneously serving in executive positions which nevertheless required a pilot but did not involve active flying on a crew. It was like expecting a company president to also work on a production line. Now if the proper question had been asked, McNamara would have seen why there was a pilot shortage, and he would have either trained more pilots or instructed the Air Force to try to convert some of these nonflying positions requiring pilots to positions that did not require pilots. But the correct questions weren't asked by civilian chiefs, nor were answers to questions that weren't asked encouraged of those in uniform.

Another problem was attempting to quantify the nonquantifiable. Sometimes a nonquantifiable factor was ignored completely. One example given to the Air Force as if it were being explained to a child was why the United States shouldn't try to build the best fighter airplane in the world. The analysts assumed that each airplane provided a certain amount of "combat power." They quantified this "combat power" using a compli-cated formula resulting from many factors: range, speed, rate of climb, payload, and so on. If the best fighter plane that could be built provided 100 units of combat power and a lesser fighter plane provided 10 units, it was a no-brainer that you should build the one that provided 100 units.

Not so fast. Let's throw in cost. Maybe the best airplane costs $100 million each, and the lesser airplane costs "only" $1 million. For $100 million you could buy only one super fighter airplane, but you could by 100 lesser airplanes for the same amount of money. You only got 100 units of combat power from the $100 million airplane, whereas you got 1,000 units of combat power from the lower-capability fighters bought for the same amount of money. Those analysts concocting this example were smart enough to adjust for the expenses associated with the addi-tional pilots needed, aviation fuel, maintenance, and so forth for training and flying the 100 lower-performing airplanes. Therefore, it was obvious from the example that on a cost-benefit basis, it was better to buy the 100 copies of the not as good airplane rather than one superplane.

Well, maybe not so obvious. What about the psychological advan-tage of the pilot flying the superior fighter over the pilot flying the inferior one? What about the psychological advantage of the nation owning the superfighter? Those kinds of psychological factors are hard to quantify, so they were simply ignored. That's the kind of thing Drucker was talk-ing about. Drucker knew that dependence solely on numbers could get a marketer in trouble, so he had certain rules pertaining to what should be considered in marketing research. They are not what you usually find taught in Marketing Research 101. Drucker concluded:

- If it's not yet on the market, don't do the market research.
- Expert opinion is of limited value.
- You must understand the risks and the importance of the test of reality.
- It's the customer that defines the product (or service).
- There are three kinds of information that all researchers need.
- You need to know what to emphasize when researching the customer.

If It's Not Yet on the Market, Don't Do the Market Research

Once upon a time I taught the traditional view about marketing research. Don't do it without considering the time delay in getting your product to market. Don't do it without considering that you may reveal your intentions to a competitor. Don't do it unless you're going to get information which will help you to make a decision. I don't ever remember saying, "Don't do it if it's not yet on the market." Of course it's not yet on the market. In many situations, why else would I want to do market research? Unfortunately Steve Jobs's statement was precisely correct, and Drucker had said it many times before: "One cannot do market research for something genuinely new. One cannot do market research for something that is not yet on the market."[2, 3]

People don't understand much if they can't see and put their hands on the something. They can't appreciate what you are talking about. This makes it rather difficult to know the likely reception for something before it is released to the market and it is seen and used. This is a problem, but it's not all. If market research isn't much good for something new, many would turn to expert opinion or judgment to get a general idea of market receptivity. The problem is that this is not likely to work very well either.

Why Expert Opinion May Be of Limited Value

Drucker thought that expert opinion might be the answer too. So he checked it out. Sure enough, he found many, many instances in which the experts had all lined up and agreed and later on were proven correct. The problem is that he also found many, many instances in which the experts all agreed, and they were later proven 100 percent wrong.[4] After analyzing what Drucker called the receptivity gamble he concluded, "Only hindsight can tell us whether the experts are right or wrong in their assessment," and "Opinion research is probably not just useless but likely to do damage."[5] The potential damage was the result of a propensity to risk more and risk more often when told by experts that you are right on target with your plans.

Risk and Reality

There was one type of marketing research for new items that Drucker always favored. He called it the reality test, and it was probably as close as he ever got to marketing research orthodoxy. Drucker felt that we have no choice if we're talking about knowledge-based innovation, and since there is little that isn't knowledge-based nowadays, we frequently have little choice. We must gamble on the receptivity of whatever we want to introduce in the marketplace. Fortunately, this gamble could be substantially reduced in two ways. First, we could integrate new knowledge with one of the other sources of innovation or new product or service development we talk about in Chapter 9 as supply-side innovation. Of course, it is still a gamble, caution still has to be exercised, and what we do must be organized and purposeful.[6] Even more favored to lower the risk in this gamble is "the test of reality."[7] In other words, get something out in the market and see what happens. Yes, Drucker was talking about some sort of test marketing. However, test marketing needn't be overly sophisticated.

I heard once that when Lee Iacocca thought about reintroducing a convertible into a market that had seen few convertibles over the preceding generation, he called a meeting of his design and production staff at Chrysler to discuss how to proceed. "Cut the top off one of our standard sedans," he said. And he gave his staff a day to get the job done. The next day the team met with Iacocca and presented him with plans and drawings as to how they would proceed using a current sedan model, but with new tooling to produce the body without the roof and the incorporation of a convertible feature that would fold into the trunk. The plans included cost estimates and approval points. They had worked all night to get this done in only 24 hours and were pretty proud of their accomplishment. They had it all worked out exactly how to proceed. "No," cried Iacocca. "You don't understand. I want you to cut the top off of one of our cars and have it ready for me this afternoon." According to corporate legend, if Iacocca did any quantitative analysis in this research, it was that he counted how many people waved as he drove this ad hoc "convertible" around town. This, Drucker would agree, was reality testing. Along the same lines was introduction of a limited amount of product into the market or into a limited geographical area.

A Product or Service Is Defined by the Customer, Not the Marketer

One of the surprising things that Drucker found when looking at products and services that had been introduced into the market was how frequently the marketer got it wrong. That is, the marketer thought she was introducing one thing only to discover that she was introducing something entirely different or that she introduced it into one market and an entirely different market segment that was interested in the product emerged. Drucker noticed that it was always the customer who defined the product or service, not the marketer.

DuPont introduced the product Kevlar in the early 1970s. Kevlar was a supercloth whose fibers had five times the tensile strength of steel. The engineers thought it would be an excellent substitute for the steel reinforcement in heavy duty tires. It was, but it made even better fragmentation protective body armor. When it was treated for rigidity and to protect against blunt trauma, protective helmets made of Kevlar were worn by ground combatants as well. Thus did the U.S. Army's "steel pot" of World War II fame disappear from the battlefield. Cossman, that amazing entrepreneur who seemed to be able to sell a million or more of almost any product, was amazed to find his flexible garden hose innovation being snapped up as inexpensive air conditioners for chicken coops.

Drucker was shocked to discover that some marketers didn't like it when someone either used or bought something other than where or how it was intended. Thus did Alfred Einhorn become distressed when dentists began using his anesthetic drug, Novocain? It was intended to be used by medical doctors only. He was so upset that he traveled up and down Germany discouraging the use in the same way that Macy's battled against appliance sales that weren't supposed to take place in a department store where the strength was supposed to be soft fashion goods. Both tried to make those causing the abnormality stop, even though it was in their own and their customers' best interests to exploit the unplanned and unexpected increase in sales.

In response to this mismarketing, Drucker published a warning that marketers introducing new products or services should start out with the assumption that their products or services might find uses and markets never imagined when the product was designed and introduced.[8] Well do I recall that the most effective way to get a quick shine on shoes as a West Point cadet was the application of 5-Day Deodorant pads—not under arms, but to shoe leather? This use wasn't confined to West Point. A professor of nutrition at the University of California, Davis, from the same era recently recounted from his ROTC days at UCLA: "I learned quickly how to use 5-day deodorant pads for that mirror finish on my shoes that was required for passing inspection."[9] Understandably, I don't think any marketer from the 5-Day company ever tried to exploit this additional market for this product, and I'm fairly certain the company would have been horrified had it known. Even though our shoes must have smelled pretty good, the manufacturer and the marketer would probably have fought this use of their product. However, another manufacturer did try to capitalize on the idea of using similar pads to shine shoes some years later, though today there are other alternatives for obtaining a mirror finish shine that are more effective even if they don't smell as good.

The Three Categories of Information That All Market Researchers Need

Drucker identified three sets of information that marketers need to gather and use:

1. Inside
2. Across organizations; that is, partnerships and alliances
3. External[10]

Although all three are important, Drucker thought that external research was the most important, if for no other reason than there are more prospects than customers.[11] He did not dispute the fact that companies expended tremendous effort and expense in turning a prospect into a customer. Therefore, they must not fail to please those customers who are already making purchases, so he was not saying not to ignore old customers. However, he believed that researching potential customers was extremely important. His focus was more on wanting to know what a potential customer would buy and less on researching a company's own products. Along these lines, he agreed that focus groups and similar types of marketing research were rightfully considered valuable, but he was distressed by what he considered an overemphasis on research on the company's own products as opposed to researching customers and what they bought.[12] He also felt that customer research could be even more important than researching the market. And as we will see shortly, this means that indirect competition has a special importance.[13]

What You Need to Know About Potential Customers and Their Buying

Drucker confirmed that marketers are on the right track when they seek to learn who their customers and potential customers are, what they buy, where they are, what they read or watch on television, and so on. However, he found that few marketers emphasize perhaps the most important question of all: what do customers and potential customers value? Drucker stressed this again and again in his writings about marketing. It's not what the marketer is certain about that is important and what is or is not a competitive advantage, but rather what the customer thinks is an advantage of the product or service—what does the customer value?[14] As we will see in Chapter 21 regarding quality, what the marketer defines as quality and how the customer defines it may be two entirely different things. And this is a reason why researching indirect competition may be far more important than researching your direct competitor.

By indirect competition, Drucker meant claimants on potential customers' disposable dollars for what prospects value.[15] Sufferers who take pills to cure headaches want fast, effective, long-lasting relief. So marketers compete head-to-head on this basis and on these qualities in drug products to "cure" headaches. However, vitamin supplements are growing by leaps and bounds against headache products if the vitamin products are effective in preventing headaches because avoiding the pain is what customers are trying to achieve and what they value. Similarly, no customer needs a typewriter if he can get the same job done without having to correct mistakes physically with a computer. It's indirect competition that marketing researchers need to be concerned about.

In summary, Drucker advised to do marketing research, but do it in the right way and to focus on the important, relevant issues, not on less important minor aspects of the market or marketing issues.

Chapter 16

Exploiting Demographic Change

Most Americans were appalled when American young people seemed to suddenly rebel against the beliefs and morals of the "greatest generation" and not only did they embrace drugs, free sex, communal living, "streaking," and more, but they rejected other of their parents' most sacred values with considerable enthusiasm. Many think and still think that the American way of life had suffered a unique and crushing reverse at the hands of the insanity of the post–World War II generation. Members of this generation missed the character-building challenges of the Great Depression and the sacrifices of World War II and therefore were spoiled by having life too easy and by missing lessons wrought by pain and struggle. In short, this particular generation didn't know what it was doing.

Not so, according to Drucker. He explained this period of the 1960s as a predictable phenomenon. It was a shift in demographics in which the average age of the population which had previously been centered in the twenties and thirties dropped significantly. These older age groups are traditionally ultraconservative. However the "baby boom," which began in 1946, had caused a sudden shift such that the dominant age average dropped to the teens. According to Drucker, the "youth rebellion" of the sixties which spawned the hippies wasn't a permanent shift in American values. It was just typical rebellious adolescent behavior that became representative of the times and the entire country only because there were so many more young people around relative to the general population. Drucker noted that the largest single age group at this time was seventeen-year-olds![1] Sure enough, as Drucker had predicted, the large numbers of rebellious youths grew older, and the age center of gravity drifted upward toward more conservative waters; the previous rebellious college student groups became more focused on grades and careers, and Haight-Ashbury in San Francisco faded into history to be visited only by tourists or former inhabitants seeking to recapture memories.[2]

Drucker looked at changes in population and realized that population change alone is perhaps the most important factor that a marketer can analyze to accurately predict the markets and market behaviors of the future. He found that major trends in markets, buying power, buying behavior, customer needs, and more can all be predicted with near certainty by analyzing what has already happened in population dynamics and structure.[3] What an insight—and how valuable for marketers everywhere now and in the future!

Orthodoxy and Where It Goes Wrong

There is much more to demographics than the size of the population, and these other aspects of demographics can be even more important. They include age structure, ethnic composition, employment, education, and income. Drucker thought these to be the clearest and most unambiguous of the various characteristics of population to examine for prediction. More important, these precise characteristics have the most predictable consequences for marketing.[4]

Marketing researchers usually investigate demographics to incorporate them directly into their planning, so use of demographics in and of themselves is nothing new. However, they are rarely used to predict the future. The norm is for marketers to look at demographics to determine what segments or subgroups exist in the overall population that make up the market they are analyzing. After establishing these segments, they seek to develop a detailed profile of the characteristics of a typical segment member. Such profiles combine a number of different variables such as those recommended for analysis by Drucker as well as others including ethnicity, gender, or something else. Once these profiles for various segments are constructed, they are incorporated into marketing strategy and used to develop a marketing plan.

But there is a catch. Demographics are not static. They change. Both segmentation and profile development done in this fashion are but a snapshot of an instant in time. The implicit assumption is that the demographics and resulting profiles will hold constant for the indefinite future. They won't. Remember, it was only for a few short years that the United States went from hard-core conservatism to hard-core hippiedom and back to conservatism. So it's marketer beware. The figures marketers are using are dated at the very time they are being relied on. As a result, despite Drucker's injunction that the best way to predict the future is to create it, marketers need to spend some time predicting as well as creating. To do this, they need to analyze demographics in a different way.

The Strangest Secret

So we can all agree that demographics are far from unknown to marketers. Indeed just about everyone acknowledges the really critical importance of population trends, movements, and other changes, and we see concerns about these changes in newspapers, in magazines, on the Internet, and on television all the time. Since we all agree that this is true, why don't our politicians, much less businesspeople and marketers, base their plans and strategies on these proven factors that are measurable and for the most part have already occurred? The only conclusion can be that while our brains assimilate these facts and cannot help but reason to logical conclusions, emotionally our psyches don't want to accept these conclusions, and so the reasoning never occurs or it is not accepted.

Detroit's Problems Were Predicted Years Earlier

In the late 1950s, I heard an analyst from the automobile industry lecture on the future of the U.S. automobile industry, which was then unchallenged by any country in the world. He showed us figures that proved that it would be the Japanese who would eventually not only challenge the U.S. automobile industry, but would lead in taking over the U.S. market and put tens of thousands of American automobile employees out of work. This was particularly surprising because few people considered the Japanese major challengers to the U.S. automobile industry at the time. Rather, it was the Germans and their beetle-shaped Volkswagen that were thought to perhaps create problems, although not very big ones. Of course it took another 20 years for the Japanese to actually challenge the United States, but they did—right on schedule.

If the figures were so certain, based not only on demographics but also on other known figures of production and little else, why was this not believed and acted upon? Why instead were U.S. automobile sales and production figures simply extrapolated into the future with little change expected except for growth based on an increase in usage because of a population increase? At the time, I recall the reaction to this presentation was disbelief and an overwhelming sense of, well, that's 20 years in the future. Something will happen to change in the intervening years, or what can I do about this, anyway?

Drucker thought that the primary reason was that demographic change appeared to be too slow to be relevant for any practical concern. This view is still alive today. It is as if there was a common agreement to assume that any change in demographics occurs too slowly to worry about. The resulting consensus is to simply assume constancy or continued growth, and plans, marketing and otherwise, incorporate data that are certain to be in gross error. Yet decision makers continue to repeat this error over and over.

Drucker thought that this was the most rewarding opportunity for those taking the time to do what is really a relatively simple analysis. Decision makers of all stripes—marketers, businesspeople, public servants, and government policy makers—continue to assume that demographics or the rate of demographic change occurs too slowly to be important. Yet changing demographics represent major opportunities for those who have the desire and know-how to do the analysis and take advantage of the information they derive. This opportunity is enabled by two simple facts:

1. The events causing these demographic changes have already occurred and are usually well known.
2. The lead times between these events and the demographic changes that will accrue are also known.[5]

Where and How to Start

Of course an analysis of demographic changes with Drucker's method still begins with population figures. However, absolute population is the least significant number for this type of analysis. Drucker noted that age distribution is far more important.[6] Basically, Drucker wanted us to wonder: what is happening, and what effects will this have on the population? Recall Drucker's strategic "certainties" in Chapter 12, which I recommended that all marketers consider in their plans:

1. The collapsing birthrate in the developed world
2. Shifts in the distribution of disposable income
3. New definitions of performance in an organization
4. Global competitiveness
5. The growing incongruence between economic globalization and political splintering[7]

These were all developed using Drucker's methods of demographic analysis. One looks out the window and observes what has already occurred and what this will mean demographically. The baby boom beginning in 1946 meant more toys and baby products required in the infant and childhood years. It also meant more mothers searching for information about problems with child rearing. Is it any surprise that pediatrician Dr. Benjamin Spock's book *Baby and Child Care*, published the same year that the baby boom began, became one of the biggest best-selling books of all time? Fifteen years later, this mass of live, new "terrible teens" led to the temporary social upheaval the United States saw in the 1960s. As this group enters the twenty-first century and becomes senior citizens, it means among other things increased demand for healthcare and healthcare products, the growth of which has skyrocketed and paralleled the aging of the baby boom generation.

The original process of demographic analysis and application for marketers was to segment, profile, and apply findings to plans and strategy. Drucker's process was to observe events that have occurred, to reason to logical conclusions as to results, and then to seek opportunities in the competitive advantage of having this knowledge. It does not eliminate the need for segmentation and developing appropriate profiles of the population segment members along with other important marketing analyses and decisions, but it imparts a major advantage to companies that know what is in the future marketing environment.

What Opportunities to Look For

Drucker well understood that discovering what would happen in the future in the marketplace did not end the marketer's task. Sure, these "certainties" could and should be incorporated into marketing plans instead of the simple segmenting and profiling as a onetime "snapshot" as most marketers do. However, knowing the future represents such a tremendous competitive advantage that seeking special opportunities cannot and should not be ignored, and it raises the very important question of what opportunities these developments would offer. As corollaries, the marketer must look at values of expectations and needs and wants of the demographics and age groups analyzed. With some experience of my own in Internet education for executives, I was not too surprised to note Drucker's prediction about the rise of what was then referred to as e-learning education for managers.

How to Seize the Opportunity

Drucker developed and built courses that delivered instruction, not by the standard method of the face-to-face classroom but through electronic means and the computer. This success motivated him to coauthor an article for *Training and Development* titled "The E-Learning Revolution," with Patricia Galagan, who was editor in chief of the ASTD (American Society for Training and Development) Magazine Group in 2000. Although this article was directed toward trainers of executives, it had clear implications for executive education in colleges and universities since Drucker was not only heavily involved in both, but considered both similar, and excepting his e-learning efforts, he conducted both training and education in the classroom in a very similar fashion. Drucker stated that while there would always be trainers, the growth segment was clearly in the e-learning direction.

He based this conclusion partially on demographics: the growth of numbers of knowledge workers needing advanced education was indeed one of the theories behind the PhD program in executive management he codeveloped at what is today Claremont Graduate University. But he also saw that advantages enabled by the new technology of electronic learning were irresistible. These included convenience for the learner, cost of delivery, and participant reach. No professor could possibly instruct in person as many people as could be reached by electronic means. As Drucker wrote, "But e-learning has done far more than make knowledge easy to access by a large number of people." He went on to say that the effects were nothing short of revolutionary, challenging most of the basic tenets from the classic instructional model to its strategic role.[8]

As usual, he was challenged by many. Educators said that he was far overstating his case, that nothing could replace the on-the-spot instructor in the classroom and the interaction of students. They insisted that such instruction had to be inferior to the traditional primary method of disseminating knowledge since the time of Aristotle.

However, those who looked through the window and drew the same conclusions as Drucker not only prospered, but they seized the opportunity and carried e-learning into the stratosphere. True, for undergraduate education, no one argued that four years of student attendance at traditional colleges and universities should or would be abandoned. And why should they? Students do far more than receive instruction. They become socialized to other students, make lifelong friends, join clubs, are exposed to new ideas, and frequently are introduced to their future spouses. For these students online learning fulfills only part of the reasons they attend college. However, for managers, executives, and professionals, e-learning has revolutionized education. Online education has been growing at 10 percent a year and exceeded this rate of growth for many of the past

12 years since Drucker's article in *Training and Development*. Almost 2,000 colleges and universities teach over the Internet today, including major schools such as Harvard, Stanford, and the University of Southern California. Boston University offers a doctoral program entirely online. Even in this recession year and with government cracking down on disreputable schools or practices, the industry has reached $60 billion with 6.2 million students.[9] At a conference on higher education the *New York Times* reported that two former governors argued that public universities must embrace online education for budgetary reasons.[10]

Moreover, contrary to the assertions by numerous educators, study after study has demonstrated that students learn better online than in traditional classrooms. The 2010 U.S. Department of Education's "Review of Online Learning Studies" found that students who took all or part of a course online performed better, on average, than those taking the same course through traditional face-to-face instruction.[11] Confirming this, a meta-analysis study conducted by Drs. Mickey Shachar and Yoram Neumann that analyzed 20 years of research, 125 studies, and over 20,000 students found that in 70 percent of the cases, students who took distance-learning courses outperformed their counterparts who took courses in a traditional environment.[12]

It was explained by Drucker that the focus was on the learner rather than on the instructor.[13] In practice this probably means that online students are more motivated to learn, whereas in the classroom much depends on the instructors' ability to motivate the students to learn.

However, whether you agree or disagree with these research results, there is little question that the growth Drucker predicted has occurred, it was based on his methods of analyzing demographics, and those who followed his suggestions and applied the conclusions in the correct way were successful in exploiting the opportunity that existed.

Chapter 17

Timing Isn't Everything;
It's the Only Thing

Although attributed to Vince Lombardi, legendary coach of the Green Bay Packers, UCLA Bruins coach Red Sanders said the now famed, "Winning isn't everything; it's the only thing."[1] Apologies to both. I've appropriated the quote and changed "winning" to "timing." With good reason. Timing is extremely important. William Shakespeare emphasized this almost 500 years ago. He had Brutus utter words in his play *Julius Caesar*: "There is a tide in the affairs of men, which taken at the flood, leads on to fortune."[2] As events would later prove, Brutus may have been correct about the tide's existence, but he must have missed it. However, Drucker would have agreed completely that such a tide existed and would probably have gone further to suggest that timing was mightily important even for an assignation and in handling of the events that followed. So too are happenings in modern times heavily dependent on timing for their success. An article in a leading business magazine, titled "Timing Is Everything," advised, "No matter what size your business is, the best time to buy advertising is in the first quarter—always. The next best time is the third quarter. These are the months when most radio and TV stations are hungry and offer low rates and special packages to lure advertisers who may not otherwise bother to advertise . . . and that spills over to print media." The article went on to say, "Inventory needs to be filled to make budgets, and the buyer is really in the driver's seat. Rates can drop by half in the first quarter."[3]

This is all true and the first and third quarters are the time to buy if you look only at "buying advertising." However, if you are deciding *when* to advertise, the advice must be much more "situational" and you have to consider whether your prospects will buy your product or service during that quarter, regardless of the cost of advertising. If you sell snow shovels, advertising in the spring or summer would be ill-advised unless you live in the southern hemisphere. Running a promotional campaign for a water sprinkler system in the dead of winter would also be a serious timing era for most locations.

Some years ago an entrepreneur established a web design and hosting company. Understanding the importance of segmentation, but not having read or assimilated Drucker's advice regarding researching and understanding one's customer, he discovered the hard way that March is not a good time to run a direct-mail campaign to CPAs. After spending lots of money and getting zero leads, he finally figured out that his prospects were in the middle of tax season and were too busy doing taxes to pay attention to his mail. So he reorganized his plans and spent his scarce monetary resources to promote his service to CPAs at a more favorable time of the year considering his customers. It was still the wrong timing. The year was 1999 and few CPAs were familiar with web advertising. So even though his prospects had the time to read his advertising material, the entrepreneurial web designer lost money.[4] Timing is everything.

Drucker knew that timing was critical for all management actions and said so. Moreover Drucker cautioned that there are two major challenges in timing that he thought unique to management. Both result in additional problems for marketing planners. The first challenge was that the time of development was lengthening. He pointed out that in the 1880s, Thomas Edison needed about two years from the time of work in the laboratory until a pilot plant manufacturing a new product was up and running. Drucker stated that in contrast to 100 years earlier, 15 years would not be considered an unusually long time period from laboratory to initial production today. This meant that by the time a product or service could be introduced, it might be obsolete because of other ongoing developments.

Zap Mail's Rapid Demise

FedEx has had a number of highly successful services. FedEx's Zap Mail was not one. It was withdrawn before it really got warmed up after it was launched in 1984. Zap Mail delivered faxed messages for business clients before the general availability of fax machines and at a time when fax machines were still priced fairly high. For high-volume users, FedEx installed its own fax machines on the client's premises with the electronic transmission being carried over its own private network. The company's investment and the charges to the corporate customer were both relatively high, but FedEx believed in its investment and that it was worth it for many customers to see their material delivered in hours rather than the following day. However, quality problems caused delays, and planned incorporation of final transmission by satellite had to be aborted because of the loss of the space shuttle Challenger. By then the cost of personal fax machines had been reduced considerably so customers for Zap Mail only numbered in the hundreds. When FedEx dropped the project only two years after beginning, its losses were in the neighborhood of $320 million.[5]

The Second Challenge

Drucker's second challenge that marketers face is that they must always make decisions considering not just the present but must simultaneously consider the impact of their actions on the future of the organization.[6] Or as Drucker put it: a management decision is hardly acceptable if it endangers the long-range health, if not the very existence, of the organization in the future.[7] These two dimensions are made all the more difficult to deal with because of the critical balance between being too cautious and too rash. While Drucker thought that far more problems were caused by being too cautious, acting too quickly is also a real danger.[8]

Doing the Right Thing at the Wrong Time Is Wrong

While it may seem obvious that a company should not expand exponentially until it is ready, companies sometimes try to exploit their success before they have built the necessary base. It is the right move, but rashness causes a too early action.

A health food store in Los Angeles was so successful in building sales that the manager opened 14 stores within 18 months. With insufficient financial resources, a brand name not yet established, and having not yet mastered the intricacies of the supply chain within the industry, he was bankrupt in the nineteenth month. Many e-commerce companies learned this same lesson, and like the health food store manager, also found that future potential didn't count for very much if you couldn't pay your bills in the present. Their decisions shouldn't have been considered acceptable because they endangered the organization in the future.

Webvan, the largest online grocer, went under despite 750,000 loyal customers, $800 million in investments, and having acquired rival Home-Grocer in a $1.2 billion deal. In very simple terms, Webvan expanded exponentially without ever having established that the business was in a position to make money. It exploited its failure, not its success.

Four Important Aspects of Timing

Clearly there must be a strong link between timing and strategy if you are not to waste resources and the most brilliant and innovative strategies that you may have developed. There are four important aspects regarding timing and strategy that we must consider to secure this linkage. These are:

1. When to take a specific action
2. The sequence of the actions to be taken
3. Whether the actions taken are continuous or discrete
4. Whether the actions are to be repeated

How you respond to each aspect will usually differ depending on the situation.

Understanding the major elements of timing will contribute to your ability to introduce timing elements into your marketing plans and strategies for maximum effectiveness and not simply to take actions as you happen to think of them or when you have the necessary human, capital, or equipment resources. Drucker focused on the first element. Let's see what he had to say.

When to Take a Specific Action

Knowing when to take a certain action is the basic timing decision. Take the introduction of new technology. You may think that if you develop something, you should just rush out to introduce it. This is rarely the case. If your company is known for being first with the latest cutting-edge technology, that may be your competitive advantage. If this particular advantage is important in your industry and you have the resources to support it and the risk involved, by all means introduce the technology as soon as you develop it. Clearly in this case, it makes sense to invest the resources necessary to ensure that you are the very first to develop the innovation and introduce it into the marketplace.

However, if you don't have the resources that guarantee you an immediate impact, maybe it's better to let someone else get in first and make the mistakes that you can learn from. Then you can introduce something even more advanced with less risk and a lower resource commitment.[9]

The fact is that you can sometimes be the leading-edge technology company, miss the boat in being first, and still come out smelling like a rose. IBM was the technology leader in computers when someone at IBM did the flawed marketing research study that concluded that if IBM decided to develop the technology for personal computers, a mere 1,000 customers a year would be interested in purchasing the resulting product.

Of course, this was utter nonsense, which Steve Jobs proved in founding Apple and creating an industry in the process. However, as we all know, technology-latecomer IBM did finally enter the market, with a technologically inferior product no less, and it took over the field by spotting the weaknesses in Apple's strategy of maintaining strict control over who could write computer software for its hardware. Actually, IBM wasn't just late to market; it was very late with a host of other companies getting to market before IBM showed up. This doesn't mean that being late is always the thing to do. It does, however, show that in industries in which the state of technology is not the big differentiator at the time, hanging back may have advantages. The importance of timing of entry into the marketplace illustrates both advantages and disadvantages.

Timing of Entry into the Marketplace: Being First

There are three entry timings that you need to consider. They are (1) being first, (2) being early, and (3) being late. Drucker thought up some rather imaginative names for these various timing strategies, some of which we've looked at. Being "fustest with the mostest" is just one obvious example. However he also suggested "creative imitation" and substrategies for timing when you are not being first. But let's get back to being first. Being first is inherently attractive. It connotes leadership, innovation, and being number one.

There are advantages to being first, and they are not to be dismissed easily. For one thing, a company that is first is the first to benefit from its learning curve. That is, as it gains experience and knowledge in manufacturing and marketing products, its cost of doing business goes down. Thus when competitors attempt to enter the market, the company that is first has a tremendous cost advantage, which can be translated into a price break for the customer and into increased resources for advertising, distribution, and other tactics to boost its overall strategy.

Also, there is a certain customer inertia. As long as the firm is satisfying its customers, it is going to be difficult for a competitor to woo those customers away. Third, being first gives that *first* a certain initiative and momentum as its competitors attempt to catch up with a similar product or service. The firm that is first can be moving on, either with product improvement or to additional markets. Thus, the initiative is with the firm that is first, and it has the edge always to be just a little bit ahead of its competition. Probably the greatest attractiveness of being first is the opportunity to dominate the market. This can happen for a variety of reasons associated with the factors already noted. Under some conditions an advantage is created from the process by which consumers learn about brands and form their preferences. This process can produce a preference structure that favors the first entrant. The first entry is perceived as close to the ideal, and all other brands are compared with it. This makes it difficult for later entrants to capture share from the first entry in the market.[10]

Being first is not without its problems, however. As Drucker points out in his book *Innovation and Entrepreneurship*, being first requires extreme concentration of effort. The company that is first must have one clear-cut goal and concentrate all efforts on it just to succeed. Once successful, substantial and continuing efforts are necessary to maintain leadership, or all that has been invested will be lost. The firm that is first must cut the price of its own product, process, or service, or risk encouraging and protecting competitors as they attempt to enter the market.[11]

Being Early

Being early does not mean being first, but it does mean being one of the first in the market after the first firm or the first few firms have entered the market. Sometimes early entry is really not intentional, but it happens simply because two firms are both vying to be the first and the company that was *early* really came in second or third in the race to be first. When this happens, there is usually a strong fight because of the previous commitment of resources and actions put in motion by both firms. This type of early entry requires some readjustment before proceeding and will have most of the disadvantages of being first without the advantages. On the other hand, early entry without being first can be advantageous if the organization has the resources to effectively compete with the firm that is already in the market. But be cautious here.

A weak early entry can be rather easily overcome by the established firm. However, if the new entrant has the resources and the proper strategy to take on the first entrant, an early entry can establish itself without difficulty. It actually has advantages over the firm that was first. For example, the major disadvantage of being first has to do with risk: risk in demand, risk in technological obsolescence, and risk in many other different areas where things can go wrong. It is because of this high risk that many firms do not choose to adopt a first-into-the-market timing; it is also the reason that many firms that do adopt this timing are unsuccessful.

However, there is more. Because another firm has pioneered the effort, observation, and analysis as to what has occurred in the marketplace, it gives the early entry "free" information as to what will work and what will not. It allows for a more optimum strategy with less wasted time, and, more importantly, fewer wasted resources.

It is an error to assume that because the demand for a product or service has been established that the demand is totally satisfied. At this early stage only a few other competitors are in the marketplace, so the market it is still largely untapped. Significant portions of the market have not yet been satisfied, as will be the case when the product grows more mature.

As a result, being an early entry, as opposed to being first, is an attractive alternative for many organizations. But there are two disadvantages: certain barriers to entry must be overcome, and the market opportunity may be slightly less.

Being Late

Being late involves entering the market after it is already established. There are advantages to an intentional late timing. While earlier entries are already committed to their previous investments, new entrants can include the latest technological improvements in products or processes. Later entrants may be able to achieve greater economies of scale than those that entered at an early stage. This is because the size of the market and the demand for the product can be established more accurately. Thus a larger optimal size of plant is probable, and as the size of the plant increases, corresponding costs decrease per unit sold. Later entrants may be able to obtain better terms from suppliers, employees, or customers because earlier entrants may be locked into higher costs resulting from negotiations that took place when the market was still at risk. With reduced cost for R&D and fewer marketing investments and resources wasted, later entries may be able to offer lower prices than firms already in the marketplace. As noted earlier, early entrants are obligated to reduce prices or provide a protective umbrella for new competition to enter. Yet, later entrants may be able to do this more easily or at least cancel out the advantages provided by the earlier entry going through the experience curve. Finally a late entrant can observe the entire market and niche a particular weak link, while those firms already in the market must be strong everywhere and may not be able to anticipate attempted entrance at a certain part of its market, and an effective defense may require restructuring the incumbent's entire marketing system.

Of course disadvantages are present including barriers to entry and the fact that the market opportunity could be much reduced, especially if the product has entered the maturity or even the decline stage of its life cycle.

Drucker advised two possible substrategies to the late-entry timing. These he called *creative imitation* and *entrepreneurial judo*. Creative imitation, the term actually coined by marketing expert Theodore Levitt at Harvard, involves a strategy that is imitative in its substance yet creative in that it makes better use of the basic innovation than the original product.[12]

Melvin Powers was the president of the Wilshire Book Company, a small publisher of books in various specialty fields. At any one time Melvin Powers had about 400 books in print, all trade paperbacks. Some of these were original works, and some were books that were previously published elsewhere in hard cover. For example, the Wilshire Book Company sold more than 3 million copies of *Psycho-Cybernetics* by Maxwell Maltz and more than 1 million copies of *Think and Grow Rich* by Napoleon Hill. Several years ago Melvin noted that books on the *New York Times* bestseller list included health and fitness books such as *How to Flatten Your Stomach* by Coach Jim Overroad and other books with sexual topics. Using creative imitation, Melvin imitated the idea of a book on health and fitness combined with sex through a spoof he wrote in less than two days called *How to Flatten Your Tush* by "Coach Marge Reardon." Melvin's creative imitation was his combining the two concepts of proven demand in the marketplace and putting them together in a single humorous volume. His spoof sold more than 250,000 copies in less than six months. Creative imitation works!

Entrepreneurial Judo

Entrepreneurial judo was Drucker's name for the catapulting of a company into a leadership position in an industry against the efforts of entrenched established companies by sidestepping their strength. Developed in 1947 by Bell Laboratories, Bell recognized that the transistor would eventually replace the vacuum tube; the estimated date of replacement was about 1970. Meanwhile, Akio Morita, president of Sony in Japan, read about the transistor and went to the United States and bought a license from Bell for only $25,000. Two years later the first Sony portable transistor radio entered the market. Within eight years the Japanese had captured the radio market all over the world.[13]

Richard Davis practiced entrepreneurial judo with a far less sophisticated product. Davis was the owner of a small pizzeria in Detroit. While making a pizza delivery one hot summer night in 1969, Davis was attacked and shot. While recovering from his wounds, Davis began thinking about a means of personal protection, not only for himself, but for police.

Davis found that while the police were given body armor that would stop many types of bullets, in the final analysis it provided no protection at all. The reason was that the armor was heavy, rigid, and bulky. So, it remained in the trunk of the police car, and when police were shot, they weren't wearing it. Investigating different options, Davis found that a flexible body armor vest using flexible ballistic nylon had been used by the military since the Korean War. It was also heavy and bulky and had many manufacturers. However, it was heavy and bulky primarily because it covered the entire upper torso. This was necessary because although the vest wouldn't stop the high-velocity rifle bullets prevalent on the battlefield, it would stop grenade and other shell fragments traveling at a lower velocity which, though not specifically aimed, could do damage anywhere on the upper torso. These military vests would also stop most pistol bullets, which was the main threat facing police.

Davis reasoned that two rectangles of the ballistic nylon material would protect the front and back of the torso and could even be worn under a police shirt. The two parts could be held in place by Velcro straps. This was a brilliant innovation that no one had thought of previously. Davis proved it would work by firing at a telephone book protected by his armor. The bullet didn't penetrate. Moreover, the design was easy to manufacture, and the materials were relatively inexpensive.

He built a company called Second Chance based on this innovation. The idea for his armor could not be patented and was quickly copied by others. However, not before his body armor saved many lives and the former pizza deliveryman had sold his company many years later for $45 million.[14, 15]

Any marketer must conclude, as Drucker did, that it's not enough to do the right thing. A successful marketer must do the right thing at the right time.

Chapter 18

How to Avoid Major Failure

Drucker knew how to avoid major failure in marketing. His solution may surprise you, as it meant breaking with a successful past, but in Drucker's mind, it was absolutely essential.

Why You Shouldn't Copy Past Success Forever

Drucker believed that if you continue to do what made you successful in the past, you will eventually fail. This has been true in all times and in every field including not only marketing and business but war and politics. Companies, industries, countries, and even individuals failing to understand this single principle litter history. Moreover, the error is not simply in continuing to market the same product or service without thought to its eventual abandonment. It has long been recognized that extension of a successful brand name to other products or services has significant limitations.

Recently a young woman knowing that I had authored many books asked if I would be willing to review and write a testimonial for a book on clothes and fashion that she planned on submitting to a publisher. I declined, recommending that she seek out someone whose name or company might be more influential to individuals who might be interested in buying the book. Specifically, I suggested someone in the fashion industry, such as a fashion editor of a popular fashion magazine, an instructor at a fashion school, a celebrity known for her fashion sense, an author who had written a successful book in the same genre, or anyone along those lines. Without this connection, I told her that the testimonial wouldn't help her much and that it might actually hurt because it implied that she was unable to get anyone interested who had greater knowledge about the subject she was writing about. She wanted to do an extension strategy based on simply my authorship of business books. That's not nearly close enough.

In the same vein, one might be successful in producing Honda automobiles as well as motorcycles or motorbikes. But it is unlikely that Honda Baking Powder would work very well as a brand extension strategy. So Drucker's cautionary notes about the time limits of successful products or strategies might apply to extension of brand name into other areas as well.

Aircraft and Pilot Obsolescence Predicted by Air Force's Commander

I said that Drucker's point about success not being extendable indefinitely applied to other fields, not just business. One of the most remarkable cases of a manager who recognized what Drucker meant even before Drucker publicized it was not a business or marketing executive, but an Air Force general. His name was Henry H. "Hap" Arnold. He was the commander of the U.S. Army Air Forces during World War II. After the U.S. Air Force was given independence from the U.S. Army after the war and a separate military service was created, he became the first and only five-star general that the Air Force has ever had. General Arnold had fought his entire career for an air force independent of the U.S. Army with full career opportunities for the pilots that flew the aircraft that were the essence of this new military force.

Full career opportunities had frequently not been available when the Air Force was under the control of nonflying senior Army officers. Yet with a lifetime of fighting for more and better career opportunities for his pilots, almost immediately after formation of an independent Air Force, General Arnold cautioned them: "We must think in terms of tomorrow. We must bear in mind that air power itself can become obsolete."[1] General Arnold wrote that more than 60 years ago when airplanes flown by pilots were the only weapons delivery system in the Air Force's inventory.

As the years went by the space program, missiles, and other systems took an increasingly larger share of the Air Force budget. Today, ballistic missiles, cruise missiles, and unmanned drones flown from ground stations thousands of miles away are replacing manned combat aircraft to such a degree that more missile officers, those concerned with spacecraft, and remote pilots of RPV (remotely piloted vehicles) "flying" their planes from the ground are needed than pilots flying in airplanes in the air. While air power is not obsolete, it has changed substantially from General Arnold's time, and the term "aerospace power" has largely replaced "air power."

Horror Stories from the Recent Past

In recent years in business we have seen failures of financial organizations so powerful that we would never have thought it possible. Lehman Bros., AIG, Merrill Lynch, Fannie Mae and Freddie Mac, Washington Mutual, and many others have collapsed, been taken over by the government, been acquired by others, or are coping with serious problems brought on by their failures. In every case, they were following strategies that had previously been successful, sometimes for years. Unfortunately as you read this, hundreds of formerly successful organizations, big and small, are proceeding down the same primrose path to failure in blissful ignorance that disaster awaits just around the corner. Sure, the strategies are different, but as Andrew Ross Sorkin, the author of *Too Big to Fail*, pointed out, "When the next, inevitable bubble bursts, the cycle will only repeat itself."[2] In other words, future financial crises and financial failure are certain even though the strategies these institutions use may differ. This is not the result of the present recession although we'll continue to see plenty of these types of failures too in other industries before the current financial problems have disappeared. However, I'm talking about marketing organizations that aren't even in danger now.

They operate and follow the same, formerly successful ways of the past. Drucker would say that this is a very predictable mistake.

Just recently a friend who had been a highly successful marketer told me how he had to restructure to avoid bankruptcy. During the boom years he had big buildings and several hundred employees. He thought that he had been successful with only minor fine-tuning to his marketing strategy. He was taking in $50,000 a month. Then his CPA informed him that although he was taking in $50,000 a month, he was spending $150,000 a month to do this. Now he and two employees are revamping the whole business and struggling to find a way to rebuild.

Of course the failures in the ongoing financial crisis emanate originally from derivative loans gone bad and the collapse of the housing industry. Yet financial organizations exist that took Drucker's advice and changed course before it was too late; that is, those that realized that while risk is a part of business and marketing, no success (bubbles are certainly in this category) lasts forever. In 2001, Kenneth D. Lewis became CEO of Bank of America, the largest U.S. bank. He looked at the derivative loans owned by the bank shortly after becoming CEO, and it was pointed out to him that these were profitable and highly successful. Still, he ordered Bank of America to divest these and get out of the business. Lewis may have made mistakes while heading up Bank of America, but this wasn't one of them. These few but wiser institutions got out early and got out in time, proving that it is possible to avoid the problem of following past successful actions into failure.

Horror Stories of Trying to Ride Success Forever

Classic business cautionary tales of those ignoring this concept include the demise of the buggy whip industry and everything having to do with equestrian transportation. After the automobile industry was well established, a very successful Ford Motor Company lost its market leadership to General Motors for 50 years or more when founder Henry Ford failed to notice or acknowledge that customers were prepared to ignore the highly successful Model T in a single color, black, and pay a lot more for a variety of colors and other options.

The railroad, that great invention of the nineteenth century, helped win the American West and in the process created some of the wealthiest men in America. From Europe to Asia the railroad caused major changes in the history of the world over the next hundred years. Yet the legendary and mighty companies that were the industry's stalwarts shrank to tiny shadows of their former selves when airline transportation became common and widespread. Sure they had a case of "marketing myopia," too, and considering themselves in the transportation business rather than the railroad business might have saved them, but the point here is that no success is forever. The entire billion-dollar vinyl record industry vanished almost overnight, and vinyl record manufacturers lost millions when they failed to prepare for the growing threat from compact disc technology. Slide rules were once carried by engineers worldwide. That market disappeared in a flash with the introduction of the handheld calculator.

I could go on, but you get the general idea. The point is that like a lightbulb that seems to burn its brightest just prior to complete failure, many of these companies and industries gave the appearance of being at their best just a few months prior to their bankruptcy. This is true of products and services as well as strategies and concepts. Remember the explosion of software stores of the 1980s? Where are these stores today? Even legendary Sears, Roebuck and Co., one of the first mail-order companies, the company that created the thick-as-a-bible catalog known as the "Wish Book" was forced out of the catalog business with high losses in 2003 after over a hundred years of successful operation.

Why do these marketing missteps occur? Why can't a company or an organization continue to do what has made it successful in the past in every market or opportunity? What happens is that the environment changes or is different in some critical way that invalidates all the old rules that led to previous success. For example:

- **Technology:** Something new like the automobile comes along and changes the use of a horse from a basic means of transportation to a sport or a leisure pastime.
- **Economics or business conditions:** The economy falls into depression or becomes inflationary. One condition might cause

potential customers to hold on to their money; the latter to spend more freely and in a much shorter period of time.

- **Social change:** Bathing suits covering the entire body went out of fashion. Prior to the 1950s, almost all men wore hats as a part of business dress. Men's hat shops abounded. Now they're relegated to specialty stores, and men who wear hats daily for business or on formal occasions are in the minority.

- **Politics, laws, and regulations:** What was once legal becomes illegal and vice versa. Prohibition on the sale of alcoholic beverages becomes illegal or becomes legal and causes major changes in the spirits industry. What is considered criminal behavior and what is not is hardly fixed. Many people know that Coca-Cola got its name and its nickname, Coke, from an original ingredient, no longer legal and no longer used by the Coca-Cola company or any other legal entity as part of a food or drink on sale at your corner supermarket or convenience store.

- **Actions of competitors:** A competitor is successful in an action that you have not anticipated and allowed for. Apple Computer started the personal computer industry. But IBM's strategy of encouraging rather than restricting others in making compatible software gave IBM PCs a significant advantage.

- **Unexpected major events:** The terrorist attacks on 9/11 led to increased air travel restrictions and much greater security. A major earthquake or a war can affect the environment similarly.

You might think that marketers easily anticipate and readily prepare for these changes. This is rarely the case for several reasons. Successful marketing executives are in their positions because they became successful under the old marketing paradigm. These prior actions helped their organizations thrive. They are comfortable with the old way, not some new, unproven idea or way of doing business. Some are afraid to deviate, afraid to make a mistake. They invested heavily in the old model and avoid anything that says that they must invest again and start over. These are the marketers whose prediction of the future is simply accepting a straight-line projection as to what has worked in the past and will continue to work in the future. Above all, they are afraid to risk. But risk is essential. As Drucker wrote: "Risk is of the essence, and risk-making and risk-taking constitute the basic function of enterprise."[3]

Essentially these mistaken marketers perceive no change on the horizon or perhaps forever. But change is the only certainty we have. It takes an exceptional marketer to discontinue or part with the direction of past success, or even to utter the words that imply that anything will change. Yet Drucker said that this must be done or the marketer and his project were certain to eventually fail.

How to Know When to Abandon Success

There is a challenge for those wishing to adopt Drucker's advice on abandoning former success. For example, it would be foolish, even dangerous, to abandon successful products or services without thought as to their replacements. So it is important to be able to recognize that a significant environmental change is approaching and that we must immediately take action with our products, services, or means of operating in order to be ready.

In short, we need to recognize that we have a problem, and then we need to do something about it. One of Drucker's most important questions to executives was, "What are you going to do about it?" He asked this question of Jack Welch in a famous incident described in Chapter 13 which led to considerable success for GE and Welch. In fact, this was almost a standard means of Drucker consulting: he asked questions. As reported by his colleague and coauthor Joe Maciariello in *The Daily Drucker*, even at his seminars he would conclude by telling his audience: "Don't tell me you enjoyed this; tell me what you will do differently on Monday morning."[4] However, before we take action, we must know how to know that we should. Here are a few suggestions for knowing when to abandon a former "good thing":

- Know what's going on, not only in your industry, but in the world. Familiarize yourself not only with new products, but also with anything that could remotely affect your operations. This means a regimen of continually reading trade journals, newspapers, and other relevant media. You can never stop this as a process.

- Ask yourself what is likely to happen based on current developments that have already taken place.
- Play a "what if" game with yourself. What would you do if . . .
- Watch trends and new developments closely. If sales drop over several quarters, find out why. Do not automatically assume that everything will return to normal. There is no normal.
- Recognize that nothing lasts forever, prepare yourself mentally for change, and take immediate action when necessary, regardless of your previous investment in time, money, or resources.
- While you should not change just for the sake of change, establish a program of continual review of every product, strategy, tactic, and policy. Aggressively seek opportunities to change and use change to stay ahead of the competition.
- Declare your own products, services, and strategies obsolete and look for better ways to meet demands.

Follow Drucker's method, and you'll not only avoid major marketing failure by not trying to ride an old success beyond its time of useful service, but you'll stay ahead of the competition, and you'll succeed and survive brilliantly while others plodding on in the old way will fall by the wayside.

Chapter 19

Drucker's Five Deadly Marketing Sins

From 1975 to 1995 Drucker wrote a column for the *Wall Street Journal*. On October 21, 1993, his column was titled "The Five Deadly Business Sins."[1] It was important enough that he incorporated it into his book *Managing in a Time of Great Change*,[2] and the *Wall Street Journal* published the article again in 2005. It could have been called "The Five Deadly Marketing Sins" because four of his five deadly "business" sins had to do with marketing directly and the last was an issue that marketers can hardly ignore. Here they are. Judge for yourself:

1. Seeking high profit margins and premium pricing
2. Charging what the market will bear
3. Using cost-driven pricing
4. Focusing on past winners
5. Giving problems priority over opportunities

What could Peter have been thinking? What Drucker called "deadly sins" are confirmed recommendations of much of marketing orthodoxy. However, this is Peter Drucker, so perhaps we should examine these in some detail before we dismiss any of them out of hand.

Seeking High Profit Margins and Premium Pricing

Drucker was a little stronger in his description of this first sin than my own title. He called this sin the *worship* of high profit margins and of premium pricing and said it was easily the most common of the five. I wouldn't use the term "worship," but why shouldn't marketers at least seek high profit margins? That sounds like just good common sense. And premium pricing? Here we'd better make certain that we get our definitions straight.

The common definition of premium pricing is along these lines: "Practice in which a product is sold at a price higher than that of competing brands to give it snob appeal through an aura of 'exclusivity.'"[3] I'm not certain that this common definition is what Drucker had in mind. He provided two examples to support his views, and both of these had to do with offering more so as to charge more and therefore to increase profit margins. First he cited Xerox, which invented the copy machine, but allowed the Japanese to take over the entire worldwide market. According to Drucker this unwanted result came about because Xerox kept adding features in order to raise the price and increase the profit margin. At first this idea worked just fine and Xerox profits skyrocketed. But since the consumer really just wanted a simple machine to do the job of copying without the frills, this high profit margin strategy eventually attracted Japanese competition. The Japanese entered the market with a product that did the job at a much more reasonable price and took Xerox's market with great ease.

Drucker's second example indicted the entire American automobile industry. He accused it of abandoning the market to smaller cars, again mostly to the Japanese. It did this by completely ignoring the obvious demand for small, more gas-efficient cars, a need especially noticeable beginning with the gasoline crisis of 1973. According to Drucker this was the same story as Xerox. Bigger automobile size and more gadgets meant higher profit margins. The illusion that temporary increased profits would continue into the future was just that, an illusion. And by not responding to what the consumer really wanted in price, mighty Detroit suffered loss of market share which it still hasn't regained. Both examples made plain that major disasters were in store for those pursuing premium pricing with the object of attaining high margins.

Here it becomes clear that Drucker's use of the words "premium pricing" did not mean a relatively high price as a sign of a better product, but rather the addition of add-ons or obvious attributes, such as a large size, simply to allow increased profits. His conclusion was that the notion that this would be sustainable over the long haul was nearly always a delusion. The problem is that it seems so automatic and obvious that big margins must lead to maximum profits. But this is an error. Total profit is margin multiplied by sales. So what the marketer should be seeking is an optimum profit margin that combines with sales over time to equal maximum profits. Perhaps the worst part of the whole business is that the strategy of high profit margins combined with the necessary tactics of premium pricing (as defined by Drucker) invariably creates a market for the competition.[4] So unstated in his conclusion, but obvious from his two examples, is that not only would the quest for high profit margins ultimately fail, but that it could result in the loss of the entire market to a competitor.

Charging What the Market Will Bear

How often I have heard the "words of wisdom"—charging what the market will bear. So simple, so obvious, and yet as Drucker showed, so wrong. The theory is pretty simple. You invent or discover a new product. You have total protection. Maybe this is a patent. This gives you years to do what you want. Maybe you have a secret formula, or something else that no one else can duplicate. Maybe it is just the time it took you to get the product to market and the notion that the same is necessarily true for anyone else. So you can charge whatever you want! Go ahead, charge whatever the market will bear. When your poor competition finally catches up in development, you can now use all the extra cash you have accumulated to fight off any competitors that try to enter the marketplace. You can use these excess profits to outspend these competitors in advertising. You can put the money into additional "bells and whistles." You can sink the money into research and development and make your product even better. You can even lower your price at this point and go lower than your competitors. This way, they can never catch you. Charging what the market will bear is a "sure thing" marketing strategy when you enter the market before your competition and have some leverage to keep competitors away. At least that's the conventional wisdom.

Sorry, but as Drucker claimed, the only sure thing about charging what the market will bear is that you will lose your market—and a lot sooner than you might think. The problem is that a very high price creates an almost risk-free opportunity for your competitor to jump in and seize your market. Risk is always present so that when a nearly risk-free opportunity presents itself, it is a wonderful incentive. It is almost irresistible. Moreover, the higher the price, the lower the risk to a competitor and the greater incentive to jump in and compete.

What one innovator can do, another can duplicate. So you have a patent. There is no patent and no invention that can't be designed around. At least that is what an experienced engineer who made a living by doing exactly that told me once. And he proved it right before my eyes, again and again. So sooner or later, competitors will enter the market, and with the right strategy a competitor can take the market away from you before you have time to respond.

Drucker contrasted the copy machine with DuPont's synthetic fiber innovations. Americans invented and introduced the copy machine, but the Japanese easily took the market by pricing their machines an incredible 40 percent lower than those that appeared first in the market. They did this without losing their shirts and not with cheap materials or lowering quality, but by using the learning curve to jump ahead two to three years in developing their pricing. In other words, they didn't use current manufacturing costs to price their product. Instead they leapfrogged ahead and priced it as if they had learned all the ins and outs of manufacturing and were selling it in high quantity and not at the quantities sold or cost of production as when they first started out. Of course this meant that several years in the future they had to actually learn how and actually reduce these costs, but they did this. The copy machines inventors didn't stand a chance. They lost the market almost overnight with no chance to respond.[5]

Contrast this with DuPont. It patented nylon and sold it at a price that it anticipated it would have to sell the product at five years later to undercut any potential competitor. Drucker estimated that this price was less than half of the price DuPont could have sold the product for successfully at the time. However, when competitors attempted to get into the market, DuPont had no difficulty keeping them out and keeping its market.[6] In the process DuPont made nylon affordable to millions of women and kept competitors away for years. When it finally sold its fiber business to Koch Industries to pursue faster-growing industries after years of huge profits, it received an additional $4.4 billion from the buyer.[7]

This does not mean that you need to charge such a low price that you put yourself out of business. Drucker turned to the automobile industry to find an example of an important cautionary note describing the dangers of extremes in the other direction. He recalled that the Hyundai Excel once was selling at the rate of 400,000 cars a year, the fastest of any car in the industry. A brilliant example of underpricing success. Then in two years it almost vanished completely. They cut it too close. With no profits to speak of, there was no money for promotion, service, or product improvement. Drucker quoted Henry Ford: "We can sell the Model T at such a low price only because it earns such a nice profit."[8]

Using Cost-Driven Pricing

Politicians are famous for claiming how clear they make their points. Drucker was no politician, but he did make it very clear that cost-driven pricing was ridiculous. Drucker warned that insisting on following the tenets of cost-based pricing was a sure road to disaster. Among other bad results, he blamed the loss of the consumer electronics industry and the machine-tool industry in the United States directly to this deadly sin.[9]

Frankly, I was a bit surprised when he claimed that most U.S. and practically all European companies still used cost-driven pricing, at least in 1993 when he first exposed the problem and in 2005 when the *Wall Street Journal* reprinted the article. Cost-driven pricing means that you simply add up all your costs, then add a profit, and there you are—the price you should charge. It's all very logical, but it is wrong, wrong, wrong. Drucker said that instead of cost-driven pricing, you needed to do *price-driven costing*. That is, you need to start at the other end with the right price, and then to work back from price to determine your allowable costs.

I'm well aware that the government and large organizations that are your prospects or customers frequently require you to justify your price on a form, which develops pricing in exactly the way Drucker said not to do it. Those organizations feel that this prevents excessive profits. You'll need to go through the procedure required on these forms anyway because you want to know your total costs compared to the "right price" that Drucker suggested you develop. If your costs exceed the right price, it can mean several things. It may mean that you need to develop your costs based on a higher anticipated number of unit sales by using the learning curve, just as the Japanese did with copy machines. If there is no way that you can get your costs below what you need to make a profit even using a learning curve, then you need to think of something else. Can you reduce your cost of materials, labor, or other manufacturing costs? Obviously if you lose money on each unit sold no matter what, you cannot make these losses up by selling more units. As in the case of Solyndra described in Chapter 14, you're going to lose money. Of course, Solyndra's problem was one of timing. However, if conditions change and you're faced with a new set of circumstances, cost-based pricing is always an error. And unless you're making money elsewhere or are instigating a strategy that will eventually lead to profits despite these short-term losses, before introducing any new product or service you'd better think again.

Focusing on Past Winners

I really like Drucker's colorful description rather than my more mundane title, but calling this sin "slaughtering tomorrow's opportunity on the altar of yesterday" creates a rather bizarre, nonbusiness metaphor. Anyway, though Drucker's flamboyant label is more exciting, I think mine describes more succinctly what he was talking about. There is a human tendency to assume that any success will continue forever. I've already discussed this in past chapters. But here Drucker wanted to emphasize more the sin that managers commit in the name of past successes. That is, organizations actually fritter away opportunities by focusing on past winners. Drucker pointed out that after IBM had accomplished the remarkable feat of recovering from its immense research gaffe in totaling missing the demand for PC computers and then amazingly catching up with Apple in a flash, it still insisted on subordinating its newly won PC business to its old winner, the mainframe computer. Not only did resources go mainly to the mainframes, but the new PC marketers were discouraged from selling their product to mainframe customers, lest these customers mistake what business IBM was really in. The net result according to Drucker was that IBM would not reap the fruits of its amazing achievement in coming from nowhere and taking leadership of the PC market from Apple. Instead its achievement was mainly to create IBM clones—and this act of marketing hara-kiri didn't help its mainframe business in any way.[10]

Steve Jobs, even as a young entrepreneur, owed much of his success to his continually introducing a series of new products and innovations and focusing on these to ensure their success. He rarely failed. In the early years he was accused of giving too much attention to the Mac at the expense of Apple's cash cow, Apple II. He ignored the criticism, much from experienced executives he had hired to join Apple to help bring professionalism to his company. In response he called the formerly successful Apple II "the boring project" and went on to make the Mac a great success and a worthy successor to his original hit.

Giving Problems Priority over Opportunities

Giving problems priority over opportunities is a sin in and out of marketing. There will always be problems, and some are discrete and need to be taken care of immediately. If you are being sued over a patent infringement by a competitor, you may not have the luxury of focusing on an opportunity in developing a new market in Zambia or elsewhere, even though the opportunity is terrific.

That's not what Drucker was talking about. His issue arose when he discovered that many companies he advised put their best-performing people to work solving old problems with products in decline. Meanwhile opportunities were frequently assigned to those who lacked experience or ability. So in some ways this sin is related to "slaughtering tomorrow's opportunity on the altar of yesterday" because the opportunity is frequently lost over a problem that could be easily ignored because the problem is associated with a product, service, or business that is on its way out anyway.

This frequently occurs, as is the case with many things, because we let our egos get in the way. It relates to the issue in the Introduction of Drucker admonishing the CEO of a Fortune 500 company and telling him that he should visit his partner in Osaka despite the slight handed him when the partner failed to promote a seminar given by this executive and Drucker. It is akin to what many of us might do in our personal lives.

My wife and I both own portable GPS devices for our cars, which we have used without problems since purchase. As with any system, the maps get outdated. So on a recent Saturday I decided to update my maps. I logged into the brand's website and for $89.95 plus tax updated my GPS with the latest maps and with the ability to do three more updates for the year. Sunday morning I turned the GPS on and received a message that I had no maps, new or old. Monday afternoon I called the brand's support number and spent several hours with a very nice lady who told me she was from Mexico. She told me to update again and all would be well. As the updating took some time, she hung up. However, when the updating was done my GPS still indicated no maps. So Monday evening I called again. I spent another hour or so with another individual rendering technical support. It still wasn't working. This gentleman told me that he had done all he could and that I now needed to consult with "a level 15," a technical person with greater expertise. However, customer service had closed. It operates only until 11 p.m. EST, and in California that's 8 p.m. So after work on Tuesday I called again. This time when I called I immediately got a level 15. She told me that I was very lucky because she was a level 15 and that there were only six level 15s. She worked with me for an hour or so and then told me to download something and all would be well. Now suspicious, I asked "What if it isn't?" "It will be," she assured me, but if not, I could call again. The downloading began and she hung up and told me to check the downloading in about 45 minutes. I did.

There was an error message saying that the computer could not complete my request.

I'd had enough and decided to take the whole thing to work on Wednesday so as to try my luck during the workday. As you might imagine, I was beginning to get a little irritated. Wednesday morning at my work computer I got hold of another level 15. He quickly read my log and spent 30 to 40 minutes with me. At the conclusion he told me that there was no hope. That my GPS was gone for good—wiped out permanently. "Okay," said I, "are you going to overnight a new GPS?" I was surprised to learn that this company's policy was "tough luck" unless I had bought the GPS within a year and could prove it with a sales receipt. I thought customer service might help. No. I talked to a supervisor. No. This was wrong. Their download program had destroyed my GPS. I was angry. I was upset. I was going to take them to small claims court. I was in the right, and I wanted to get those bad guys at this company. They were mismarketing and giving customer service a bad name. Then I remembered Bill Pollard's story. Heck, this GPS was a cheap one. It cost less than $100. I could spend a lot of time taking this to small claims court or whatever. Sure their policy is shortsighted, and hardly builds goodwill. But for less than $100, I could move on with my life. This was a much better move. It no longer bothered me. In fact I felt so good that I made one more try and called again in the evening. By the sheerest of good fortune, I got another level 15, and she fixed the whole thing in a few minutes. Now there are all sorts of lessons here, but the one I want to get across confirms Drucker's point: In marketing this is like sinking a lot of resources, money, and people to fend off someone's encroachment into one of your established markets. Sure it may be declining, but this is your turf, right? So your ego is involved, and you allocate all sorts of time to defending what may be barely worthwhile, while your real opportunity in Zambia or elsewhere is picked up by a competitor.

When Drucker claimed there was a sin, he wasn't exaggerating. Sinners take heed!

Chapter 20

The Only Way to Set a Price

In the last chapter we began to look at Drucker's thoughts on pricing. In many cases these were clearly at odds with what many corporations, organizations, and small businesses do, or even what is taught in our business schools about pricing and marketing today. He thought that these differences were important enough to begin this discussion by calling them "deadly sins." Even before that, way back in 1955, he wrote: "Pricing is really the darkest Africa of management."[1] Now that we know why he so strongly opposed some of the commonly accepted practices, we are in a better position to look at some of his other ideas about pricing.

The Myth of the Irrational Customer

I was all of 10 years old when I was warned that customers were irrational and not to be trusted. My father, then an Air Force major, had recently been assigned to Hickam Field, near Honolulu in Hawaii. An advertisement had appeared in one of the two major Honolulu newspapers for a newspaper boy to deliver its product. The parents of the previous newsboy had recently been reassigned back to the States. The paper was the *Honolulu Star-Bulletin*, which was in second place to the number one *Honolulu Advertiser*, which finally acquired the former in 2010 to form the *Honolulu Star-Advertiser*. The requirements for the position were honesty, reliability, and the possession of a bicycle. The bicycle was a necessity since all newspapers were delivered in this manner, not by automobile and adults as is the norm in most localities today. My father had started working in Morgantown, West Virginia, at a much earlier age and so had put me to work the previous year selling a short newspaper for five cents a copy and published once a week in Dundalk, Maryland, when we were living near Washington, D.C. There were no paper routes for that job. We bought what we thought we could sell for two cents each, and we went from house to house, knocking on doors, wherever we thought we had a good chance of a sale. What we couldn't sell we were stuck with, so this was a wonderful motivator for learning persistence as a newspaper sales boy.

I interviewed with the manager at the *Star-Bulletin* who was impressed with my ability to make money selling at three cents profit. He told me that the number of subscribers had been declining on the route that I was being assigned and asked me if I would be able to increase the number of subscribers inasmuch as some customers were "irrational." Therefore, I needed to be careful because the chances of gaining new subscribers for those in this category were not very good. I said that I would build up my route by soliciting additional subscribers. I had no idea what irrational meant, but I was afraid to display my ignorance and perhaps lose the job. I thought irrational was something like "contaminated" and was a little concerned about that aspect of meeting and persuading these contaminated customers to purchase subscriptions to the newspaper I was representing. However when I started visiting prospects, all the people who came to the door looked and behaved more or less like everybody else. I thought maybe that I was just lucky in not having any irrational customers on my news route, and I went on to build up the number of subscribers as I had promised.

However, years later, I did find it interesting that Drucker compared the notion of a marketer calling the customer irrational because of failing to respond to a marketing campaign he had launched to a physician calling a disease irrational when it failed to yield to an antibiotic the doctor had administered. Drucker stated boldly that if something fails to respond to what the theory predicts, it is not a demonstration of irrationality. Rather, something is wrong with the theory, and it has to be changed.[2]

There are many reasons why a potential customer may not buy in addition to price. As Drucker confirmed, price is only one measurement of value.[3] However, price is probably one of the most important elements for illustrating so-called customer irrationality and debunking it. Moreover, price can be successfully set only by first determining its relative importance to the customer.[4]

In some cases this is not difficult. It is fairly easy to explain why customers insist on paying more for a product when lower-priced products of equal or better quality are available. The explanation is that when there is limited information available about the product or it was previously nonexistent and potential customers have no experience with it, it is perfectly rational to assume that the most expensive product is of the highest quality whether this is actually true or not. Similarly, if a price reduction fails to increase sales, maybe the reduction is too small relative to the original price to attract much attention. Or other factors may be seen as far more important, such as reputation for reliability or other things, not irrationality. On the other hand, is it irrational that points awarded for purchasing leading to awards of varying types generally do increase sales even if this amounts to only a few cents when we convert the value of the awards to money? This is psychological motivation of getting something for nothing, not irrationality. Drucker's lesson is that the customer is not irrational and that marketers must examine these issues from the customers' perspective to uncover the real issue so that it can be dealt with.

What Suppliers Want to Sell May Not Be What Customers Want to Buy

According to Drucker, the marketer must start with price and what the customer wants to buy rather than what the supplier wants to sell. For many years foreigners saw more pictures of one American than any other. No, it was not a picture of George Washington found on our $1 bill. It was not a famous general, a religious leader, or a founding father. Rather, it was a man who sold safety razors. He wasn't the first to sell a safety razor, and he didn't invent the safety razor. His razor wasn't any better than anyone else's, and it was more expensive to produce. However, despite the costs of manufacture, Drucker said that the man pictured practically gave the razor away. Yet the razor was much less expensive than any of its competitors'. As a result, millions all over the world bought the razor and used its blades. In fact, once they purchased the razor, they really didn't have much choice. It used a patented blade, and the razor was designed so that it was the only brand of blade that could be used. The man in question was King Gillette, and his picture was on the packaging of every blade. Every blade cost him less than one cent, and he sold each for five cents. That's a nice markup, but it was a win-win. Since the blade could be used at least six times, the buyer got a shave for less than one cent. That was one-tenth of the going rate for a shave in a barber shop in those days. So who cared if the razor used only one brand of blade.

Gillette wasn't stupid. He priced his razors at about 10 percent of the price of his competitors' safety razors and positioned his buyers to enjoy a tremendous cost savings at the same time. He realized that the customer was not really much interested in buying either razors or blades. That's only what Gillette's company was manufacturing. The customer was buying shaves.[5]

Pretty clever, Peter. Now if we could just figure out how we can connect the price to what the customer sees as value, we can make some money. Drucker said that we can do this if we start with:

- The utility; that is, efficacy, convenience, usefulness, and so on as seen by the customer
- The kind of product that the customer buys
- The customers' realities as they see it
- What the customers value

According to Drucker, this is what marketing is all about. Any marketer willing to base pricing or any other marketing action on these factors is likely to acquire industry leadership almost without risk.[6, 7] Of course to accomplish this also implies that we understand all the dynamics. We can master the dynamics by considering both sides of the purchase equation. While many marketers simply start with the costs and tack on what they feel is a suitable profit, Drucker maintained that you had to start with the right price first and then work to come up with the right costs. We have already seen that we can affect price by an understanding of how the customer sees the world. Only then should we begin to look at cost. This includes both our cost and seeing how cost may look to our customers. Let's look at some examples.

The Concept of Chain Costing

There is much more to price than simply the cost of the product. Got a favorite gasoline station where the price difference is as high as five cents a gallon? If the drive is a mere five miles across town versus the gas station one block away, you may be better off paying the additional five cents. Yet frequently the obvious is completely ignored. Look at the figures. Let's say that your car gets 15 miles a gallon while driving in town. To get back to your starting point is 10 miles. If the gasoline costs $3.50 a gallon at the cheaper gas station, this additional drive will cost you two-thirds of a gallon × 3.50, or $2.33. If your car holds 15 gallons, you saved 75 cents. Not bad. Your drive was a net loss of only $2.33 – 0.75, or $1.59. But wait. If your little trip across town took 15 minutes and was made during work hours, you had better factor that time in. How much do you make on an hourly basis? Let's make it easy and use round numbers regardless of your actual income.

If your salary and benefits total $100,000 a year and you have 2,000 productive work hours in a year, that's $50 an hour or another negative $12.50 for the 15 minutes. I'm leaving out insurance costs, wear and tear on your tires and engine, and so on. In my own city, one of the local radio stations always announces the cheapest gasoline in town. It's always a few cents a gallon less, and saving this money sounds good, especially in difficult times. But heck, even if the gasoline was a dollar a gallon cheaper, you'd barely break even.

Congratulations, you have just grasped the importance of chain costing which says simply that you need to consider all the costs in the chain. The importance of looking at the entire economic chain is hardly new. According to Drucker, this concept was first expressed by Alfred Marshall, perhaps the greatest economist of his time. His time was the 1890s.[8] Marshall's book *Principles of Economics* was the dominant economic textbook in England in those days. He was no slouch. He was the one who brought the basic concepts of supply and demand, marginal utility, and costs of production into one coherent theory. Drucker was against favoring theory over practice, but when theory and practice were in agreement, Drucker was happy to acknowledge it. Unfortunately, many practitioners thought Marshall's work was exactly that, pure theory that could be safely ignored as having no practical application. Drucker thought differently, and he urged marketers to adopt Marshall's theory.

The notion of chain costing is representative of your total costs for a particular product or service, but it may also reflect costs that your customers may be paying that they may or may not understand, such as the attraction of saving a few cents at the gas pump. But as smart marketers setting price, it should be understood by us if we are to really understand the entire pricing picture. Regarding our costs, it may also help us in understanding the advantages, as well as the challenges, in vertical integration of the entire process of getting the product from planning and design to sales actions whether or not this is even seen by the ultimate consumer.

Drucker pointed out that once upon a time, Coca-Cola was a franchisor with independent bottlers putting everything together. Not so today. But who cares? Even drinkers of Coke who know the whole story don't consider this an important issue.[9] To put it in Drucker's terms, "What matters in the marketplace is the economic reality, the costs of the entire process, regardless of who owns what."[10]

The Importance of the Learning and Experience Curves

Drucker liked to point out that we are frequently too quick to assume that present costs will be the same forever as we introduce a new product, whereas smarter marketers and price-setters steal our markets again and again by doing things differently. We would be well advised to ask not what our costs are in producing or providing a handful of whatever it is we are just introducing to the marketplace, but what the costs would be if we sold this product or service in multitudes which may take several years to achieve.

Drucker said U.S. companies just don't price this way, but they should. However, he was wrong in this particular statement, because some U.S. companies do price this way. As a matter of fact, an American developed the methodology. The idea is that the more times a task will be performed, the more we learn about doing the task, and many elements such as costs are reduced in the process. All of this came about resulting from Boeing's production of the B-17 and analysts at Wright-Patterson Air Force Base in the late 1930s. The B-17 was an expensive piece of equipment. However, analysts found that every time total aircraft production doubled, labor decreased by 10 to 15 percent. Naturally costs went down. Subsequent empirical studies from other industries and products yielded different values. However, the curve of decline could be determined and used to predict future costs. The whole method was good enough to be employed throughout World War II and is still required of those bidding on government defense contracts today. The experience curve is supposed to be broader in scope, including far more than labor costs, but frequently today the two terms are used interchangeably. There is a nice discussion of the whole idea and its application on Wikipedia at http://en.wikipedia.org/wiki/Experience_curve_effects. A number of books have also been published on the concept, so we're not dealing in anything mystical here. The fact is that future costs can be determined fairly accurately. Of course, if your number estimates are off, this will significantly affect your results. However, this doesn't say that Drucker was in error in calling this to our attention and indicating that we had better pay attention lest we lose our markets to competitors who take this approach to enable substantial reduction in prices today, based on eventual costs in the future.

Life Cycle Costing

In a sense, life cycle costing is the reverse of the experience curve because it recognizes that costs may be greater than anticipated on a product under development or if numbers planned for purchase are reduced. However, it is definitely related to the chain costing concept. Life cycle costing came into practice when Robert McNamara was Secretary of Defense. If McNamara erred in other ways in management concepts, with this concept he was right on the button. Prior to McNamara, armed forces chiefs presented an annual budget. Such a budget might include costs for development and procurement of a new rocket or missile system. But the costs were for the upcoming year. They failed to include the costs of maintaining the system or other follow-on costs after purchase such as training or storage.

In marketing, life cycle costing might apply to new production facilities or equipment or other projects you might dream up. Again, it is important in pricing to consider costs incurred by the seller as well as what the buyers see if they buy your product rather than a competitor's. According to Drucker life cycle costing is being applied more and more to business operations and is a concept that must also be factored into pricing decisions.[11]

Can we sum up these various ideas? Drucker felt strongly that to assign the correct price, one must first look at prospective customers and how they see the product or service in the context of the market. Once one has the price, it is only prudent to look at costs to ensure that the product can be sold profitably. No good marketer should forget that a product or service envisioned can't be sold without considering both sides of this equation and remembering always that the driving side is the customer and his or her perceptions, not the supplier's.

Part V
Drucker's Unique Marketing Insights

Chapter 21

Quality According to Drucker— It's Not What You May Think

Q uality is a very necessary and important part of the product or service that you offer, whether the product is an automobile or an airplane, potential candidates for a job, or due diligence accomplished by a consultant, attorney, or accountant prior to an acquisition. Yet too many marketers either don't understand what quality is for their customer, or they don't know how to express it to prospects in presenting it as an advantage to a customer, or both. Yet quality and its presentation are very important aspects of marketing. Durability is part of quality. So is the speed at which your service is provided and the other advantages you provide above those offered by your competitors—your "competitive advantages." All these are examples of quality. Or are they? Before we proceed, we should be clear that Drucker viewed quality as a feature defined wholly by the customer, not the supplier. In other words, one might have an excellent product or service, one superior in many ways, and it still might not be considered quality by the customer.

What Drucker Considered Quality

Drucker wrote without equivocation that quality in a product or service is not what the supplier puts in. It is what the buyer gets out of it and is willing to pay for.[1] Customers pay only for what they can use and what gives value to them. I emphasize "to them." Value is as they perceive it, not what the supplier may think. Quality is part of that value. Therefore, it is foolish for the seller to spend money, time, and effort in developing quality as he sees it if the buyer does not have the same definition. Further, it is equally foolish for the marketer to promote a durable product that will last forever, products or service that are provided fast, or something that is 100 percent reliable in manufacture if that is not what is desired or not appreciated as something desirable by the customer. It gets back to the importance of supplying what the customer values.

I once worked for a company that made oxygen breathing masks for military aviators. It supplied them to the government in quantities of upwards of 40,000 at a time. Many companies tried, but no competitor ever succeeded in getting into this market. It was all because of a single valve used in the oxygen mask. No matter how much "quality" the manufacturer built into the valve, a significant number of valves failed to perform as specified during quality testing of production batches. It turned out that the quality built into the valve as defined by the manufacturer was meaningless. Competitors developed some pretty "high-quality" values made of expensive and exotic materials. They were frequently far more expensive than those made by the company I worked with. Yet unfortunately for them, there were still always a significant number that failed the government quality control tests. Consequently they could never guarantee the quality of the valves so that the government would purchase them. Yet my company always had a 100 percent success rate on the valves in the oxygen masks that were delivered to the customer. What was its secret?

The secret was well-guarded, but it wasn't complicated and it didn't require a valve built of higher-quality materials than was the norm. The company I worked with didn't have a better success rate in production than its competitors. In fact, in many cases my company's production success rate may have been worse. But this company realized that the government didn't care whether or not the valves were consistent in meeting production standards. Quality for the government was whether the valves delivered quality standards in its own government quality tests, not whether the company produced a valve in which quality standards were met as defined by the company. In fact, our production chief told me that he didn't think anyone in the world could produce valves in such a way that every single valve in a batch met the quality specifications. Yet, except on very rare occasions, every single valve he turned over to the government easily passed government specifications. How did he do it? The solution was simple, but unthought of. The company didn't test a percentage of valves in a batch to ensure reliability. It tested every single one of the valves sent to the government, be it 40 or 40,000 valves. Those that failed were simply tossed out as waste. This was probably more expensive than if production could develop a valve that consistently passed the government's quality test *after* production, but it fulfilled the customer's definition of quality which was quality on delivery, not the supplier's definition, which was quality on manufacture, and that was Drucker's point.

Even speedy service can be a quality negative under certain conditions. A major aircraft manufacturer needed a number of ejection seats for a jet fighter it was developing. Thinking that it was doing the aircraft company a favor, the ejection seat subcontractor developed and produced the needed seats six months earlier than the contract called for. Without coordinating with the aircraft manufacturer and thinking that the manufacturer would be pleased, the seats were shipped out immediately. The aircraft manufacturer was frantic. It didn't have facilities for storing and protecting the seats until they were needed. Moreover, the contract it had with its own customer required some close scheduling in production to make the delivery time. It had used the preproduction estimate from the ejection seat manufacturer in calculating its figures. The earlier delivery made a mockery of these calculations and when the ultimate customer learned of it, it caused the aircraft developer and the ejection seat manufacturer to lose credibility.

Another Kind of Quality

Drucker was not trying to recommend that suppliers offload poor workmanship or performance because that's what the customer wanted, a defense one hears occasionally from publishers, television producers, newscasters, or in other industries developing product as to why "quality" products are no longer provided to the buyer or consumer in that particular industry. Drucker wrote that the definition of quality and trying to quantify it is far easier than it appears, especially when it comes to quality results from work by a knowledge worker. Even the old saw about "knowing it when I see it" can be misleading. Although exceptions exist, quality by itself is nearly impossible to quantify. He used the example of a surgeon as being one exception where quality could actually be quantified. Except under specific conditions such as a general emergency with a high number of casualties that must be treated, proper quantifying certainly wasn't the number of operations performed, but the number of operations performed successfully. That, Drucker said, was an exception by which the quality of the knowledge worker might be measured. But, in most cases he stated that knowledge worker quality could not be calculated so easily.[2]

Drucker went on to state that while one might quantify, and thus measure, performance or productivity even with knowledge workers, this is not the problem. The problem is the difficulty in deciding on the task of the job being performed. Look at the wrong task in the product or service, and you get the wrong answer. Drucker then proceeded to demonstrate a prime example: public schools in the inner city.

The Problem of Measuring Quality of Performance and Productivity

Clearly inner city schools are for the most part not a success story. However, right next to them in the same areas and under the same conditions of crime and poverty exist private schools. These are not private schools in the sense of boarding schools or schools catering to the wealthy or the elite. Most are religious schools, and even though parents are not wealthy, they scrape together enough money to send their children to these schools or they try to get their children scholarship admissions. These students come from the same backgrounds as the students going to the regular inner city schools. Yet while the public schools next door complain of indifferent students, crime, and lack of discipline, the atmosphere in these other schools is the opposite.

Several years ago, I saw firsthand the outstanding performance output in quality of these schools located in the Los Angeles inner city. However, these were not inner city schools. As a general officer in the Air Force, I participated in the ceremonial flagging of junior Air Force ROTC in several of these schools. My duties were to show up in uniform, say a few words, and participate in the ceremony in which the school officially received its flag identifying and certifying it as an Air Force ROTC school. In the process I met and talked with school administrators, teachers, parents, and, of course, students. The grounds of many of the regular inner city schools appear to be in a war zone, and as an administrator of such a public school once told me, "After sundown, your life wouldn't be worth a plug nickel here." On the other hand, the schools I visited were neat and well cared for, in part by the students themselves. Students were courteous and respectful, whether they were involved in ROTC or not.

According to Drucker while there were many reasons for the differences between these two classes of schools in the same areas, the primary one was how each defined its tasks. Most inner city schools define their tasks as helping the underprivileged. The private schools, like the ones I visited, defined their tasks as "enabling those who want to learn, to learn."[3] Clearly how tasks are defined influences quality, and this is not only true in these schools but at all levels of education. A professor teaching at a state university once contrasted output as he saw it at his school versus some of the more prestigious schools in his geographical area. Both offered similar degrees. A parent who had a student in this particular state university and another in an Ivy League school had sat in on classes at both and remarked that he was amazed to discover that there was very little difference in teaching quality that he could discern. Yet the professor at this school made a profound observation. "Prestige schools teach success," he said. "We teach survival." These differing definitions of one's tasks are true in providing any product or service, and they affect the observed "quality" output.

Quality Is a Condition, Not a Restraint

According to Drucker, work performance means quality for many jobs and therefore also describes the output in quality of product or service produced. Moreover, the quantity of results from these jobs may be quite secondary to their quality.[4] However, this is not so simple. There are other jobs in which both quality and quantity together define performance and thus task definition. Many sales jobs provide a near perfect example. An unfortunately large number of organizations define mere quantity as a definition of a salesperson's quality—so many units sold or such and such level of dollars sales reached. However, even this obvious definition of units defining quality of sales needs to be carefully analyzed.

There is an old story of two tired salesmen seated next to each other on a train ride home after a hard day's work. After learning that they both are in sales, one asks the other, "How did it go today?" "Not so bad," responds the individual questioned. "I took wholesale orders for over 12 dozen men's shirts. How about you?" "I sold two," answers the first salesperson. "Oh too bad," his new friend commiserates, "I'm sure you'll have a better day tomorrow." "It wasn't a bad day," responds the salesman whose sales were so few in numbers. "I sell locomotives."

However, even this example doesn't begin to explain the complexity of quality definition, especially for a sales job. Some very adept salespeople whose dollar and quantity figures may be very satisfactory may fail in the long run by not properly servicing the accounts of sales made, and thereby hurting the company or brand's good name and losing sales to competitors in the long run. Thus, they overlook the fact that it is far easier and less expensive to obtain sales from established customers than to find and convert prospects into new customers.

This caused Drucker to believe that in order to maximize, or more accurately to optimize, quality, this goal had to be injected into the production or development process at the start and not relegated to the end of the process when the product or service was to be sold. It caused him to make a statement that was surprising to some—that the quality control was in the design stage[5] and that quality was a condition, and not a restraint. However, to understand this condition and thus what quality of the work performed really meant required thinking through what category of work the job fit into and the requirements and its relationship with quantity.[6]

Quality Requires Two Different Lenses

In summary, Drucker knew that we had to look at quality in a product or service in two ways. One way is through the eyes of our customer. Only our customer can define what quality is. We do this by looking not at what we value and consider important, but at what our customer considers of value and can use and is therefore important. Once we get that right, we can proceed to measure performance and productivity in that area. This in turn will help us to build quality into our output at the very beginning, when we design our product and service. Only in this way we can truly optimize quality, and it is the only way that a marketer can accurately proclaim that her product or service has quality.

Chapter 22

Integrity Is Critical to Marketing

In the 1980s, someone in Chicago laced a popular over-the-counter pain killer medication with cyanide. Seven customers who bought the poisoned product died. This resulted in nationwide panic. One hospital received 700 queries from people suspecting that they had been poisoned with the tainted product. People in cities across the country were admitted to hospitals on suspicion of cyanide poisoning. The Food and Drug Administration (FDA) investigated 270 incidents of suspected product tampering. While some of the products had been tampered with, although not poisoned, in most cases this was pure hysteria with no basis at all in fact. However, as panic set in, some state health departments banned all forms of the company's branded products, while others banned only serial numbers associated with the poisonings. It didn't make much difference. The product's brand name and reputation were virtually ruined by the poisoning scare, and sales would have been reduced to almost nothing had it not been for a response that is seen all too infrequently by corporations when things go wrong.

Unlike many organizations' actions in time of tragedy, responsible or not, the company responsible for the product, Johnson & Johnson, took an immediate action that surprised everyone. It assumed full responsibility even before the cause of the poisoning or who was to blame was known.

I suspect that this was absolutely counter to the advice given by corporate lawyers who invariably caution clients not to admit to anything or do anything that would indicate acceptance of responsibility lest this come back to haunt the corporation later, guilty or innocent, in legal action. But executives at Johnson & Johnson plunged ahead anyway and took a variety of public actions only days after the initial poisoning was discovered. It issued a nationwide alert to the public, doctors, and distributors of the drug and also issued a massive recall of 31 million bottles of product. This immediately set the company back almost $125 million. Then the company established a crisis hotline so that consumers could obtain the latest information direct from Johnson & Johnson on what was going on. At the same time it launched an open investigation of the factories where the tainted bottles were produced to see if cyanide had somehow entered or was intentionally put into the capsules during production.[1] It spent hundreds of thousands of dollars advertising and demarketing the product, urging its customers not to buy or use the product under any circumstances until Johnson & Johnson could guarantee the product's safety.

First the media, then the population in general, began to support the company without reservation, and Johnson & Johnson received kudos for its forthright actions. Still, every marketing expert queried about the potential future of the product predicted its inevitable demise. According to them, it could never return to the marketplace despite the company's acts and the product's previously high standing and whatever measures for safety would be initiated by Johnson & Johnson. One well-known advertising guru was quoted in the *New York Times* as saying, "I don't think they can ever sell another product under that name. . . . There may be an advertising person who thinks he can solve this and if they find him, I want to hire him, because then I want him to turn our water cooler into a wine cooler."[2] An article in the *Wall Street Journal* commented sadly that the product was dead and could not be resurrected; any other notion was a marketer's pipedream. A survey of "the man on the street" found almost no one who would buy the product despite high regard for the company and regardless of what the company did to guarantee the product's safety or promote its sale even though all admitted that the famous brand had become tainted through no fault of the product itself or its manufacturer.

Despite all this Johnson & Johnson retained the product and kept its brand name. Other organizations faced with similar dilemmas tried to avoid responsibility at all costs. It invariably ended in disaster. As a result of the integrity of its actions, sales of this product, once dismissed by every advertising and marketing expert queried, began a steady climb only a few months after the product's return to the marketplace. The product, which is of course Tylenol, returned to become the number one analgesic controlling 35 percent of a $2 billion market.

Sadly, as if to emphasize the lesson of the 1980s, not too long ago the Tylenol brand went into denial regarding something that was making customers nauseous. In 1982, it had taken six days to issue a total recall. In 2010, it took 20 months and pressure from the Food and Drug Administration which called the recall "long overdue." This cost the company millions of dollars in real cash and a lot of goodwill even though no deaths were involved. As an article in the *Christian Science Monitor* on the situation concluded, "Still, no matter what the economic environment, the best time to face up to your problems is immediately."[3] In other words, practicing integrity is always recommended regardless of circumstances, and the sooner the better.

Drucker's Journey from Ethics to Integrity

The concepts of integrity, ethics, morality, and honor are all closely related, but they are not the same. Integrity means adherence to a moral code and has to do with adherence to standards of ethics and doing "the right thing." Drucker defined honor as demonstrable integrity and honesty, adding that an honorable man stood by his principles.[4] All of Drucker's books contained evidence of his considerable concern with these concepts for the practicing manager.[5]

Among his many writings, Drucker analyzed and rejected a commonly held view of business ethics; to wit that the ordinary rules of ethics do not apply. Drucker disagreed. He wrote that personal values of right and wrong should *not* be separated from values put into practice at work.[6] However he took an entirely different tack from what most experts wrote about business ethics. This of course led to his conclusions about integrity. Let's look at how he got there.

Drucker's Analysis of Business Ethics

Drucker began with ethical authorities from the western tradition found in the Bible. He found an important point of agreement with this foundation: that there is only one ethical standard, one code of individual behavior for which the same rules apply to everyone. Moreover he agreed that the situation might modify the application of this code. For example, clemency might be granted to a violator who commits violations of the code under extenuating circumstances. "Thou shalt not steal," is one of the Ten Commandments. Yet a mother stealing to feed a starving child might be excused. Although "Thou shalt not kill" is another commandment; it too is excused in war or for self-defense. Differences resulting from different social or cultural mores might also be accepted. That is, practices of questionable morality in one locality might not only be considered acceptable elsewhere, but they might even be considered ethical.[7] Drucker illustrated this with a story about a Japanese CEO building a plant in the United States who was amazed that it was considered corruption for companies benefiting from government officials could not reward them for their actions after their retirement from government service. Drucker explained that in Japan such officials were poorly paid and that repayment after their retirement was considered the benefited company's ethical duty.

Extortion or Bribery

Drucker noted that bribery was hardly desirable from the viewpoint of the victim, and it had recently been made illegal in the United States by a law prohibiting the payment of bribes to obtain foreign contracts. Drucker thought it was stupid to pay bribes. But he did not agree that paying them was a case of business ethics. Most countries have laws against bribery. Yet it is a fact that bribery is routine and expected in all business in some countries. Some people would perceive that the promise, or at least the understanding, of the Japanese CEO that his company would reward government officials who helped his company while they were in office to be a form of bribery. But everyone in Japan understands the difference. Other countries that expect "baksheesh" as part of the traditional way of doing business in their countries may enact laws that prohibit these activities, but frequently this is just "window dressing" to satisfy countries that do not have these activities as part of their culture.

According to Drucker, a private citizen who was extorted to pay a bribe to a criminal might be considered stupid or a helpless victim of intimidation. And certainly paying extortion is never desirable. But this was not an ethical issue on the part of the individual forced to pay. Drucker strongly objected to these "new business ethics" which asserted that acts that are not immoral or illegal if done by private citizens became immoral or illegal if done in the context of a business organization without examining the circumstances. They might be stupid, they might be illegal, and they might be the wrong thing to do. However, they were not necessarily business ethics.

This was 1977. So-called business ethics laws had recently been passed by Congress to curb bribes that were made by American firms to foreigners to help them to secure contracts. Drucker predicted that the laws enacted to penalize American firms from making these payments abroad would largely be ignored. His prediction was accurate. A 2002 article in *World Tribune.com* pointed out that the U.S. government ignored a record of bribery connected to defense contracts in the Middle East, when by its own policy it should not be dealing with U.S. defense contractors with a record of bribery. It reported that the Washington-based Project On Government Oversight said the government has violated its policies that contracts be awarded only to responsible contractors that have a satisfactory record of integrity and business ethics. But the report said 16 of the top 43 contractors chosen during fiscal 1999 had been fined billions of dollars for past "business ethics" violations.[8]

The Ethics of Social Responsibility

Drucker next turned to ethics for the greater good. Essentially a CEO, a king, a president, or anyone in power has a higher duty if their behavior confers benefits to a majority of others. So it is wrong to lie personally, but in the interests of "the country" or "the company," or "the organization," it sometimes has to be done for the greater good. Drucker called this "the ethics of social responsibility." This sounds very high-minded, but Drucker maintained that it was too dangerous a concept to be adopted as business ethics because it would become a tool of a business leader to justify what would clearly be unethical behavior for anyone else.[9] Drucker looked further on his list.

The Ethics of Prudence

To be prudent means to be careful or cautious. It is a rather unusual philosophy for an ethical approach, but admittedly it has some benefits to it.

Drucker wrote that Harry Truman, at the time a U.S. Senator, gave this advice to an army witness before his committee in the early years of World War II: "Generals should never do anything that needs to be explained to a Senate Committee—there is nothing one can explain to a Senate Committee."[10]

This may be pretty good advice for staying out of trouble, but it is not much of a basis for ethical decision making by a marketing executive. For one thing, it doesn't tell you anything about the right kind of behavior. For another there are decisions that a leader must make that are risky and that may be difficult to explain, especially if things go wrong. Yet they may be the correct decisions to make.

The Ethics of Profit

Drucker also thought through what he called "the ethics of profit." Drucker did not say anything about limiting profits. Much to the contrary, Drucker wrote that it would be socially irresponsible and most certainly unethical if a business did not show a profit at least equal to the cost of capital because failing to do so would waste society's resources.[11] Rather, this is looking at the basis for the old explanation that anything goes in business because that is the nature of business.

Drucker believed that the only logical rationale for the justification for "profit" was that it was a cost. He exhorted business leaders as follows: "Check to see if you are earning enough profit to cover the cost of capital and provide for innovation. If not, what are you going to do about it?"[12]

Drucker stated that profit as an ethical metric rested on very weak moral grounds as an incentive and could be justified only if it were a genuine cost and especially if it were the only way to maintain jobs and to grow new ones.[13]

I found it interesting that the rise in gas prices (prior to their dramatic fall) in 2008 produced the following response from one refining company CEO when challenged by a Congressional investigating committee: "There is no 'profit'. Every dollar goes into exploration or research and development and is needed to run this business." Drucker would have agreed, although this would have probably been extremely difficult for someone not in the oil business to understand or accept, and it clearly did not satisfy the committee, confirming Truman's advice to his generals.

Confucian Ethics

Drucker called Confucian ethics "the most successful and most durable of them all." In Confucian ethics the rules are the same for all, but there are different general rules that vary according to five relationships based on interdependence. These five are superior and subordinate, father and child, husband and wife, oldest brother and sibling, and friend and friend. The right behavior in each case differs in order to optimize the benefits to both parties in each relationship. Confucian ethics demand equality of obligations, of parents to children and vice versa; of bosses to subordinates and vice versa. All have mutual obligations. Drucker points out that this is not compatible with what is considered business ethics in many countries including the United States where one side has obligations and the other side has rights or entitlements. Though he clearly admired Confucian ethics which he called "the ethics of interdependence," they cannot be applied as business ethics because this system deals with issues between individuals, not groups. According to Confucian ethics, only the law can handle the rights and disagreements of groups.[14]

Even doing things in business that are "clearly unethical" did not define business ethics according to Drucker. "Hiring call girls to entertain visiting executives does not make you unethical," he wrote. "It merely makes you a pimp."[15]

Drucker concluded that business ethics as defined by most are not "business ethics" at all. If ever business ethics were to be codified, Drucker thought they ought to be based on Confucian ethics, focusing on the right behavior rather than misbehavior or wrongdoing. In summary Drucker believed that the moral code of the manager or marketing executive should incorporate:

- The ethics of personal responsibility from the physician Hippocrates: "Primum Non Nocere," which in English means, above all (or first) do no harm.[16, 17]
- The mirror test: What kind of person do I want to see when I look into the mirror every morning?[18]

In short this means that integrity means adherence to this code.

Marketing Integrity

Personal integrity had to be linked to this code, and this adherence was required under all conditions and regardless of whether anyone else was aware of a deviation from it. Moreover, it is critical because as Drucker said, "The spirit of an organization is created by the people at the top."[19] The proof is uncompromising integrity of character.[20] This will permeate the organization, and it is certain to resonate with an organization's customers as well.

How Integrity Saved a Company

In 1979, the Chrysler Corporation was in danger of bankruptcy. The president of Chrysler, Lee Iacocca, is rightfully given the overall credit for saving the corporation. He was the man in charge, and he came from a sales, marketing, and engineering background in the automotive business. He was helped in this accomplishment by his straight-from-the-shoulder ads in print and TV as well as his public interviews and testimony that won over the man on the street, and eventually Congress to guaranteeing the loans for Chrysler that saved the day. He spoke with absolute integrity. Moreover, it was the ad campaign developed by advertising risk taker Leo-Arthur Kelmenson, a decorated ex-Marine who had to convince Iacocca to be the company's spokesperson and to both run and participate as spokesperson in these ads. Iacocca was under a lot of pressure already, and being the spokesperson in these ads was not his original intention at all. Kelmenson approached him and was soundly rejected. He risked Iacocca's wrath and his own dismissal by his persistence. Kelmenson had already risked his company by abandoning Ford Motor Company to take the Chrysler account. However, Kelmenson had a history of doing what he believed to be right regardless of consequences. According to the *Los Angeles Times*, Kelmenson's ads combined with Iacocca's straightforward delivery, both conceived in the context of "integrity first," gained the support of the public and brought about the government bailout that saved the company.[21] And though it was Iacocca's integrity that the public saw, it was Kelmenson that convinced Iacocca to let everyone see the real Iacocca, warts and all, and the combination saved the company just as surely as Johnson & Johnson had saved the Tylenol product and brand.

Drucker's View on Marketing Integrity

Drucker's views on integrity in marketing follow:

- You can make many mistakes that will be forgiven by people inside the company and customers and the government outside your organization—but a lack of integrity will not be forgiven.
- Maintaining your integrity may cost you, but it is worth it.
- Be true to yourself and to your values and beliefs. As Shakespeare wrote: "This above all: to thine own self be true, And it must follow, as the night the day, Thou canst not then be false to any man." (*Hamlet*, act 1, scene 3)

Chapter 23

The Dangers of Marketing Professionalism

More than 50 years ago Drucker reported on the allegory of the three stonecutters.[1] According to Drucker, these three workers were approached and asked what they were doing. The first answered: "I'm earning a living by cutting stone." The second one didn't even pause to look up when the question was asked. This stonecutter continued to work, but eventually took the time to respond: "I'm a stonecutting professional: I'm doing the best job of cutting stone of anyone in my profession." The third stonecutter had a visionary look on his face as he replied, "I'm building a cathedral."

I heard that delivered by a nationally known motivational speaker. While this speaker suggested that the third stonecutter had the ideal approach, he suggested that the second one came pretty darn close to what was desired and that if the worker or manager did not have the vision for the project, at least he was going to do the absolute best job professionally that he could.

Why Drucker Said That the Motivational Speaker Was Wrong

Drucker came to a very different conclusion, and this difference has a significant impact on the way we look at marketing, perform marketing tasks, and engage in marketing in any organization. Drucker wrote that we would get useful work from the first stonecutter. His philosophy was clearly something along the lines of a "fair day's work for a fair day's pay." Of course unless this stonecutter changes his thinking and his attitude, he is not managerial material, and he has career limitations that he probably does not understand himself, because no one can advance in any organization by merely doing a fair day's work for a fair day's pay. As Mary Kay Ash, that sales and marketing genius who founded the billion-dollar Mary Kay Cosmetics Company, liked to say: "Success comes from doing what is expected of you *and then some*." But as far as the project of building the cathedral goes, we can get useful work from a stonecutter or a marketer like this who does a fair day's work for fair compensation, and his is certainly an ethical philosophy.

Drucker also agreed that the third stonecutter was ideal both for the immediate job and most importantly for the organization and its future. Moreover, this stonecutter also had potential as a future manager of other stonecutters. In today's terminology, we would probably say that this fellow was fully engaged.

However, Drucker disagreed strongly with the motivational speaker regarding his conclusions about the second stonecutter. He said that this man was not only a problem, but was even potentially dangerous to the organization and to the project. Of course good work skills and good professionalism are essential and should be encouraged. At the same time, according to Drucker, there is a great danger if the worker places professionalism as his primary goal above all else. This is because anyone proclaiming technical proficiency or professionalism as his *primary* goal will not put the goals or the mission of the organization first. He might believe he was accomplishing something toward organizational goals when, in fact, all he was doing was cutting stone, albeit to the best of his ability and in the best possible way. Drucker equated this with the "gun for hire" manager who would go anywhere and do anything, not for the customer or the organization's goals, but because he considered his first allegiance to his achieving "top gun" rank with the status, perks, and benefits that go along with it. Drucker wrote that while good skills should always be encouraged, it must always be related to the needs of the whole organization and especially to the organization's mission. The goal of the organization must come first, and everything must be done to support this goal as long as it is done with integrity. Or to quote stonecutter number three in this instance, as long as it is done with the goal of "building a cathedral."

Professionalism, Not Always the Best Thing?

The German army of the 1930s gives us a fair example of how professionalism can be misguided and even destructive. The military in Germany was known for its professionalism. It put this professionalism above all else, and despite its relatively small size after World War I, it maintained a reputation as, man for man, one of the best armies in the world. However, individually, German officers put their professionalism above the state with which they were entrusted with defending.

When Hitler gained total power in Germany after the death of President Hindenburg in 1934, he recognized the extreme professionalism of the German Army and decided to take advantage of it to further his own political ambitions. He did this by having the members of the Army take a loyalty oath, not to the German constitution as in the past, but to the person of the Fuehrer, or Leader, Adolf Hitler. For the professionally minded German Army, this represented a tremendous dilemma later when the extent of Hitler's depravity and evil intentions became apparent. By the Army's interpretation of honor and professionalism, German officers could not rebel against Hitler since they had sworn "by God a sacred oath to the Leader of the German empire and people, Adolf Hitler." As a result, even though his atrocities became common knowledge among senior officers of the German armed forces, they felt they could do nothing against him less they impugn their professional honor. It was not until July 20, 1944, that a major attempt to assassinate Hitler to end the crimes committed in the name of the German people was made in "Operation Valkyrie." The attempt failed, and the horrors of World War II were played out to the bitter end both within and without Germany for another nine months.

Other Types of Misguided Professionalism

Drucker criticized both workers and managers for the direction in which professionalism sometimes led them. He pointed out that in every contract negotiation with management, the union was expected to achieve more and more benefits. This was the union's professional goal. I read recently that because of the current recession, benefits and high salaries won over several decades through the unions were being lost or eroded. But these benefits were always "won" at the expense of the corporation, and maybe the customer, since productivity and the company's interests were not simultaneously considered and did not benefit from the union's professionalism. Drucker was one of the first to propose that union leaders be appointed to the boards of corporations so that they would share in the responsibility of the decisions made in the corporation's development and performance and also share in accountability—increasing benefits and compensation without corresponding increased productivity.

But Drucker did not spare management his criticism or his wrath. The continued increase in compensation of top-level professional managers, who rotated to increased salaries from one company to another, resulted in salaries many times the average salaries of their employees. He considered this an abomination and clear evidence of these managers' devotion to a management "profession" and not the primary welfare of the organizations that were entrusted to them and for which they were responsible. "Society will eventually pay a terrible price for this abomination," he declared. And of course, he was right.

Giving Up Professionalism for the Good of the Organization

Surrendering professionalism for the greater good of the organization is never easy. It means that sometimes a subordinate organization or an individual is denied the resources needed to be number one in the interest of other subordinate organizations or individuals being able to make contributions so that the overall organization reaches its goals. It is avoiding corporate suboptimization. This avoidance is a measurement of the engagement of your employees with the organization. This is easily seen in sports where, for example, the champion star basketball player who is well on his way to setting a new individual record in baskets scored gives the ball to a teammate who can score more easily or with less risk in order to ensure a victory for the team.

What This Means for Individual Professionals in Marketing

As individual professionals, we avoid the hazards Drucker notes by putting the goals of the organization first. This may mean that hard-pressed marketers or salespeople give of their own valuable time to help or train the neophyte, new hire, or just someone who is less experienced. This may hurt the individual performance and record of the professional who does this, but it is immensely valuable to the organization as it seeks to "build a cathedral."

You may remember the 1982 movie *An Officer and a Gentleman* that starred Richard Gere, Debra Winger, and Louis Gossett, Jr. In the film, Richard Gere plays a young aviation cadet attending Navy Officer Candidate School, which would lead to his commissioning as a naval officer and is a prerequisite for his attending flying school in the Navy. Every officer candidate must pass this demanding course and become an officer before he can begin flight training. In the school Gere demonstrates poor judgment in almost every aspect of his training and repeatedly gets into trouble. The only positive element in all of his activities during Officer Candidate School is his ability to run the obstacle course better and faster than anyone else. In fact, he is so good at this that it is expected that he will set a record in completing the obstacle course while his classmates must prove themselves by running the course against a time limit prior to graduation. However, Gere commits an act so grievous that he is almost certain to be dismissed without graduating. While the authorities debate whether to dismiss Gere, the class is scheduled to run the obstacle course against this time limit. If an individual has passed all other requirements and completes the course within the time limit, he will be allowed to graduate. It is the final test that all must pass before graduating. Their instructor, a Marine drill sergeant, has set the goal of everyone completing the obstacle course within the time limit to successfully complete this final graduation requirement. Failure to complete it within the time allotted also means dismissal. Of course, Gere has no fear of not completing the obstacle course within the time requirement. After all, he has the ability to set a record. However, one of Gere's female classmates has had a great deal of difficulty with the obstacle course and particularly in getting over one of the obstacles. Whether she can get over this obstacle and success-fully complete the course within the requisite time allotted is questionable. The obstacle run begins, and of course Gere is far ahead of everyone. Then he passes the obstacle that has given his classmate so much trouble. Far ahead and on to set the record, he glances back and sees that his female classmate is once again hung up on the obstacle and cannot get over it.

This presents him with a critical decision. Should he continue on to set a record which may lead to the authorities allowing him to graduate despite his poor record and his latest escapade which a Board of Officers is still debating, or should he stop, go back, and help his classmate so that she can finish, complete the course, and graduate. In terms of profession-alism, he might decide to continue and set the record, thereby convincing the Board of Officers that he should be allowed to graduate because of his individual proficiency and professionalism. However, the organiza-tion's goal, set by the Marine drill instructor, is to get everyone through this final test. After some hesitation, Gere stops and goes back. He helps his classmate to negotiate the obstacle successfully and both finish the obstacle course as required. Of course because Gere has gone back to assist his classmate, he sets no record. However, it turns out that it is his drill sergeant's testimony, based not on his performance in running the obstacle course but on his decision to sacrifice his performance to help his classmate complete the course, the organization's goal, that convinces the Board to allow Gere to graduate despite his other transgressions.

Gere's personal physical fitness and performance on the obstacle course, elements of professionalism, were considered of less importance than the organization's goal of "building the cathedral," in this case meaning all candidates passing this last test.

Beware the Marketing Hired Gun

It is the leader of the marketing organization who is responsible for avoid-ing the marketing "hired gun" syndrome. It is one of the most difficult challenges for the leader of the marketing organization to maintain high standards of personal performance and marketing or sales professionalism in all employees while avoiding the trap of building individuals who see themselves as supermarketers or supersalespeople. I would say that this is especially challenging in sales where performance is explicit, some competition is desirable, and results are measured in numbers critical to the organization and the company. One can see that there are many challenges that Drucker sought to overcome by avoiding the creed of the second stonecutter.

Overcompetitiveness and Unprofessionalism Can Result from Too Much Professionalism

Overcompetitiveness to such a degree that other employees and the organization's goals are hurt by the actions of the "professional" is a major danger. You can see this where individuals, or sometimes even organizations, compete with each other in a no-holds-barred approach, and helpful information is not passed on and anything and everything may be done not in the interest of the company or the customer but only for the individual "professional" or the professionalism of a subunit. Paradoxically this can lead to very unprofessional conduct.

Recently I went shopping with my wife to a major department store in Beverly Hills. While she was trying on a dress in a fitting room, we overheard an incident in an adjoining room. A customer had been helped by a saleswoman in another part of the department but then apparently had wandered off when the saleswoman went to find a different size of a dress in which the customer expressed interest. Another saleswoman had approached the customer as the customer became interested in yet another dress. The saleswoman failed to ask if she were already being helped and instead guided the customer to the fitting room next to ours.

When the original saleswoman found out, she angrily and publically confronted both the customer and the second saleswoman, telling both that they had acted unprofessionally. I'm certain that this confrontation was against every policy of the store. I'm also sure that the second saleswoman was supposed to ask if the customer was already being helped. I don't know whether her failure to do this was intentional or not. Regardless, I do know that the confrontation initiated by the first saleswoman did no one any good. The first saleswoman was technically correct. But she was overly competitive and too much a stickler for her rights to the customer. It would have been far better if she had considered her store and the customer first and handled things differently.

Here are the dangers of professionalism that Drucker wanted to avoid:

- Suboptimization by which one individual excels but others fail because of this individual's performance
- High compensation being the sole motivation for performance
- High turnover in the organization because of people seeking the goal of higher and higher compensation in other organizations or companies
- Functional work as an end in itself where high sales goals in the short run are not followed up with good after-sales customer service, so in the long term the company suffers
- Promotions in the organization resulting from individual skills rather than contribution to the enterprise as a whole

These problems intensify through technological advances where both the number of highly educated specialists increases at the same time as their importance and the level of their technical performance. This increases the tendency to make the specialized function the worker's goal. To get it right, there is a necessity for all specialists to see exactly where their contribution fits in with others to result in achievement of company objectives.[2] Of course, accomplishing this and finding the proper balance is up to the marketing leaders, be they marketing managers, sales managers, or whatever the title. Only in this way can workers honestly claim that they are building cathedrals and not merely polishing stones. This is how they can avoid the dangers of marketing professionalism.

Chapter 24

Why Buying Customers Won't Work

Drucker was always thinking about the future, and much of his reputation and success was the result of his uncanny ability to predict
almost exactly what was going to happen. In *The Daily Drucker*, published in 2004, he wrote: "Of the top marketing lessons for the highly
competitive twenty-first century, the most critical one is that *buying customers doesn't work.*"[1] Even though we're well into the twenty-first century today, the original version of this sentence was one that he wrote
even earlier for an article in the *Wall Street Journal* appearing in 1990.
It was published again in his book *Managing in the Future* two years
later. In both publications this read, "Of the top marketing lessons for
the highly competitive '90s, the most crucial one may well be that buying customers doesn't work."[2] The point is that not only did Drucker
not change his declaration much in the ensuing 14 years between 1990
and 2004, but he actually became more emphatic in restating his opinion. Note the italics in the version from *The Daily Drucker*. These are
Drucker's italics, not mine.

Ways of Buying Customers

Drucker identified several ways of buying customers, none of them recommended by him despite their popularity in the marketing community. One way was to price so low that there was little if any profit, but since the whole idea was not profit, but to buy the customer, who cares? This made severe underpricing an acceptable tactical alternative. Or one could be more (or maybe it's less) subtle: offer discounts, cash bonuses, low- or no-interest financing, or some other incentive (read bribe).[3] I'm sure you know of others. All of these means are supposed to allow one the privilege of raising price to an equitable level at some future possible date.

Now is as good a time as any to consider exactly what Drucker was talking about by "buying customers." Since there were situations when Drucker recommended pricing based on future lowered costs, he must not be talking about simply low pricing, but rather low pricing based not on what the customer considers value, but on low price as a bribe to get the customer to purchase the product or service. There is a difference. Assuming that marketers understand their costs, why would they want to bribe customers to buy their product anyway?

Why Do Marketers Want to Buy Customers?

Drucker emphasized that buying customers usually came from the desire on the part of marketers to break into an established market or to fend off competitors they were losing market to in a market in which the marketers were already established. The situation is that the established market buys at a certain going rate. Marketers realize that the customer must have some reason to purchase the marketer's product or if they're losing share to the competition, to defend their share. They decide that the easiest way to create an advantage is if they can lure customers to purchase their product by presenting the market with a substantially lower price than the going rate. According to this thinking, customers will now buy their product. This will allow the marketers to establish or reestablish themselves, and it is assumed that they can raise the price later. As I indicated previously, we need to distinguish between buying into the market in this fashion from creating a market so low from the start that the market is based on this low price as valued by the customer and demonstrated in razors by King Gillette in Chapter 20.

The problem with this strategy of buying customers to break into an established market is not that the marketers can't get business. In the short run they can. They may even be able to survive over a longer period if profits aren't too small. One problem with this "solution" is that they have established themselves in this low-priced niche. Frequently, it is a niche that the marketers cannot easily climb out of. So buying customers may be the beginning of a lingering illness for the business which can eventually lead to the business's or product's demise. Moreover, it ignores other problems that may be present including quality, service, image, and so on that may be the real problem. That's what Drucker was very much concerned about. However, before we examine this part of the problem, let's look at simply trying to climb out of a low-priced niche, something common to many start-ups with issues of long-term product and even company survival.

Some years ago a young accountant working for Blue Cross did a little moonlighting during tax season. To break into this established market part time, he charged the bargain price of $75 an hour when the going rate in his geographical area was about twice that. Of course in marketing, we have an official name for this. We call it *penetration pricing*. But just because we have a name for it doesn't make it right. Did this moonlighting accountant get clients? Absolutely! Since he was employed full time, he considered this once-a-year foray into a small business pure gravy. Being an excellent accountant, his seasonal tax practice grew every year. Ten years later he had the opportunity to purchase a private accounting practice and leave his full-time employer. His former clients in his part-time business would make up about 20 percent of his new independent practice. However, he had a problem. He had two classes of clients, one paying $150 an hour and the other $75. This young accountant assumed that his part-time clients knew they were getting a tremendously good deal owing to his full-time employment with Blue Cross, and maybe they did.

However, when he contacted them, announcing his new full-time practice and that they would now be charged $150 an hour, every single one of them dropped him. More than a few were angry. Most immediately approached other tax accountants—some not as experienced, a few even untried. These former clients had no idea whether their new CPAs were as good as their previous one or not. Yet they happily paid these others more than $75 an hour, some even $150 an hour. They just wouldn't pay their former low-priced accountant this amount.

The same applies with products or services sold by large corporations. It doesn't seem to matter much if you've been giving your customers a tremendously good deal or not. Assume that you have been buying customers and want to break the habit. You had better spend some time thinking through how you are going to do this, because raising prices is never easy no matter who or what the product or service is.

Anthem Blue Cross in California provided a cautionary warning for all in 2010 when it announced increases in premiums of up to 39 percent based on the hard facts of the weak economy causing many customers with good health to drop out, leaving those with more serious medical problems to share the insurance burden. In an attempt to be proactive and maintain profits, the corporation's president instantly raised prices enough to make up for his losses. It made front-page newspapers around the country. The increases were eventually retracted, but not before they caused reverberations from President Obama on down.[4] It's not much of a stretch with the riots in Greece. Here's a country in which every citizen knows that government spending absolutely must be reduced to avoid bankruptcy. Still there are riots and destruction of ancient buildings with rioters demanding that the government benefits they have received previously not be revoked. Such is human nature.

Why Drucker Was Even More Concerned

Drucker was even more concerned about the issue of buying customers. He took the automobile industry as an example. First he looked at the Hyundai Excel. It was Hyundai's first foray into the U.S. market, and it entered the market with a bang with an eye-opening low price, helping it to be voted one of the best new products of the year and listed as such in *Fortune* magazine. It set a record for first-year imports, and Excel's cumulative production exceeded 1 million within two years. Drucker said that it had the fastest growth of any automobile in history. The problem was that to accomplish this, Hyundai had pulled out all the stops and shaved costs to the bone. The company made little money with this product. Suddenly and immediately the car disappeared from the market. Quality problems played a part. However, as Drucker noted, a marketer must have sufficient profits to reinvest in the business, including correcting quality problems in design and on the production line.[5]

Drucker didn't just pick on Hyundai. He said that America's "Big Three"—Ford, GM, and Chrysler—did the same in attempting to ward off the Japanese brands that were encroaching on their market shares. Initially, rather than address the quality issue, all three offered all sorts of sales incentives to woo customers to buy their cars. This included discounts, cash bonuses, and on and on, and they did it again and again. Did these things work? Yes, they did. In every case and for every program, sales went up. The problem was that when each offer expired, sales nosedived to a lower level than they were before the incentive started, and all three lost substantial market share to the Japanese. Drucker said that the real results of these purchase incentives were:

1. Customers who had already decided to buy a domestic car from one of the three simply waited for the next incentive to do so.
2. For *potential* customers, these bribes were a negative. These incentives gave the impression that they were an admission that the products offered by these companies were inferior. The big issue during this period was quality and that U.S. cars (and about everything else) were inferior to the equivalent Japanese product. Remember Japanese Management and Theory Z? So this might have actually affected the opinion negatively of formerly satisfied customers who had already decided to buy a car from one of the Big Three U.S. manufacturers.

Also, while Drucker didn't explore this issue further, there is a very real third psychological reason that would tend to further decrease sales in the first and second categories above. If potential customers missed the deadline of the incentive program's expiration, these customers were likely to feel cheated, just as the accountant's old clients deserted him when he upped their prices and went elsewhere. Both old and potential customers are fully capable of doing the same.

The bottom line according to Drucker was that the bribes intended to buy customers attracted few, if any, new customers. Worse overall, both GM and Chrysler lost substantial shares to the Japanese while Ford was barely able to maintain its position.[6]

Think Before You Buy

Before any marketer decides to buy customers, I think it's important to reflect on the objective and how it's going to play in the marketplace. Yes, I know. A sales incentive or any strategy for buying customers is supposed to allow you to temporarily lower the price without affecting your product's image or ability to raise the price later. Is this true in every situation? I doubt it. We've already established in a previous chapter that customers are not irrational. They are not stupid, either. The Johnson Smith Company is an old mail-order catalog house that originated in Australia at around the turn of the twentieth century selling novelties. Its catalog once reached 576 pages, and over 100,000 copies were published. In fact, I remember as a preteen, it was fun to read the catalog and to visualize the colorful images the descriptions invoked. In those days, the Johnson Smith Company carried a motto: "We are in business for fun." I don't think any customers or catalog readers took this motto literally, if they considered it at all. However, today the company's motto is the more accurate: "Things you never knew existed." The point is that if your customers or prospects simply always seek the lowest price and that is the only reason for them buying from you, you might just as well lower your price permanently now. Customers or prospects know that you are not "in business for fun" nor are you granting discounts or whatever because you like their looks or because it is a holiday. You can buy customers, and you will increase sales temporarily. But if buying customers is your object, as soon as your discounting or other incentive program has expired, your customers are going elsewhere to find the lowest price again.

I don't think that Drucker was against sales incentives or other discount programs designed to accomplish a specific objective. But bribing customers should not be done on a routine or permanent basis. So first you need to think through the question: Why aren't you getting more sales at your current pricing? Or, if your objective is to break into an established market, exactly how can you do this and still not trap yourself in a low-priced niche?

How to Avoid Entrapment in a Low-Priced Niche

With penetration pricing, the marketer seeks to enter a market with a low price to capture as large a market share as possible. Pricing is emphasized as a major differential advantage over the competition. Once the product is established in the marketplace, the price is raised to be more on a level with that of the competition, or the price can be raised even higher. However, don't forget our young accountant. The issue here is to think through exactly how you intend to raise prices. A good example of this is Datsun/Nissan. Introduced into this country as a sports car in the early 1970s, the Datsun 240Z was underpriced compared to similar sports cars offered by other manufacturers. Then, as market share was captured and the product became well established in the U.S. market, the price was raised. Ten years after its introduction, its price was on the high side for its class. Moreover, even with the low price, the car was good enough to compete, and the Datsun folks made money.

Considering this example, what might our young accountant have done? He might have raised his prices with his part-time clientele 10 percent a year. Assuming it was five years between his initial foray into the market and when he bought an accounting practice and went on his own, he would have charged $75 plus $7.50 or $82.50 an hour the second year, $90.75 the third, $100 the fourth, $110 the fifth, $121 the sixth, and $133 the seventh. By year eight he would have been at market level, and he would have had no difficulty with his new clients.

Business Bribes Are Always Wrong

As with many of Drucker's concepts, we must dig deeper to appreciate his full meaning. His deeper intent was to induce marketers to think things through and decide exactly what they were trying to do in their pricing before they did it. They need to be sure that lower pricing could help them achieve their ultimate objective and the need for profit—to create a customer and sustain and grow the business. He knew that there were many ways of doing this and that there are many environmental factors that impact a pricing decision, even a temporary one disguised as a loan or some other sales incentive and that there are many other ways of creating a differential advantage over competitors that would result in permanent increase in market share besides what he chose to term "buying customers." Most important, he wanted marketers to avoid covering up other problems by the too easy and too temporary solution of simply lowering price. That, to Drucker, was buying customers.

Chapter 25

With Drucker into the Future

P eter Drucker spent a good deal of his life writing about and predicting the future. Much has been covered in this volume on this subject because one cannot look at Drucker and avoid his particular brand of unique management fortune-telling. Drucker himself understood this, probably because there is little doubt that being able to predict the future and knowing "the shape of things to come," fair or not, constitute a significant competitive advantage for any marketer, indeed for any manager. However, we should not talk about Drucker's spectacular success as a management fortune-teller without first noting that his initial public prediction was a bust. It was a prediction published shortly before the stock market crash that preceded the Great Depression beginning in 1929. In this case he predicted a rosy future and a bull market. He ate crow a few weeks later and was forced to begin his career as a newspaperman with an article on the stock market crash published in the *Frankfurter General-Anzeiger* titled "Panic on the New York Stock Exchange." That must have been difficult for him, and it was the last time he attempted to predict the stock market. It may also have been the root of his well-known cautionary note that, "The best way to predict the future is to create it." Drucker could do little to create a bull stock market, so he stayed away from stock market predictions in the future. Nevertheless as explained throughout this volume, he made successful predictions again and again on just about everything else by using the methods we've looked at. As the cover story for *BusinessWeek* written shortly after his death reported, "He was always able to discern trends—sometimes 20 years or more before they were visible to anyone else."[1]

The Future Has Arrived and Is Proceeding— but with Drucker?

What of Drucker's insights, values, principles, and concepts? Are his ideas something that extend out into the future, or have they ended with Drucker's death? Has their value already begun to diminish and started to fade? Is Drucker now a footnote to management and marketing rather than a prime mover? A dean of the Drucker School most infamously once told a media interviewer even while Drucker was still alive and a member of his faculty: "This is a brand in decline."

But a prime mover Drucker was, affecting marketing both directly and indirectly. Shortly after his death business journalist John Byrne attempted to assess Drucker's contributions and strived to explain "why Drucker's ideas still matter." Byrne's list of Drucker's major accomplishments included:

- It was Drucker who introduced the idea of decentralization, a concept that became basic to every large organization in the world. Drucker thought that brilliant idea up more than 70 years ago, and its basic to how companies selling in many varied geographical locations market today all over the world. But let's face it, its basic to many organizations. As with most of Drucker's ideas, this is so obvious that we might wonder whether no one understood this previously, but the fact is that apparently no one did.
- In the 1950s Drucker became the first to assert that workers should be treated on the asset side of the ledger and not listed as liabilities. In fact it was one of the main conclusions of his

1946 book, *Concept of the Corporation*. Previously, the idea was to focus on efficiency resulting from technology primarily to reduce worker "cost." Even TV science fiction shows of the era frequently underlined the terrible but apparently the inevitable event of losing one's job to a future technology when machines replaced people. These predictions are still reported in the media today, but perhaps not so frequently except during a recession. Witness the 2011 movie *Real Steel* starring Hugh Jackman. Jackman's character is a down-on-his-luck former champion boxer who's now the manager of a robotic metal fighter after human boxing has been outlawed as too primitive and dangerous. Drucker however came up with the then peculiar notion that the corporation needed to be considered a community built on trust and respect, and not just a machine for profit maximization. This community of men and women, properly led, resulted in new opportunities and was a significant asset, not a cost.

Not to overuse the word metaphor, but technology and machines would therefore increase people's productivity, not replace them. It's the sort of notion that I once saw an economist use to explain why commercial fishing was better for the single person who once struggled with only a hook, line, pole, and bait with which he might successfully feed his family for a day, being replaced with a community of like-minded people working in concert with machines not just to feed their individual families, but to export their catch to an entire world.

- Drucker went on to complete the decade by expounding the revolutionary idea that since there was no business without a customer, the purpose of a business was not profit at all, but to create a customer. You may recall that we took on and explained that thought in Chapter 2.

- It was Drucker who wrote about the contribution of knowledge workers, and in fact he invented the term, long before anyone knew or understood how knowledge would be of importance above other corporate inputs to productivity. Until Drucker, no one knew how knowledge and those who worked with it could optimize the organization or how the application of knowledge in organizations would help to gain advantage over those that did not.[2] So for better or worse we can blame everything from the Internet to information overload at least partially on Drucker's brilliance and unending imagination.

Byrne's compilation of Drucker's contributions related more to Drucker's contributions to management rather than marketing directly. Three marketing academics, including well-known marketing researcher Jagdish Sheth, documented Drucker's direct contributions to marketing a couple of years later. These included the following:

- He was first to state the marketing concept of creating value for customers, the foundation of modern marketing. This he did in 1954 in his book *The Practice of Management* with his definition of business purpose as discussed in Chapter 2 of this book.
- Then he wrote, spoke, and argued for broadening the role of marketing in society such that today many people speak of the age of societal marketing including corporate social responsibility, consumerism, marketing of nonprofit enterprises, and even lessons for for-profits from nonprofit organizations.
- He made extraordinary contributions to strategy from making clear the starting point ("What business are you in?") to Byrne's notation previously mentioned that it was Drucker who moved the worker from a debit to an asset in the corporation. Also included was Drucker's cautionary warning to beware of growth for growth's sake and a reminder that "business enterprise is an entrepreneurial institution" with attendant strategy implications.
- It was Drucker who championed today's well-known term "innovation and entrepreneurship," and he further developed the sources of innovation success described earlier in this book. And he did not skimp on this. He devoted an entire book to this "dynamic duo" under that title in 1985.

- Finally, it was Drucker who foresaw the growth of globalization and of nonnational enterprises.[3] Older readers will recall that the term globalization was little used in marketing and that the term "international marketing" was in vogue and was deemed a somewhat mysterious process in which only something like 7 percent of U.S. companies participated, let alone were such radical concepts as multinationalism used.

Throughout, Drucker used history to assist him in analyzing his ideas concerning what was likely to work and what was not. He effortlessly went back and forth from the past to the present and the future. When asked what business books Drucker read during his 70-plus-year tenure of management exploration, declaration, and mastery, it was not too surprising to learn from Doris Drucker, Peter's widow, that he generally didn't read any. True, he read business magazines and newspapers. However, he only scanned business books; he read and assimilated much through the other books at his bedside, all of them on history. Clearly Drucker would have been a fan of the *History Channel* on television had it been available during the period of his greatest productivity. As he several times declared, his concepts of leadership were 2,000 years old and came originally from the ideas of Xenophon, a successful Greek general and author writing about battlefield leadership almost half a millennium before Jesus. For many years Drucker refused to write specifically on leadership as a separate subject, telling those who asked for his insights on this topic that they should consult the ancients and read history, since so-called modern techniques were all cutting edge 2,000 years earlier.

Can Drucker Help Us Today?

I think that Drucker can help us today, but we have more responsibilities that we must accept in order to get maximum value from Drucker's work. Drucker never stressed how to do things. Rather he suggested what to do and had us work through the details of how to get them done on our own. Drucker didn't tell Jack Welch he should dump profitable GE companies. He asked whether there were profitable businesses that

GE owned that Welch would rather not be in, and if so what did Welch intend to do about it? It was Welch who decided that if a GE company wasn't number one or two in the industry, even if it was profitable, it had to go. Drucker's questions led to Welch's solutions. Of course doing this hereto unheard of action freed up money and resources for Welch to get into far more profitable businesses for GE, leading to GE's phenomenal growth and Welch's reputation both as the CEO of the decade and as Neutron Jack, the guy who forced GE employees to go elsewhere.

So what's the difference today? Obviously Drucker is no longer with us to ask these questions, to get us thinking, and to force us to make the decisions that all managers must make. His concepts, principles, and values are still present, and they are still valid and still guide us through directions, insights, and demands to make the decisions that marketing executives must involve themselves in daily, including assuming the risks associated with these decisions.

So, yes, Drucker is gone, but his spirit, values, concepts, principles, and ideas live on, forcing us to think through our issues and to make decisions in all management areas. This too is an opportunity. It compels us to build on the foundations Drucker has given us and to continue to develop them. Only in this way can other Jack Welches, Andrew Groves, and the outstanding CEOs of major corporations, government executives, not-for-profits, entrepreneurs, and small businesses continue to build, prosper, and sustain their organizations and their enterprises and continue to create customers and serve society. Only in this way is it likely that those who have been led by Drucker's ideas into the future can truthfully say, it was all because of Drucker's views on marketing.

Notes

Introduction

1. Drucker, Peter F., "Selling Will Become Marketing," *Nation's Business*, November 1955, vol. 43, no. 11, p. 79.
2. Speech by C. William Pollard on installation of Deborah Freund as president of Claremont Graduate University on September 15, 2011, and e-mail with additional information from C. William Pollard, November 15, 2011.
3. Henry To quoted in "China Embraces Old School Business Guru," *Wall Street Journal*, June 18, 2008.
4. Drucker, Peter F., "The Way Ahead," *Executive Excellence*, May 2004, p. 3.

Chapter 1

1. Drucker, Peter F., *Management: Tasks, Responsibilities, Practices* (New York: Harper & Row, 1974), p. 64.
2. E. Jerome McCarthy, a professor at Michigan State University, developed the concept of the four Ps of marketing—product, price, promotion, and place—by reducing the many elements of the marketing mix to these four in 1960.
3. Drucker, *Management*, p. 63.
4. Ibid., p. 62.
5. Ibid.
6. Ibid., p. 63.
7. Drucker, Peter F., in Rick Wartzman, ed. *The Drucker Lectures* (New York: McGraw-Hill, 2010), p. 242.
8. Drucker, Peter F., *Innovation and Entrepreneurship* (New York: Harper & Row, 1985), p. 77.
9. Zeithaml, Carl and Valerie A., "Environment Management: Revising the Marketing Perspective," *Journal of Marketing*, vol. 48, Spring 1984, pp. 50–51.
10. Drucker, *Innovation and Entrepreneurship*, p. 58.

Chapter 2

1. Drucker, Peter F., *Management: Tasks, Responsibilities, Practices* (New York: Harper & Row, 1973, 1974), p. 60.
2. Ibid.
3. Naisbitt, John, and Patricia Aburdene, *Reinventing the Corporation* (New York: Warner Books, 1985), pp. 85–86.
4. Allison, Melissa, "Starbucks Has a New Growth Strategy—More Revenue with Lower Costs," *Seattle Times*, May 15, 2010, http://seattletimes.nwsource.com/html/businesstechnology/2011861321_starbucksstrategy16.html, accessed March 31, 2011.
5. Drucker, *Management*, p. 61.

Chapter 3

1. Drucker, Peter F., *The Practice of Management* (New York: Harper Collins, 1954, 1986), p. 37.
2. Drucker, Peter F., *Management: Tasks, Responsibilities, Practices* (New York: Harper & Row, 1973, 1974), p. 103.

Chapter 4

1. Drucker, Peter F., *Managing the Non-Profit Organization* (New York: Harper Collins, 1990), pp. 83–84.
2. Drucker, Peter F., *The Practice of Management* (New York: Harper Collins, 1954, 1986), pp. 38–39.
3. Drucker, Peter F., *The Five Most Important Questions You Will Ever Ask About Your Organization* (San Francisco: Jossey-Bass, 1993, 2008).
4. Drucker, Peter F., *Managing for Results* (New York: Harper and Row, 1964), p. 93.
5. Mathews, Jay, and Peter Katel, "The Cost of Quality," *Newsweek,* September 7, 1991, p. 48.
6. Fisher, Anne B., "Morale Crisis," *Fortune,* November 18, 1991, p. 70.
7. Drucker, Peter F., *The Effective Executive* (New York: Harper Collins, 1967, 1985, 1996, 2002, 2006), p. 79.
8. Levitt, Theodore, "Marketing Myopia," *Harvard Business Review*, vol. 38, no. 4, July–August 1960, p. 50.

Chapter 5

1. Drucker, Peter F., *Management Challenges for the 21st Century* (New York: Harper Business, 1999), p. 21.
2. Drucker, Peter F., meeting with the author, November 7, 1997.
3. Hemmings, Robert L., *How to Jump-Start Your Career* (Chicago: Racom Communications, 2011), pp. 3–4.
4. Poe, Richard, "A Winning Spirit—It Takes Integrity to Lead Franchises to Victory," *Success,* vol. 37, no. 6, August 1990, p. 60.
5. Ibid.
6. Barack Obama, Matt Lauer interview, *The Today Show,* NBC Television, January 13, 2009.
7. McWilliams, Gary, "Whirlwind on the Web" *BusinessWeek,* April 7, 1997, p. 132.
8. Ibid., pp. 132, 134, 136.
9. No author listed, "Company Facts," Dell, http://www.dell.com/content/topics/global .aspx/about_dell/company/leadership/collaborate_communicate?~ck=ln&c=us&l=en& lnki=0&s=corp.
10. "Supercuts, Inc.," *Funding Universe,* http://www.fundinguniverse.com/company-histories/Supercuts-Inc-Company-History.html.
11. Bongiorno, Lor, "The McDonald's of Toiletries," *BusinessWeek*, August 4, 1997, pp. 79–80.
12. No author listed, "Beth M. Pritchard," Forbes.com, http://people.forbes.com/profile/beth-m-pritchard/28320.

Chapter 6

1. Drucker, Peter F., *Innovation and Entrepreneurship* (New York: Harper & Row, 1985), pp. 130–132.
2. McLellan, Dennis, "Inventor of Powerful Adhesive Super Glue," *Los Angeles Times,* March 31, 2011, p. AA4.
3. Schultz, Harold, with Katie Couric on CBS TV *Sunday Morning,* March 27, 2011.
4. For a complete and detailed discussion of the Wrights' innovative processes in inventing the airplane, see Wright, Orville, *How We Invented the Airplane* (Mineola, New York: Dover Publications, 1988).

Chapter 7

1. Drucker, Peter F., *The Practice of Management* (New York: Harper Collins, 1954), p. 69.
2. Drucker, Peter F., *The Essential Drucker* (New York: Harper Collins, 2001), p. 273.

3. Drucker, Peter F., *Classic Drucker* (Boston: Harvard Business School Publishing, 2006, 2008), pp.78–79.
4. Quinlon, Michael, "More Than One Way to Skin a Cat," *World Wide Words*, July 17, 2011, http://www.worldwidewords.org/qa/qa-mor1.htm, accessed August 17, 2011.
5. Drucker, Peter F., *Managing the Nonprofit Organization* (New York: Harper Collins, 1990), pp. 70–71.
6. Lienhard, John H., "No. 1525: Liberty Ships," *Engines of Our Ingenuity*, http://www .uh.edu/engines/epi1525.htm, accessed August 18, 2011.
7. Drucker, Peter F., *Innovation and Entrepreneurship* (New York: Harper & Row, 1985), pp. 134–138.

Chapter 8

1. No author listed, "Silly Putty," *Inventor of the Week*, http://web.mit.edu/invent/iow/ sillyputty.html, accessed September 7, 2011.
2. Drucker, Peter F., *Innovation and Entrepreneurship* (New York: Harper & Row, 1985), p. 36.
3. No author listed, "Silly Putty," http://www.chem.umn.edu/outreach/Sillyputty.html, accessed September 7, 2011.
4. Drucker, *Innovation and Entrepreneurship*, pp. 37–38.
5. No author listed, "William Lloyd Warner," *New World Encyclopedia*, http://www. newworldencyclopedia.org/entry/W._Lloyd_Warner, accessed September 6, 2011.
6. Ibid., p. 51.
7. Oliver, Myrna, "E. J. Cossman, 84; Ant Farm, Spud Gun Made Him Fortune," *Los Angeles Times,* December 19, 2002, http://articles.latimes.com/2002/dec/19/local/ me-cossman19, accessed September 6, 2011.
8. Cossman, E. Joseph, telephone interview with the author, November 24, 1997.
9. Drucker, Peter F., *Managing for Results* (New York: Harper & Row, 1964), p. 147.
10. Ibid., pp.147–148.

Chapter 9

1. Drucker, Peter F., *Innovation and Entrepreneurship* (New York: Harper & Row, 1985).
2. Ibid., p. 209.
3. General Nathan Bedford Forrest Historical Society, "Quotes by General Forrest: Origin of First with the Most," http://www.tennessee-scv.org/ForrestHistSociety/quotes.html, accessed April 18, 2011.
4. Drucker, *Innovation and Entrepreneurship*, p. 210.
5. Ibid., pp. 215–217.
6. Baseball-Reference.com, *http://www.baseball-reference.com/leaders/batting_avg_progress .shtml?redir*, accessed April 18, 2011.
7. Drucker, *Innovation and Entrepreneurship*, pp. 220–225.
8. Brown, Mike, "A Strategy of Surprise and Least Resistance," in *Brain Zooming*, BusinessWeek.com, October 1, 2007, http://bx.businessweek.com/strategic-marketing/ view?url=http%3A%2F%2Fbrainzooming.blogspot.com%2F2007%2F10%2Fhit-em -where-they-aint-strategy-of.html, accessed April 18, 2011.
9. Ibid., pp. 227–229.
10. No author listed. "Ecological Niche," Answers.com, http://www.answers.com/topic/ ecological-niche, accessed April 21, 2011.
11. Drucker, *Innovation and Entrepreneurship*, pp. 233–242.
12. Drucker, Peter F., *The Practice of Management* (New York: Harper & Row, 1954), p. 37.
13. Drucker, *Innovation and Entrepreneurship*, pp. 243–252.

14. "The History of Ice Cream," Zinger's Ice Cream, March 2008, http://www.zingersicecream .com/history.htm, accessed April 24, 2011.
15. Drucker, *The Practice of Management*, p. 85.

Chapter 10

1. Drucker, Peter F., with Joseph Maciariello, *Management*, rev. ed. (New York: Collins, 1973, 1974, 2008), p. 113.
2. Drucker, Peter F., *On the Profession of Management*, from the preface (Boston: Harvard Business Review Book, 2003), p. ix.
3. Drucker, Peter F., "The Information That Executives Truly Need," *Harvard Business Review*, January 1995, vol. 73, p. 54.
4. No author listed, "The Story of Soichiro Honda," *The Reading Room*, http://www .bspage.com/1article/peo23.html, accessed November 3, 2011.
5. American Honda Motor Company, "Honda's First Dreams," 4Strokes.com Honda Articles, http://www.4strokes.com/articles/honda/1stdream.asp, accessed November 3, 2011.
6. Drucker, Peter F., *Managing for Results* (New York: Harper & Row, 1964), p. 203.

Chapter 11

1. Drucker, Peter F., with Joseph Maciariello, *Management* (New York: HarperCollins, 1973, 1974, 2008), p. 26.
2. Drucker, Peter F., *Managing the Nonprofit Organization* (New York: HarperCollins, 1990), p. 7.
3. Ibid., p.146.
4. Isidro, Isabel, "Soapworks: How a Family Need Spurred a Profitable Business," *PowerHomeBiz.com*, http://www.powerhomebiz.com/vol135/soapworks.htm, accessed September 9, 2011.
5. Manas, Jerry, "Napoleon's Six Winning Principles," *PM World Today*, vol. x, no. 2, February 2008, p. 2.
6. Schine, Eric, and Peter Elstrom, "Not Exactly an Overnight Success," *BusinessWeek*, June 2, 1997, p. 133.
7. "Qualcomm," *Wikipedia*, http://en.wikipedia.org/wiki/Qualcomm, accessed September 9, 2011.
8. Drucker, Peter F., *The Practice of Management* (New York: HarperCollins, 1954, 1986), p. 37.

Chapter 12

1. Drucker, Peter F., *Management Challenges for the 21st Century* (New York: Harper Business, 1999), p. 43.
2. Drucker, Peter F., *Innovation and Entrepreneurship* (New York: Harper & Row, 1985), p. 251.
3. Drucker, Peter F., *Managing the Future* (New York: Truman Talley Books, 1992), p. 100.
4. Drucker, *Management Challenges for the 21st Century*, pp. 43–44.
5. Ibid., p. 69.
6. "Japan Birthrate Fall World's No. 1," *Kyoko News*, April 18, 2009, http://search. japantimes.co.jp/cgi-bin/nn20090418a5.html, accessed August 3, 2011.
7. Drucker, Peter F., "The Changing World Economy," in Rick Wartzman, ed., *The Drucker Lectures* (New York: McGraw-Hill, 2010), p. 186.
8. Drucker, *Management Challenges for the 21st Century*, pp. 47–50.
9. "Sullivan Act," *Wikipedia*, http://en.wikipedia.org/wiki/Sullivan_Act, accessed October 2, 2011.

10. Drucker, *Management Challenges for the 21st Century*, pp. 50–58.
11. Ibid., p. 60.
12. Ibid., p. 59.
13. Ibid., pp. 60–61.
14. "Global Competitiveness," World Economic Forum, http://www.weforum.org/issues/global-competitiveness, accessed May 4, 2012.
15. Drucker, *Management Challenges for the 21st Century*, p. 62.
16. Reich, Robert, "G20 Failure Moves Global Economy to Brink of Protectionism," *The Christian Science Monitor*, November 10, 2010, http://www.csmonitor.com/Commentary/Global-Viewpoint/2010/1115/G20-failure-moves-global-economy-to-brink-of-protectionism, accessed August 3, 2011.
17. Drucker, *Management Challenges for the 21st Century*, p. 64.
18. Ibid., p. 67.

Chapter 13

1. Mulligan, Thomas F., and James Flanigan, "Prolific Father of Modern Management," *Los Angeles Times, Business Section*, November 12, 2005, p. A-1, http://articles.latimes.com/2005/nov/12/business/fi-drucker12, accessed September 13, 2011.
2. Heller, Robert, "The Drucker Legacy," Thinking Managers, http://www.thinkingmanagers.com/management/drucker, accessed September 13, 2011.
3. Drucker, Peter F., *Managing for Results* (New York: Harper & Row, 1964), pp. 143–146.
4. "The Model T Ford," Frontenac Motor Company, http://www.modelt.ca/background.html, accessed September 13, 2011.
5. "Ford Model T," Wikipedia, http://en.wikipedia.org/wiki/Ford_Model_T, accessed September 13, 2011.
6. Drucker, Peter F., *On the Profession of Management* (Boston: Harvard Business Review Book, 1963, 1964, 1966, 1985, 1987, 1989, 1991, 1992, 1993, 1994, 1998), pp. 116–117.
7. Drucker, *Managing for Results*, p. 221.
8. Drucker, Peter F., with Joseph Maciariello, *Management* (New York: HarperCollins, 1973, 1974, 2008), pp. 163–166.
9. Drucker, Peter F., *Classic Drucker* (Boston: Harvard Business School Publishing, 2006, 2008), p. 29.
10. Drucker, Peter F., *Management Challenges for the 21st Century* (New York: Harper Business, 1999), p. 74.
11. Drucker, *Managing for Results*, p.143.
12. Ibid., p. 144.
13. Drucker, Peter F., *Innovation and Entrepreneurship* (New York: Harper & Row), p. 155.
14. Drucker with Maciariello, *Management*, p. 61.
15. Drucker, *Managing for Results*, pp. 144–145.
16. Drucker, *Management Challenges for the 21st Century*, pp. 74–76.
17. Drucker, *Managing for Results*, p. 145.
18. Drucker, Peter F., "Putting More Now into the Internet," Forbes.com, May 15, 2000, http://www.forbes.com/global/2000/0515/0310092a.html, accessed September 14, 2000.
19. Drucker, *On the Profession of Management*, pp. 25–26.
20. Drucker with Maciariello, *Management*, pp. xxvi–xxvii.
21. Drucker, *Innovation and Entrepreneurship*, pp.154–155.
22. Drucker, *Management Challenges for the 21st Century*, p. 79.
23. "Gale Encyclopedia of Biography: Jack Welch," Answers.com, http://www.answers.com/topic/jack-welch, accessed September 16, 2011.

Chapter 14

1. "Dictionary," *Resource Library*, http://www.marketingpower.com/_layouts/Dictionary .aspx, accessed September 22, 2011.
2. Wood, Robert E., quoted in A. D. Chandler, Jr., *Strategy and Structure* (Cambridge, Mass.: MIT Press, 1962), p. 235.
3. Leonnig, Carol D., and Joe Stephens, "Lawmakers Accuse Solyndra Execs of Ripping Off Taxpayers," *Washington Post Politics*, September 9, 2011, http://www .washingtonpost.com/blogs/2chambers/post/solyndra-executives-to-appear-before-house -committee-friday-morning/2011/09/22/gIQAF0vCqK_blog.html, accessed September 21, 2011.
4. "Solyndra," Wikipedia, http://en.wikipedia.org/wiki/Solyndra, accessed September 21, 2011.
5. "Great Lessons from the Great Depression," *CPIFinancial.net*, August 10, 2009, http:// www.cpifinancial.net/v2/print.aspx?pg=fa&aid=333, accessed September 27, 2011.
6. "Successful Companies and Industries During the Great Depression," *Google Answers*, http://answers.google.com/answers/threadview?id=178334, accessed September 27, 2011.
7. "P&G Sponsors its First Daytime Serial," *Old Time.com*, http://www.old-time.com/ commercials/1930%27s/OOMP.htm, accessed September 27, 2011.
8. "Swatch," Wikipedia, http://en.wikipedia.org/wiki/Swatch, accessed September 27, 2011.
9. "The Swatch Marketing Strategy," Marketing and Global Research Center, http:// moneymantras9.blogspot.com/2010/02/swatch-watch-marketing-strategy.html, accessed September 27, 2011.

Chapter 15

1. Hiltzik, Michael, "A Tech Visionary: Comparing Jobs to Edison Doesn't Quite Capture It," *Los Angeles Times*, October 6, 2010, p. AA8.
2. Drucker, Peter F., with Joseph Maciariello, *Management*, rev. ed. (New York: Harper Collins, 2008), p. 347.
3. Drucker, Peter F., *Management Challenges for the 21st Century* (New York: Harper Business, 1999), p. 86.
4. Drucker, Peter F., *Innovation and Entrepreneurship* (New York: Harper & Row, 1985), pp. 126–128.
5. Ibid., p. 128.
6. Ibid., p. 129.
7. Drucker, *Management Challenges for the 21st Century*, p. 87.
8. Drucker, *Innovation and Entrepreneurship*, pp. 191–192.
9. Grivettit, Louis E., "Dialog: Recent Vietnam Stories Since the War," http://www.pbs .org/pov/stories/vietnam/bios/grivetti.html, accessed October 12, 2011.
10. Drucker with Maciariello, *Management*, rev. ed., pp. 354–355.
11. Drucker, *Management Challenges for the 21st Century*, pp. 131–132.
12. Ibid., p. 131.
13. Drucker with Maciariello, *Management*, rev. ed., p. 465.
14. Drucker, Peter F., *Managing the Non-Profit Organization* (New York: Harper Collins, 1990), p. 100.
15. Drucker with Maciariello, *Management*, rev. ed., p. 465.

Chapter 16

1. Drucker, Peter F., *Management: Tasks, Responsibilities, and Practices* (New York: Harper & Row, 1973, 1974), p. 90.
2. Drucker, Peter F., *Innovation and Entrepreneurship* (New York: Harper & Row, 1985) p. 88.
3. Drucker, *Management: Tasks, Responsibilities, and Practices*, p. 90.
4. Drucker, *Innovation and Entrepreneurship*, pp. 96–97.

5. Ibid., p. 93.

6. Ibid., p. 95.

7. Drucker, Peter F., *Management Challenges for the 21ˢᵗ Century* (New York: Harper Business, 1999), pp. 43–44.

8. Galagan, Patricia A., and Peter F. Drucker, "The E-Learning Revolution," *Training and Development,* vol. 54, no. 12, p. 24.

9. "Abstract" from Online Education: An Industry & Competitor Analysis published by MarketData Enterprises, Inc., August 2011, http://www.giiresearch.com/report/md208742-online-education-industry-competitor-analysis.html, accessed October 20, 2011.

10. Ruiz, Rebecca R., "The Debate Over Online Learning," *New York Times,* education section, October 20, 2011, http://thechoice.blogs.nytimes.com/2011/10/06/online-ed/, accessed October 20, 2011.

11. Bush, Jeb, and Jim Hunt, "New Higher Education Model," *Inside Higher Education,* October 6, 2011, http://www.insidehighered.com/views/2011/10/06/bush_hunt_essay_on_why_public_universities_need_to_embrace_online_education.

12. Shachar, M., and Y. Neumann, "Twenty Years of Research on the Academic Performance Differences Between Traditional and Distance Learning: Summative Meta-Analysis and Trend Examination," *Journal of Online Learning and Teaching (JOLT),* vol. 6, no. 2, June 2010, http://jolt.merlot.org/vol6no2/shachar_0610.pdf, accessed October 23, 2011.

13. Galagan and Drucker, "The E-Learning Revolution."

Chapter 17

1. "Winning Isn't Everything; It's the Only Thing," Wikipedia, http://en.wikipedia.org/wiki/Winning_isn%27t_everything;_it%27s_the_only_thing, accessed December 20, 2011.

2. Shakespeare, William, *Julius Caesar,* act 4, scene 3, pp. 218–224.

3. Kobliski, Kathy J., "Timing Is Everything," *Entrepreneur.com,* February 1, 2001, http://www.entrepreneur.com/article/37592, accessed October 25, 2011.

4. McCall, Kimberly, "Crash and Learn," *Entrepreneur.com,* October 2000, http://www.entrepreneur.com/article/32078http://www.entrepreneur.com/Your_Business/YB_SegArticle/0,4621,279211,00.html, accessed October 25, 2011.

5. "Zap Mail," Wikipedia, http://en.wikipedia.org/wiki/Zapmail, accessed October 25, 2011.

6. Drucker, Peter F., *People and Performance* (Boston: Harvard Business School Press, 2007), p. 33.

7. Drucker, Peter F., with Joseph Maciariello, *Management,* rev. ed. (New York: Harper Collins, 2008), p. 30.

8. Drucker, Peter F., *Managing the Nonprofit Organization* (New York: Harper, 1990), p. 24.

9. Aiello, Albert, Jr., "Timing Is Everything," *CIO Magazine,* September 1, 1997, http://www.cio.com.au/article/123514/timing_everything/.

10. Carpenter, Gregory S., and Kent Nakamoto, "Consumer Preference Formation and Pioneering Advantage," *Journal of Marketing Research,* August 1989, p. 298.

11. Drucker, Peter F., *Innovation and Entrepreneurship* (New York: Harper & Row, 1985), p. 209.

12. Ibid., pp. 220–232.

13. Ibid., pp. 225–232.

14. "Second Chance (Body Armor)," Wikipedia, http://en.wikipedia.org/wiki/Second_Chance_(body_armor), accessed October 26, 2011.

15. "Second Chance Body Armor Company," Wikipedia, http://en.wikipedia.org/wiki/Second_Chance_Body_Armor_Company, accessed October 26, 2011.

Chapter 18

1. Arnold, H. H., *Global Mission* (New York: Harper & Row,1949), p. 615.
2. Sorkin, Andrew Ross, Quoted in Michael Connor's Book Review, "Andrew Ross Sorkin's 'Too Big to Fail,'" *Business Ethics*, November 24, 2009, http://business-ethics .com/2009/11/24/too-big-to-fail-an-inside-story-guaranteed-to-make-you-angry/, accessed May 5, 2012.
3. Drucker, Peter F., *Management: Tasks, Responsibilities, Practices* (New York: Harper & Row, 1973, 1974), p. 511.
4. Drucker, Peter F., and Joseph Maciariello, *The Daily Drucker* (New York: Harper Business, 2004), p. xiii.

Chapter 19

1. Drucker, Peter F., "Drucker on Management: The Five Deadly Business Sins," *Wall Street Journal*, October 21, 1993, p. A18.
2. Drucker, Peter F., *Managing in a Time of Great Change* (New York: Truman Talley Books/Dutton, 1995), pp. 45–50.
3. "Premium Pricing," *BusinessDictionary.com*, http://www.businessdictionary.com/ definition/premium-pricing.html, accessed November 9, 2011.
4. Drucker, "Drucker on Management: The Five Deadly Business Sins."
5. Ibid.
6. Ibid.
7. Wash, Juliann, "DuPont to Sell Synthetic-Fibers Unit," SunSentinel.com, http://articles .sun-sentinel.com/2003-11-18/business/0311170385_1_dupont-nylon-koch-industries, accessed November 10, 2011.
8. Drucker, "Drucker on Management: The Five Deadly Business Sins."
9. Drucker, Peter F., *Managing for the Future* (New York: Truman Talley Books/Dutton, 1992), pp. 251–252.
10. Drucker, "Drucker on Management: The Five Deadly Business Sins."

Chapter 20

1. Drucker, Peter F., "Selling Will Become Marketing," *Nation's Business*, November 1955, vol. 43, no. 11, p. 80.
2. Drucker, Peter F., *The Age of Discontinuity* (New York: Harper & Row, 1968, 1969), p. 164.
3. Drucker, Peter F., *Management: Tasks, Responsibilities, Practices* (New York: Harper & Row, 1973, 1974), p. 65.
4. Ibid., p. 85.
5. Drucker, Peter F., *The Essential Drucker* (New York: Harper Business, 2001), p. 183.
6. Ibid., p. 188.
7. Drucker, Peter F., *Innovation and Entrepreneurship* (New York: Harper & Row, 1985), pp. 243–252.
8. Drucker, Peter F., *Management Challenges for the 21st Century* (New York: Harper Business, 1999), p. 115.
9. Drucker, Peter F., "The Information Executives Truly Need," *On the Profession of Management* (Boston: Harvard Business School Publishing, 2003), p. 87.
10. Drucker, *Management Challenges for the 21st Century*, p. 114.
11. Drucker, Peter F., with Joseph Maciariello, *Management*, rev. ed. (New York: Harper Collins, 2008), pp. 333–334.

Chapter 21

1. Drucker, Peter F., *The Essential Drucker* (New York: Harper Collins, 2001), p. 172.
2. Drucker, Peter F., *Management Challenges for the 21st Century* (New York: Harper Collins, 1999), pp. 145–146.

3. Ibid., p. 146.
4. Drucker, Peter F., *Managing for the Future* (New York: Truman Tallbooks/Dutton, 1992), p. 104.
5. Wartzman, Rick, ed., "Peter F. Drucker On Globalization" in *The Drucker Lectures* (New York: McGraw-Hill, 2010), p. 217.
6. Drucker, *Managing for the Future*, p. 105.

Chapter 22

1. Bell, Rachael, "The Tylenol Terrorist," truTV's Crime Library, http://www.trutv.com/library/crime/terrorists_spies/terrorists/tylenol_murders/index.html, accessed May 5, 2012.
2. Knight, Jerry, "Tylenol's Maker Shows How to Respond to Crisis," *Washington Post*, October 11, 1982, referenced in Tamara Kaplan, "The Tylenol Crisis," http://www.aerobiologicalengineering.com/wxk116/TylenolMurders/crisis.html, accessed September 11, 2011.
3. Belsie, Laurent, "With Tylenol Recall 2010, a Corporate Icon Stumbles," *Christian Science Monitor*, January 15, 2010, http://www.csmonitor.com/Business/new-economy/2010/0115/With-Tylenol-recall-2010-a-corporate-icon-stumbles, accessed September 10, 2011.
4. Cohen, William A., *A Class with Drucker* (New York: AMACOM, 2008), p. 114.
5. For a more complete analysis of these struggles, see Schwartz, Michael, "Peter Drucker and the Denial of Business Ethics," *Journal of Business Ethics*, November 1998, vol. 17, no. 15, pp. 1685–1693. I disagree with the author that Drucker denied "business ethics." It is just that Drucker's definition of what constituted business ethics was different from that of others; in fact he created his own.
6. Drucker, Peter F., and Joseph A. Maciariello, *The Daily Drucker* (New York: Harper Business, 2004), p. 129.
7. Drucker, Peter F., *The Changing World of the Executive* (New York: Times Books, 1982), pp. 235–237.
8. Author unknown, "U.S. Ignores Bribes for Mideast Defense Contracts," *Worldtribune .com*, June 13, 2002, http://www.worldtribune.com/worldtribune/WTARC/2002/ss_military_06_13b.html, accessed September 11, 2011.
9. Drucker, *The Changing World of the Executive*, p. 245.
10. Ibid.
11. Drucker with Maciariello, *The Daily Drucker*, p. 126.
12. Ibid.
13. Ibid., p. 86.
14. Ibid., pp. 248–254.
15. Drucker, Peter F., *Management: Tasks, Responsibilities, Practices* (New York: Harper & Row, 1973). p. 367.
16. Ibid., pp. 366–375.
17. Although Drucker, and others too, declares "first, do no harm" to be part of the Primum Non Nocere part of the Hippocratic Oath, this is not true. See "Primum non nocere," Wikipedia, http://en.wikipedia.org/wiki/Primum_non_nocere, accessed September 11, 2011.
18. Drucker, Peter F., *Management Challenges for the 21st Century* (New York: Harper Business, 1999), pp. 175–176.
19. Drucker, *Management: Tasks, Responsibilities, Practices*, p. 612.
20. Drucker with Maciariello, *The Daily Drucker*, p. 3.
21. Nelson, Valerie J., "Adman's Work Helped Save Chrysler," *Los Angeles Times*, September 6, 2011, p. AA5.

Chapter 23

1. Drucker, Peter F., *The Practice of Management* (New York: Harper Collins, 1954, 1986), pp. 122–123.
2. Ibid., p. 123.

Chapter 24

1. Drucker, Peter F., with Joseph Maciariello, *The Daily Drucker* (New York: Harper Business, 2004), p. 225.
2. Drucker, Peter F., *Managing in the Future* (New York: Truman Talley Books, 1992), p. 251.
3. Ibid., p. 252.
4. Helfand, Duke, "Obama Official 'Very Disturbed' by Anthem Blue Cross Rate Hikes," *Los Angeles Times*, February 9, 2010, http://articles.latimes.com/2010/feb/09/business/la-fi-anthem-obama9-2010feb09, accessed January 6, 2012.
5. Drucker, *Managing in the Future*, p. 251.
6. Ibid., p. 252.

Chapeter 25

1. Byrne, John, "The Man Who Invented Management," *BusinessWeek*, November 28, 2005, http://www.businessweek.com/magazine/content/05_48/b3961001.htm, accessed February 3, 2012.
2. Ibid.
3. Uslay, Can, Robert E. Morgan, Jagdish N. Sheth, "Peter Drucker on Marketing: An Exploration of Five Tenets," *Journal of the Academy of Marketing Science*, Spring 2009, vol. 37, pp. 53–60.

Index

About the Author

William A. Cohen, PhD, a retired Air Force major general, has written two previous books on Drucker. He was the first graduate of the PhD program Drucker developed and taught for practicing executives at the Peter F. Drucker and Masatoshi Ito Graduate School of Management at Claremont Graduate University where Cohen now serves on the Board of Visitors. He writes a monthly column, "Lessons from Peter Drucker," for several Internet newsletters including Human Resources IQ and is president of the California Institute of Advanced Management, located in El Monte, California.